Living in Christ

The Sacraments

Encounters with Christ

Joanna Dailey

saint mary's press

The Subcommittee on the Catechism, United States Conference of Catholic Bishops, has found that this catechetical high school text, copyright 2012, is in conformity with the *Catechism of the Catholic Church* and that it fulfills the requirements of Course V: "Sacraments as Privileged Encounters with Jesus Christ" of the *Doctrinal Elements of a Curriculum Framework for the Development of Catechetical Materials for Young People of High School Age.*

Nihil Obstat: Rev. William M. Becker, STD
                   Censor Librorum
                   October 11, 2011

Imprimatur: † Most Rev. John M. Quinn, DD
                   Bishop of Winona
                   October 11, 2011

The nihil obstat and imprimatur are official declarations that a book or pamphlet is free of doctrinal or moral error. No implication is contained therein that those who have granted the nihil obstat or imprimatur agree with the contents, opinions, or statements expressed, nor do they assume any legal responsibility associated with publication.

The publishing team included Gloria Shahin, editorial director; Joanna Dailey, development editor; Maura Thompson Hagarty, PhD, contributing editor and theological reviewer. Prepress and manufacturing coordinated by the production departments of Saint Mary's Press

Cover Image: © The Crosiers / Gene Plaisted, OSC

The publisher also wishes to thank Rev. Richard Ginther, MA, who advised the publishing team and reviewed the work in progress.

Printed in the United States of America

1151 (PO4169)

ISBN 978-1-59982-091-0, Print

Contents

Section 3: The Sacraments of Christian Initiation: Part 2

Section 4: The Sacraments of Healing

Section 5: The Sacraments at the Service of Communion

Introduction

You may be familiar with the hymn "O Come, O Come, Emmanuel." We usually sing this hymn during Advent, when the Church is preparing for Christmas. It comes from this passage in the Book of Isaiah: "The young woman, pregnant and about to bear a son, shall name him Emmanuel." (7:14).

In his Gospel, Matthew quotes this verse from Isaiah in describing the birth of Jesus, and explains the meaning of *Emmanuel* by adding, "which means, 'God is with us'" (1:23). Jesus Christ, our Savior and Redeemer, is Emmanuel, God-with-us.

But before I had ever read the Prophet Isaiah, when I was just a grade-schooler, I read the following phrase, painted in the dome above the altar of my parish church: "GOD WITH US." These words were like a marquee over every Eucharist, every Sacrament celebrated in that sacred space. What were these words telling me? What did they mean? Something very important, for sure, or they would not have been written there, high above the altar, in fancy, beautiful letters, for all to see.

Gradually, I realized that "GOD WITH US" written above the altar meant the Eucharist itself, and indeed every Sacrament. For in the Sacraments, we, as unique individuals, encounter Emmanuel, Jesus Christ, who is himself God.

So that we might know the Father's love, he sent his only Son to live among us. When Jesus walked on earth, he was limited to one place and one time. But at his Resurrection, he broke the boundaries of time and space. He first appeared to Mary Magdalene (see John 20:11–18) and to the disciples on their way to Emmaus (see Luke 24:13–35). He then walked through locked doors to offer the greeting of "Peace!" to his Apostles and disciples (see John 20:19–20). The Ascension marked the end of these extraordinary appearances. But, most wonderfully for us, Jesus had entrusted the Sacraments to his Church so that we could meet him, through the power of the Holy Spirit, in our time and in our place, right where we are.

But to meet Christ in the Sacraments, we need faith. We received this gift of faith at Baptism (united with the faith of the Church, which comes before our own individual faith and which enriches our faith), but faith needs to be nurtured. So I hope you read this book as more than an academic exercise. I hope that as you read about the meaning, history, and practice of the Sacraments, your faith will be nurtured and strengthened, and you will find more reasons for hope and joy.

Because Jesus Christ loves you, he wants to be with you as your Source of life and peace. You may not always feel his presence, but he is with you in the Sacraments, offering you what he offered his Apostles and disciples so long ago: the saving gift of his friendship. As the Apostle Peter wrote: "Even though you do not see him now yet believe in him, you rejoice with an indescribable and glorious joy" (1 Peter 1:8). May you too find deep joy in your encounters with Christ in the Sacraments.

In the name of Jesus,
Joanna Dailey

An Introduction to Liturgy and the Sacraments

Part 1

Liturgy

What gives meaning to human life? What shapes our existence, our journey, here on Earth and beyond? Through the centuries, answers to these questions have been communicated through the actions and the words of the Church's worship. In the liturgy and in the Sacraments, the grace of God, the life of God, becomes available to our hearts, minds, and senses. The answer to the ultimate question of meaning is not a *what* but a *Who.* In acknowledging God in the liturgy and thanking him for his gifts to us (especially the gift of his Son, Jesus Christ), we discover who God is. In the liturgy we discover that God is near to us, that he penetrates our lives with his life and his grace. The Jews of ancient times marveled, "For what great nation is there that has gods so close to it as the Lord, our God, is to us whenever we call upon him?" (Deuteronomy 4:7). We who hold in our hands the Bread of Life, the Body of Christ we receive in the Eucharist, can marvel all the more. As we celebrate together, the liturgy shapes us and guides our journey, because through the celebration we encounter the living Christ.

The topics covered in this part are:

Article 1 What Is Liturgy?

liturgy

The Church's official, public, communal prayer. It is God's work, in which the People of God participate. The Church's most important liturgy is the Eucharist, or the Mass.

The word *liturgy* has ancient roots that can help us to understand the Church's worship today. Picture this:

> A Roman centurion on horseback rides through a crowded pathway leading to the market. "Make way! Make way! Make way for the *leitourgia!*" he announces. He is followed by a road crew carrying picks and axes. They will remove the large stones from the path, smooth it out, lay handmade bricks, and make a real road.

This is a *leitourgia*—a liturgy. The literal meaning of *leitourgia* is "the people's work." The Church adopted the word *liturgy* as her own. The **liturgy** is the Church's official, public, communal prayer. It is God's work in which the People of God participate. And, of all the liturgies the Church celebrates, the Eucharist is the most important. When we gather to carry out Jesus' commandment to "do this in memory of me" (Luke 22:19), we are responding to God's invitation and his gracious love.

Not every public gathering for prayer is liturgy. A group prayer service is public and communal, but it is not liturgy because it is not official—that is, it is not governed by the Church. Private prayer is important, but, because it is not official or public, it is not liturgy.

An entrance procession, with an Entrance Chant or song, is usually part of the Introductory Rites of the liturgy. The Introductory Rites prepare our hearts and minds to participate fully in the celebration.

© Bill Wittman / www.wpwittman.com

Let us define a few terms. When we say "the liturgy," we mean the liturgy as a whole— all the Sacraments, including the Eucharist, as well as liturgies that are not Sacraments, such as the Liturgy of the Hours (see the sidebar "Liturgical Books") and Catholic funerals. When we say "a liturgy," we mean a particular Mass or liturgical celebration.

The Work of God

The liturgy is primarily the work of God (in Latin, *opus Dei*), in which we participate. What does this mean? God sent his Son, Jesus Christ, who is himself God, so that we might become, in the Holy Spirit, his adopted children and thus sharers in his own divine

Liturgical Books

Liturgical books are indispensable to the liturgy. In keeping with the solemnity and significance of the liturgy, liturgical books are beautifully designed and printed, sometimes with gold or red leather covers. You may have noticed at least a few of the following books:

- *Roman Missal* (or *Sacramentary*): This is the book the priest uses at the altar and at his chair. It includes all the prayers of the Mass.

- *Lectionary for Mass:* This book contains the readings of the Mass, including the Gospels, with the Responsorial Psalm and the Gospel acclamations.

- *Book of the Gospels:* This is a large book, containing only the Gospel readings from the *Lectionary.* It is often carried in procession. The Gospel is read from this book.

- *Rite of Baptism for Children:* You may have seen this used at Baptism. This rite and other rites are taken from *The Rites of the Catholic Church,* volume I and volume II. Volume I contains the rites for all the Sacraments (except the Eucharist and Holy Orders). Volume II contains the rites for ordinations, blessings, and consecrations of persons, and blessings of objects and places. If used in the liturgy, each of these rites is bound as a separate book.

- *Liturgy of the Hours:* This is printed in various forms, but is usually several volumes, one for each Church season of the year. It includes the hymns, readings, and prayers for each of the seven "hours" (or prayer times) of each day.

life. Wounded by Original Sin, the sin of our first parents, we, humanity, needed God's help. Even though human beings lost the original state of perfect, loving communion that Adam and Eve enjoyed, God has been working throughout history to restore that state to us. He called Abraham to be the father of a Chosen People and formed a sacred Covenant with them. He gave them a divine Law, the Old Law, to teach them how to live. He gave them rituals and a priesthood and sent judges, kings, and prophets to guide them. Unfortunately, sin and death prevailed until God's ultimate saving act, the sending of his Son, Jesus Christ. When the right time came, God intervened—not with yet one more prophet, but with his only-begotten Son, who gave his life for the forgiveness of sins and made new life for us possible. Through his Passion, death, Resurrection, and Ascension—the Paschal Mystery—Jesus Christ accomplished our redemption. Through Christ's work, we received a New Law, which is the fulfillment of the Old Law. The New Law, a law of love, grace, and freedom, is the grace of the Holy Spirit. Whenever we gather for liturgy, especially the Sacraments, we celebrate, above all, Christ's Paschal Mystery and we receive the grace of the Holy Spirit, which enables us to live according to the New Law.

God—Father, Son, and Holy Spirit—continues to intervene. "God . . . is the 'living God'[1] who gives life and intervenes in history" (*Catechism of the Catholic Church* [*CCC*], 2112). Through the Church and in the liturgy he is at work bringing about our salvation. As God's work, the liturgy involves his action, but it involves our action too. The liturgy is the "action" or work of the whole Christ: "It is the whole *community,* the Body of Christ united with its Head, that celebrates" the liturgy (*CCC,* 1140). The Church gathers for liturgy in response to God's call, and when we participate in the liturgy, our words and actions express the spiritual work that God is doing.

The liturgy is the focal point of our participation in God's work, but it is not the Church's only way of cooperating in his work in the world. Teaching and preaching the Gospel prepares good soil for the seed of faith and worship to grow in God's People. In faithful word and action, the liturgy truly bears good fruit in our lives.

Catholic Wisdom

Christ Is Present in the Liturgy

Pope Saint Leo the Great gave a sermon in which he taught that Christ is with us in the liturgy and in the Sacraments. He described Christ's Ascension into Heaven and then declared: "And so that which till then was visible of our Redeemer was changed into a sacramental presence, and that faith might be more excellent and stronger, sight gave way to doctrine" (Sermon 74). We no longer see Christ in the flesh, but he is present in the liturgy.

Liturgy, Scripture, and Tradition

All of the Church's Sacraments and liturgies have Christ as their origin, yet he did not dictate all aspects of the liturgy. So where does liturgy as we know it today come from? It comes through liturgy, Scripture, and Tradition. The essential elements of the liturgy have been handed on to us through Scripture and Tradition, while other elements that we call traditions (lowercase *t*) have emerged over time. Scripture and Tradition are distinct, yet very closely related. Both transmit the Word of God. Together they form a single sacred Deposit of Faith. The Deposit of Faith, the treasure of the Church handed on from the time of the Apostles and contained in Scripture and Tradition, makes clear the truths that cannot be laid aside because they are part of God's Revelation, truths like these: Jesus Christ is true God and true man, the Pope is the successor of Saint Peter and the head of the Church, and the Trinity is one God in three Divine Persons. The Deposit of Faith does not change. The **Magisterium**, the living teaching office of the Church (all bishops in communion with the Pope) is responsible, under the guidance of the Holy Spirit, for interpreting the deposit of faith.

Magisterium
The Church's living teaching office, which consists of all the bishops, in communion with the Pope.

The traditions, with a small *t,* that have influenced, and continue to influence, the liturgy are customs, things we do because they are part of our history and culture. They can be incorporated into liturgical celebrations when they express within them the great Tradition of the Church. For example, the priest washes his hands after receiving the gifts of bread and wine at the Preparation of the Gifts. Originally he washed his hands because the gifts he was receiving included the offerings of the faithful toward the upkeep of the parish church and for the relief of the poor. These were usually food and other farm products. The hand-washing remains in the Eucharist in an abbreviated form, and is accompanied by the priest's prayer for purification: "Wash me, O Lord,

© Bill Wittman / www.wpwittman.com

The washing of hands has been preserved in the liturgy even when there is no longer a practical reason for it. Consider the words the priest speaks to understand why the washing of hands is still symbolically important.

Tradition

This word (from the Latin, meaning "to hand on") refers to the process of passing on the Gospel message. Tradition, which began with the oral communication of the Gospel by the Apostles, was written down in the Scriptures, is handed down and lived out in the life of the Church, and is interpreted by the Magisterium under the guidance of the Holy Spirit.

Trinity

From the Latin *trinus,* meaning "threefold," referring to the central mystery of the Christian faith that God exists as a communion of three distinct and interrelated Divine Persons: Father, Son, and Holy Spirit. The doctrine of the Trinity is a mystery that is inaccessible to human reason alone and is known through Divine Revelation only.

from my iniquity and cleanse me from my sin" *(Roman Missal).* The change in the role of hand-washing occurred over centuries, yet in this change, Tradition was preserved.

Like the truths of faith, the liturgy is guided by the Magisterium. This is what makes the liturgy the official worship of the Church. Essential elements handed on through Scripture and Tradition are always retained, while aspects of our liturgical celebrations that come from traditions can be kept, modified, or eliminated under the guidance of the Magisterium. Within these guidelines, your parish may make its own decisions about such things as particular hymns or songs to sing.

Handed On from Christ

The word **Tradition** comes from a significant word in our lives of faith: *traditio.* It is a Latin word, meaning "to hand on or to give over." Our liturgy has been handed on to us from Jesus, first when he "took bread, said the blessing, broke it, and *giving it* to his disciples, said '"Take and eat; this is my body"'" (Matthew 26:26, italic added), and then later, when he died and "*gave up* his spirit" (Matthew 27:50, italic added) to his Father, and to us. In Saint Paul's account of the words of Jesus at the Last Supper, the earliest account of the words of institution found in Scripture, he notes: "I received from the Lord what I also *handed on* to you, that the Lord Jesus, on the night he was handed over, took bread . . ." (1 Corinthians 11:23, italics added). Our liturgy has been *handed on* to us, as it was to Saint Paul, as the richest inheritance of the Church. ✝

Article 2 The Holy Trinity and the Liturgy

The Church's liturgy is Trinitarian. In the liturgy the three Divine Persons of the **Trinity**—the Father, the Son, and the Holy Spirit—are at work, and through the liturgy the mystery of the Holy Trinity, the central mystery of the Christian faith, is more deeply revealed. As a sign of this, every liturgy begins, "In the name of the Father and of the Son and of the Holy Spirit." And every liturgy ends with the celebrant's asking for the blessing of the Holy Trinity.

The Rublev Icon of the Holy Trinity

(Andrei Rublev, 1425)

Some treasures of the East have been discovered by the West. The artistic expression of faith in the Western Church usually takes the form of statues, frescoes, murals, paintings, and stained-glass windows. In the Eastern Churches (both those Churches united with the Catholic Church as well as the Eastern Orthodox Church, sadly separated from the Catholic Church by schism), artistic expressions of faith commonly take the form of icons.

The word *icon* is from a Greek word meaning "image." An icon is an image of Jesus, Mary, or one of the saints. An iconographer is the painter or "writer" of the icon. Writing an icon is a spiritual process that involves preparing by praying and fasting.

The Rublev icon is particularly revered because it has layers of meaning. On the surface, it is an icon of the three angels welcomed by Abraham, the patriarch of the Jews and "our father in faith" *(Roman Missal)*. In the Book of Genesis, chapter 18, Abraham meets unexpected visitors and shares a meal with them.

The three angels symbolize the Trinity: God the Son is in the center (his two fingers symbolizing that he is true God and true man), God the Father is at the left, and God the Holy Spirit is on the right. The thin staffs they carry symbolize that they all have the same authority; they are equal.

The next layer portrays the Eucharist: God—the Father, the Son, and the Holy Spirit—has laid a table for us. The sacrificial lamb, the Lamb of God (the Body of Christ), is set in the middle of the table.

As we look at the icon, we see an open space at the table. There is no barrier between the Trinity and the viewer looking on. This open space is an invitation. We are drawn in, invited to sit at the table and to share the life and love of the Trinity.

© Bill Wittman / www.wpwittman.com

At the Concluding Doxology, we pray with the priest, "Through him, and with him, and in him . . ." and proclaim our Amen. How can this Doxology and Amen shape our Christian lives? How can we live each day in and with Christ?

Each Person of the Trinity is involved in the Church's liturgy. We acknowledge the Father as the source of all the blessings of creation, and salvation, especially the gifts of his Son, Jesus Christ, and the Holy Spirit. Jesus Christ, who became incarnate in order to redeem us, is central in the Church's liturgy, because in every liturgy Christ's gift of himself for the sake of our salvation is made present to us, here and now, by the power of the Holy Spirit.

Jesus Christ, the Second Person of the Trinity, took on a human nature without losing his divine nature in order to save us from the tyranny of sin and death. He showed us the depths of God's love, enabling us to share in his divine nature. When we participate in liturgy, we celebrate the work of salvation that Christ accomplished for us through his Passion, death, Resurrection, and Ascension.

Something that makes Christ present to us is called a sacrament; thus we say that liturgy and Christ's work within it are sacramental. The Body of Christ, the Church, is also a sacrament, because the Holy Spirit also works through her to make Christ present in the world and to be the instrument of grace and salvation for all. The Church is thus the sacrament of the Holy Trinity's communion with human beings. In every liturgy, especially the Seven Sacraments, the Church encounters God—the Father, Son, and Holy Spirit. Through this encounter and the outpouring of God's grace, we are justified, which means we are freed from sin, and we are sanctified, which means we are made holy and share in the divine life.

Sharing in God's life means that we are drawn into communion with the Trinity. During our life on earth, we are united with God in a profound way through the Sacraments. And we live with the hope that during our life after death, we will experience perfect communion and happiness with God forever in Heaven.

When we celebrate the liturgy, we celebrate with not only the people we can see with us but also with all the angels, saints, and those who have gone before us in faith. The saving work of Christ extends our liturgy on earth into Heaven. In the liturgy the boundaries of time and space are broken, and we are one in Christ. In every liturgy, we participate in, and also anticipate, the heavenly liturgy that is our ultimate goal.

In the liturgy we remember the saints in Heaven—first of all the holy Mother of God, then the Apostles, the martyrs, and other saints—on fixed days of the liturgical year, not for their own accomplishments but for Christ's work of salvation in them. Their trials and final victory encourage us as we journey to the Father in Christ. Thus the Church on earth is united with the liturgy of Heaven.

How, then, is Christ present in the liturgy? He is present in the priest, who acts in the person of Christ. He is present in the assembly, because we are the Body of Christ. He is present in the Word of God, the Scriptures. God's Word is an essential element of every liturgy and is proclaimed during the Liturgy of the Word. In the Sacrament of the Eucharist, Christ is present, in a special way, in his Body and Blood, which we receive during Communion.

The Holy Spirit is active in the liturgy, preparing us to encounter Christ. The Holy Spirit reveals Christ's presence in the assembly, in Scripture, and in the sacramental actions of liturgical celebrations. By his transforming power, the Holy Spirit makes the saving work of Christ present and active, here and now, for us. When we leave the liturgy, we carry the message of God's love to all we meet, through the work of the Holy Spirit.

It is important to understand what it means to say that "the saving power of Christ is present and active, here and now." In the liturgy and the Sacraments, we do not merely remember and celebrate the past, because the liturgy and the Sacraments are the means by which the saving power of the Risen Christ is made available to us today. Christ is alive and is not limited by time and space. In the liturgy his power is just as available to us as it was to the Apostles and the disciples. Of course, he is with us at all times, but in the liturgy and the Sacraments, in a special way, he keeps his promise to be with us always.

This Trinitarian dimension of liturgical prayer is summed up in the Concluding Doxology (from the Greek *doxa*, meaning "praise") that we are invited to affirm with the Amen:

> Through him [Jesus Christ],
> and with him,
> and in him,
> O God, almighty Father,
> in the unity of the Holy Spirit,
> all honor and glory is yours,

for ever and ever.

People: Amen.

(*Roman Missal*)

If we live our lives in Christ, with Christ, and through Christ, our fountain of goodness and love will never run dry, as promised in the Book of Isaiah:

> They that hope in the LORD will renew their strength,
>> they will soar on eagles' wings;
> They will run and not grow weary,
>> walk and not grow faint.

(40:31) ✝

Article 3 The Liturgical Year

In southern Indiana, there is an underground river, appropriately called the Lost River. At several points in its pathway, it simply disappears. It dips underground and gurgles beneath the surface for miles, only to arise again, sometimes in quiet pools, sometimes in plumes of water, depending upon the limestone caves, caverns, and channels underground through which it travels. It has been called one of America's natural wonders.

Look at the chart pictured here. What liturgical season is the Church celebrating now? In what season does your birthday usually fall? The birthdays of family and friends? Why are liturgical colors important to the seasons?

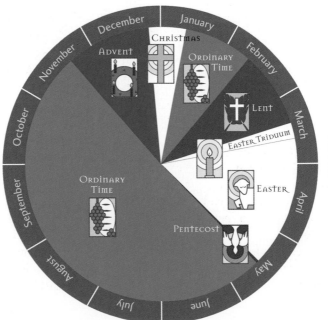

© Saint Mary's Press

A Liturgical Pilgrim

We know much about the early liturgy of the Church through the writings of Egeria, either a nun or laywoman who spent much time on pilgrimage from her home in Spain or France to the Holy Land. The Church in Jerusalem had the privilege of celebrating the liturgy at the very places where Jesus lived, healed, taught, died, and was risen. Through Egeria's writings we discover that, by the fourth century, the liturgy of the Church in Jerusalem was well established. Egeria writes of the liturgical celebrations on Sundays and holy days, like Epiphany and the Feast of the Presentation (February 2). We can recognize our traditions in her description of the Lenten fast and our Passion or Palm Sunday procession in her vivid account of it. She describes the procession with the bishop and all the community from the Mount of Olives to Jerusalem: "And all the children of the neighborhood, even those who are too young to walk, are carried by their parents on their shoulders, all of them bearing branches, some of palms and some of olives, and thus the bishop is escorted in the same manner as the Lord was of old" (Egeria's Description of the Liturgical Year in Jerusalem: Translation).

We owe this liturgical pilgrim a debt of gratitude for using her excellent skills of observation and expression to bring our ancient roots alive for us today.

For many people the **liturgical year** is like an underground river. The liturgical year gurgles beneath the surface of our days, and then, suddenly, it's Advent! or Christmas! or Lent! or Easter! The liturgical year rises to the surface of our consciousness, and we catch up to it, at least for a little while.

But the liturgical year is always there, and is always *now*. The liturgical year celebrates God's time, and is therefore timeless. The liturgical year provides a structure in which the universal Church throughout the world celebrates the whole mystery of Christ—from his Incarnation and birth, through his life, suffering, death, Resurrection, and Ascension, to Pentecost—and prays in anticipation of Christ's coming again at the end of time. All of these saving events are re-membered (put together again) and made present to us now.

Let us follow this calendar—as if following a life-giving river—from season to season. How does it nourish our lives and help us to grow as members of the Body of Christ?

liturgical year
The annual cycle of religious feasts and seasons that forms the context for the Church's worship. During the liturgical year, we remember and celebrate God the Father's saving plan as it is revealed through the life of his Son, Jesus Christ.

Advent

The liturgical year begins in Advent. This season begins on the fourth Sunday before Christmas. Advent is the time of preparation before Christmas and lasts four weeks (the fourth week is typically not a full week). Its liturgical color is purple, to signify waiting. Advent is a time of hope, of waiting, and of preparing. What are we preparing for?

© Saint Mary's Press / Mara Fenske

In our culture, preparation in this context often has one dimension: we are preparing for Christmas Day. But as Saint Bernard of Clairvaux, a twelfth-century monk, writer, and teacher, explained, our waiting and preparing has three dimensions: (1) We are waiting to celebrate the Word Made Flesh at Christmas; (2) We are waiting to celebrate the birth of the Word of God in our own hearts at Christmas; and (3) We are waiting for the final coming of Christ in glory at the end of time. Our waiting is an active waiting. We are preparing to be visited by our Savior. We are waiting and preparing for our Redeemer. We are making room in our hearts and in our lives for the One who was sent away because there was no room for him in the inn. And we are waiting for Christ's second coming, his final advent, when all things will be fulfilled in him (see Ephesians 1:7–10).

Christmas

Laney looked around at the chaotic family room. The Christmas tree glittered in the corner, and under it lay mounds of torn wrapping paper and ribbon—the evidence of the successful endeavors of her younger brothers and sisters to open their gifts in the shortest amount of time possible. Of course she and her parents had also joined in the fun. Laney smiled a little sadly. It had been a good Christmas, but now it was all over.

Laney could not have been more wrong! The Christmas season begins on December 25 and lasts until the Solemnity of the Baptism of

© Saint Mary's Press / Mara Fenske

the Lord (the third Sunday after Christmas Day). Its liturgical color is white or gold, to signify joy. During this time the Church reflects on the wonder and meaning of the Incarnation. The Word of God Made Flesh certainly takes more than one day to celebrate!

One solemnity of particular note during this season is the Feast of the Epiphany. Originally celebrated on what is now the twelfth day of Christmas (January 6), the Epiphany celebrates the Revelation of the Savior to the Gentiles (the people of the non-Jewish world). In many parts of the world, Epiphany is the day for parties and gift-giving. Epiphany has been moved to the Sunday preceding January 6, to give us the opportunity to celebrate it with our parish communities.

Ordinary Time

Ordinary Time is not called ordinary because the Church considers it "nothing special." It is called ordinary because its days are numbered with ordinal numbers (that is, the First Sunday in Ordinary Time, Second Sunday in Ordinary Time, and so forth). There are two blocks of Ordinary Time in the liturgical calendar: The first one is between the Christmas season and Lent, and the second one, which is longer, is between Pentecost and Advent. The liturgical color of Ordinary Time is green, symbolizing hope.

© Saint Mary's Press / Mara Fenske

In Ordinary Time the Church reflects on the life of Jesus Christ—his mission, his miracles, and his teachings. During this time we have the opportunity, day by day and week by week, to know Christ better, to internalize his teachings and values as we encounter him in Word and Sacrament.

Lent

Before Christ came into the world, we were like sheep without a shepherd. But Jesus came, redeemed us through his suffering and death, and led us back to the Father. During Lent we recall Christ's Passion—his suffering and death on the cross. Lent, the most solemn and reflective time of the year, begins on Ash Wednesday. Its liturgical color is purple,

symbolizing penance. During Lent the Church encourages us to perform three Christian practices in a more focused way: prayer, fasting, and almsgiving. The whole Church, as the Body of Christ, commits to these works together, supporting one another in our efforts to remember Saint Paul's question: "Do you not know . . . that you are not your own? For you have been purchased at a price" (1 Corinthians 6:19–20). During Lent we recall that Christ redeemed us through his death, and we prepare to celebrate his Resurrection on the most glorious day of the year, the Solemnity of Solemnities: Easter.

Easter Triduum

The week preceding Easter begins on Palm (Passion) Sunday and is called *Holy Week*. During this week we remember in the most intense way possible the sufferings and death of Christ.

The last days of the week, called the *Triduum* (meaning "Three Days") are the most solemn of the entire year. A liturgical "day" always begins at sundown (or Evening Prayer) on the night before. Our liturgical celebration of Sunday really begins at Evening Prayer on Saturday evening. This follows the Jewish custom and is part of our Jewish inheritance. In the same way, the *Triduum* begins on Thursday evening and ends on Sunday evening.

On *Holy Thursday* we celebrate the Mass of the Lord's Supper in the evening, and we commemorate Jesus' gift of himself in the Eucharist. A foot-washing ceremony reminds us that, as followers of Jesus, we are to serve one another (see John 13:14-15) On this day we also recall the institution of the priesthood.

On *Good Friday* we remember Jesus' Passion and death. We venerate the cross in some way. We receive Holy

Communion, reserved from the Mass of the Lord's Supper, but there is no Mass today. Every Eucharist is a sacrifice because it makes the sacrifice of the cross present. The only sacrifice we offer on Good Friday is the spiritual offering of Jesus' sacrifice on Calvary.

On *Holy Saturday* we eagerly prepare for the Easter Vigil, which begins at night. This is the greatest night, the most beautiful night, of the year. "The Church, keeping watch, awaits the Resurrection of Christ and celebrates it in the Sacraments" (*Universal Norms for the Liturgical Year and the Calendar*, 21). We celebrate with fire, candles, water, the singing of the Exsultet, readings, and the welcoming of the elect (those preparing to become Catholic) into the Church as they celebrate the Sacraments of Christian Initiation (Baptism, Confirmation, and the Eucharist).

Pray It!

Praying with the Seasons

The best way to pray with the Church's seasons is to participate in daily Mass. Also try some of the following seasonal prayers and practices:

Advent
Help your family set up an Advent wreath at home and light one more candle each week.

Christmas
Each day after Christmas, choose a Christmas card your family has received and pray for its sender.

Ordinary Time
Choose a Scripture reading from the next Sunday's liturgy to pray with and to focus on as you prepare for Sunday Mass.

Lent
Give up something for Lent, and choose one way to *give* during Lent. Each week do something positive, individually or with others, to help those in need.

Easter
Go to the Easter Vigil! (The vigil fulfills the Sunday obligation, but think about going to the Sunday celebration as well. It's Easter!) Each day of the Easter season (until Pentecost), find one way to bring joy to a person in your life.

Pentecost and Ordinary Time
Make plans to share the gifts the Holy Spirit has given you, especially during the summer.

Easter Season

On *Easter Sunday* we continue our celebration of Christ's Resurrection in all its splendor, with the fullest joy. Easter Sunday begins an entire week of celebration, for each day of Easter week, like Easter Sunday itself, is celebrated as a solemnity of the Lord. Easter Sunday also marks the beginning of the Easter season, a fifty-day period that ends on Pentecost. The season's liturgical color is white or gold. During this time the liturgical readings focus on the Risen Jesus and on the growth of the Church in the Acts of the Apostles. In the northern hemisphere, the season of Easter coincides with spring. (The word *Easter* is a form of the name of the goddess Estre, the Greek goddess of spring.) The liturgy and the world itself speak of new life, and the evidence is all around us. Death has been overcome by life, the life of the Risen Christ. His Resurrection is the pledge of our own—that our own personal lives and the lives of our loved ones will never end. Because of Christ's Resurrection, we live with the hope that one day we will be united with God in Heaven forever.

© Saint Mary's Press / Mara Fenske

At Pentecost the coming of the Holy Spirit seals the work of Jesus Christ in our lives and reminds us of all that Jesus has taught us. At Pentecost we join the Apostles, the disciples, and the Mother of the Lord in the Upper Room and together we celebrate the gift of the Holy Spirit. With the disciples of Jesus, we are sent into the crowds to proclaim God's salvation in Jesus Christ and to help carry out his mission of love for all humankind. ✝

Article 4 Liturgical Rites and Traditions

A bell clangs in the morning air, inviting you to walk through the doors into a small church. Most of the assembly is standing in prayer, although some people are lighting candles at the front. In the dim light, a deacon carrying a smoking censer walks around the entire space, incensing the icons on the walls. You look for the altar, but instead you see a wall of icons. Suddenly, the chandelier above you bursts into light. The middle doors open, and the deacon emerges. He turns and faces the open doors, through which the priest can now be seen, facing the altar. The deacon sings out, "Bless, Master!"

The priest sings in reply, "Blessed is the Kingdom of the Father, and of the Son, and of the Holy Spirit, now and ever and unto ages of ages." The choir and people sing "Amen" in response.

The Ambrosian Rite

The Ambrosian Rite is named after Saint Ambrose, who was bishop of Milan, Italy, in the fourth century. It is celebrated today by approximately five million people in the Archdiocese of Milan and surrounding areas. At the time of the Second Vatican Council, this rite was in danger of being suppressed, but due to the sympathetic influence of Pope Paul VI (a former archbishop of Milan) the Ambrosian Rite was reformed and has survived.

Let's compare the Ambrosian Rite to the Roman Rite. In the Ambrosian Mass, the entrance procession pauses in the middle of the nave (the middle aisle) for the singing of the *Kyrie eleison* (Lord, have mercy) twelve times. For most of the Mass, the altar servers stand in front of the altar, facing it, until they are needed. The priest washes his hands immediately before the consecration, not at the Preparation of the Gifts, as in the Roman Rite. There is no *Agnus Dei* (Lamb of God). During Lent a litany is sung in place of the *Gloria*. Passion (Palm) Sunday, which begins Holy Week, is called Olive Sunday, because olive branches are more accessible in Italy than are palms.

A bishop of the Eastern Catholic Church blesses the assembly with the dikerion (double-branched) and trikerion (triple-branched) candlesticks. Behind him is the iconostasis (icon-screen) and altar table.

© Saint Elias Ukrainian Catholic Church, Brampton, Ontario, Canada / www.saintelias.com / Andrei Komar

You are now a little confused. You were told that this was a Catholic Church! And it is. It is one of the twenty-one **Eastern Catholic Churches**, which, after the schism of 1054, either chose to remain united with the Catholic Church or later reunited with it. To this day each Eastern Catholic Church follows its own ancient tradition, with its own bishops, liturgical language, and liturgical customs. All of these Churches, with the Roman Catholic Church, make up twenty-two Churches united under the Bishop of Rome, the Pope. These Eastern Churches celebrate the liturgy according to one of these various liturgical rites: the Antiochene Rite, the Chaldean Rite, the Byzantine Rite, the Alexandrian (Coptic or Ethiopian) Rite, or the Armenian Rite.

Within the Catholic Church can also be found other Latin Rites (besides the Roman Rite), which are celebrated in various places, according to ancient customs. Of course the Roman Rite is celebrated by most of the Roman (Latin) Church. These other Latin Rites celebrated alongside the Roman Rite are the Ambrosian Rite (in and around Milan, Italy); the Mozarabic Rite (in the Cathedral of the Archdiocese of Toledo, Spain, and six surrounding parishes); the Bragan Rite (in the Archdiocese of Braga, Portugal); and three rites associated with religious orders: the Dominican, the Carmelite, and the Carthusian Rites.

All of these diverse rites, in both the East and the West, are legitimate expressions of the liturgy of the universal

Catholic Church. They all make present the saving power of God and the saving mysteries of Christ. Because they make present and express the same mystery of Christ, they show us that the Catholic Church is truly catholic (universal). Therefore, even in diversity, the Church remains one body. This is because we follow the teachings of Christ as we have received them from the Apostles and their successors, the bishops. Our unity, in the midst of the diversity of rites, is assured by Apostolic Succession. ✝

Eastern Catholic Churches
The twenty-one Churches of the East, with their own theological, liturgical, and administrative traditions, in union with the universal Catholic Church and her head, the Bishop of Rome.

Article
5 Celebrating the Liturgy

The first World Youth Day was instituted on December 20, 1985, at the request of the late Pope John Paul II. Since then convocations of youth have been held in Rome and also in several cities and countries around the world—cities like Buenos Aires, Argentina; Denver, Colorado; Manila, Philippines; and Paris, France. Pope Benedict XVI hosted World Youth Day in 2005 in Cologne, Germany, and in 2008, over 300,000 young people traveled to Sydney, Australia, for the worldwide meeting. For the meeting in Madrid, Spain, in 2011, the Spanish capital hosted 1.5 million young people! In 2014, Pope Francis, a native of South America, will lead the celebration of World Youth Day in Rio de Janeiro, Brazil.

Unquestionably, a liturgy with the Pope and 1.5 million young people would probably be the most exciting and wonderful liturgy imaginable. Yet, in essence, this liturgy is no different than the liturgy available to you every Sunday morning (or Saturday night).

How can this be? How can a liturgy celebrated by the Pope and attended by so many people be the same as one that is celebrated in our parish churches every day? It is the same because Jesus Christ is the same, yesterday, today, and forever. It is Jesus Christ whom we encounter in every liturgy, no matter if there is music or not, if there are crowds of people or just a few, or if it is celebrated in a great cathedral, a stadium, or a small chapel. Jesus Christ died and rose for us, and it is always he whom we meet in the liturgy.

That being said, the Church, through its documents and directives, encourages all of her members to help make the liturgy as beautiful and as meaningful as possible. We can-

© Bill Wittman / www.wpwittman.com

Looked at from the outside, like a movie, liturgy can seem boring at times. But by putting your faith and your heart into it, the liturgy becomes the true story of your life in Christ. How can you prepare for your next episode?

not be satisfied with the minimum needed for a celebration. We must make every effort to make the liturgy the best it can be.

But what if you are not on the parish liturgical committee or in the choir? How can you contribute to the celebration of the liturgy? Let us speak particularly of the Eucharist for the moment, as that is the Sacrament we celebrate most frequently and the one that unites us in a special way with Christ and with others. Consider these ways to contribute:

1. Make every effort to be present and accounted for, mentally and spiritually as well as physically. Prepare in advance by examining your conscience in light of the Word of God. Once Mass begins, pay attention to what is going on.

2. Pray to the Holy Spirit. We have learned that the role of the Holy Spirit is to help us fully participate in the liturgy. Ask him to help you to focus and to give thanks for Jesus Christ and for all the good things in your life.

3. Listen to the prayers. In some cases, they have survived thousands of years. Put yourself in the prayers. Find their value.

Live It!

Step Up to the Liturgy

Every liturgy is not, humanly speaking, perfect. Our human efforts at perfection often falter. This does not diminish the saving power of the Holy Trinity that we encounter in every Sacrament. But we do want every liturgy to be a beautiful sign of Christ's presence with us. A liturgy that seems ill-prepared can discourage and distract us. But as members of the Body of Christ, we can help. Perhaps the choir needs a few more members to sound as good as it could be. Perhaps a few more good readers are needed to proclaim the first and second readings with energy and clarity. Maybe your parish needs Extraordinary Ministers of Holy Communion to distribute the Body and Blood of Christ during the Liturgy of the Eucharist or a few more reliable parishioners to carry the Body and Blood of Christ to those who are homebound. Step up! Take your place in the work of the liturgy and participate in the work of God.

World Youth Day

World Youth Day is celebrated on a diocesan level every year, usually on Passion Sunday. The Pope welcomes youth to Rome in a special way on that day. In some years World Youth Day is celebrated internationally and is held in a chosen city outside Rome, usually in the summer, to enable more youth to participate. World Youth Day has been celebrated in the following cities and years since the first one in Rome in 1986: Buenos Aires, Argentina (1987); Santiago de Compostela, Spain (1989); Czestochowa, Poland (1991); Denver, Colorado, USA (1993); Manila, Philippines (1995); Paris, France (1997); Toronto, Canada (2002); Cologne, Germany (2005); Sydney, Australia (2008); Madrid, Spain (2011).

On the first World Youth Day in Rome, Pope John Paul II gave the young people a large wooden cross, which has since been taken "on pilgrimage" to every World Youth Day international gathering. In 2003 he gave an icon of Mary to the World Youth Day gathering. When the cross and icon are not displayed at World Youth Day gatherings, they are kept in the San Lorenzo Youth Center in Rome.

© Bill Wittman / www.wpwittman.com

4. Listen to the readings. Try (with the help of the Holy Spirit) to allow the words to touch your mind and heart.

5. Pray during the General Intercessions. Pray for the Church, the world, and those who suffer. Pray for your family and friends. Pray for yourself, particularly if you are going through a challenging time.

6. Sing. Music opens up our hearts and our spirits. It opens us up to God. As Saint Augustine said, "He who sings prays twice." There is no need for embarrassment or pride. We do not sing at the Eucharist to show off our voices but rather to give glory to God with whatever voice he gave us!

7. Say the responses and think about the meaning of the words you say.
8. Use your body. When you make the Sign of the Cross, make it thoughtfully. When you kneel, hold yourself up straight. When you stand or walk, stand up straight. Our bodies help us to pray when we truly participate in the action asked of us.
9. When you receive Communion, concentrate on the reality of Christ's presence in the Eucharistic species and the gift of grace you are receiving, which gives you strength to lead a moral life.
10. When you are dismissed from Mass, resolve to go forth to live in a way that is pleasing to God. Strive to do what is good and avoid what is evil. This includes carrying out works of mercy, loving actions that help others with their physical and spiritual needs.

The liturgy is a two-way street: God communicates with us and we communicate with him. Communication is difficult if one of us (and guess which one that might be) is missing in action! ✞

Part Review

1. What is the original meaning of the word *liturgy?*

2. What does the Church mean by the word *liturgy?*

3. What is the Magisterium of the Church?

4. What is Tradition?

5. What does it mean when we say that the Church's liturgy is Trinitarian?

6. How are we in union with the Trinity?

7. What is the liturgical year?

8. How does the Holy Spirit help us to celebrate the liturgy?

9. Explain why every liturgy is a participation in, and anticipation of, the heavenly liturgy.

Part 2

Sacraments

If you are like most Catholics, the Sacraments have been part of your life for as long as you can remember. You probably don't remember your Baptism, but you will probably never forget the excitement of your First Communion! If you've celebrated Confirmation, you have had the opportunity to affirm the faith you were given as a gift in Baptism and to receive the fullness of the Gifts of the Holy Spirit.

But you may have questions about these and the other Sacraments. Where did they come from? How do they work? Why do we have them? These are excellent questions, because they keep us from taking the great gift of the Sacraments, "God's masterpieces" (*Catechism of the Catholic Church [CCC]*, 1091), for granted.

In this part we approach the Sacraments from with a wide-angle lens. We look first at symbols and rituals in general. Then we apply those concepts to the Sacraments as signs of Christ's presence in the Church. Next we explore the Sacraments as active signs of grace and redemption for us. Last we take a look at the praying Church, including sacramentals and popular expressions of faith, as a help to our relationship with God and to our everyday Christian living.

The topics covered in this part are:

Article 6 Symbols and Rituals

We use symbols and rituals every day, almost without realizing it. In this article we discuss some of these everyday symbols and then apply our understanding to the symbols and rituals of the Sacraments. One good example of a set of symbols we use every day is language. When people have a shared language, they have a shared understanding of what words mean. If we share the meanings of words, we can communicate our thoughts and ideas. Through language we can turn what is within us (our thoughts and feelings) into something outside of us that can affect or influence others. It is hard to imagine how different our lives would be without language.

Yet, however wonderful language is, sometimes words are not enough. Where our deepest thoughts and feelings are concerned, we all sometimes need to be *shown* the meaning of words. And this is not a bad attitude to have. Saint John, the beloved disciple of Christ, wrote to his community in the first century, "Children, let us love not in word or speech but in deed and truth" (1 John 3:18). Love is a verb. Love is not only thinking and feeling but also *doing.*

© Eric Thompson / iStockphoto.com

A sign conveys one message: Go. Stop. This Way Out. A symbol conveys a web of meaning, often without words. Think of some symbols we often see and use that convey deep meaning.

Making Symbols, Doing Rituals

Because we have a need to act out our deepest thoughts and feelings, we are natural-born symbol-makers and ritual-doers. On Valentine's Day, saying "I love you" is not enough for us. We want to share something tangible like a card and flowers or a box of candy. When we meet someone, we use both words and gestures (a handshake or another kind of ritual) to show our friendliness. When we have finished a course of studies, we could just receive a certificate in the mail that says our studies are complete, but instead we have a graduation ceremony, complete with songs, speeches, invited guests, and a personal handing over of a beautifully printed diploma (probably with a handshake as well). Words are not always enough. We are human. We need action. We need symbols and rituals to act out what we really mean.

Symbols and Rituals Defined

Symbols and rituals are related, but they are not exactly the same thing. The word *symbol* comes from a Greek word meaning "to throw together." A symbol "throws together" the literal meaning of an object or action with other meanings that it evokes. For example, in the Sacrament of Baptism, water is water. It is a combination of hydrogen and oxygen. But it also evokes other meanings, like washing, cleansing, and purifying. Thus water becomes a symbol of something more than itself. The symbol of water invites us to look beyond the liquid to its deeper meanings.

A **ritual** is an established pattern of actions, usually including words. The words and actions have symbolic meaning, so "symbolic action" is another way to refer to a ritual. Rituals can be simple, like a handshake, or a wave, or the Sign of the Cross. They can also be more complex, such as the opening ceremonies of the Olympic Games or the inauguration of a president. Because the liturgy and the Sacraments involve symbols with words and actions, we call them *rituals*.

Sacraments, Symbols, and Rituals

Why are we symbol-makers and ritual-doers? Because God made us this way. When God communicates with us, he does not use words alone. And when we respond to him, we do not use words alone. One of God's best ways of communicating with us is through liturgical celebrations, especially the Sacraments. And our participation in the Sacraments is one of the best ways we can respond to him. ✝

symbol
An object or action that points us to another reality. It leads us to look beyond our senses to consider a deeper mystery.

ritual
The established form of the words and actions for a ceremony that is repeated often. The actions often have a symbolic meaning.

Catholic Wisdom

Julian of Norwich (1342—c. 1416) was an anchoress (a solitary nun) in England. Her teachings are simple but profound. Here is an example:

> For as the body is clad in the cloth, and the flesh in the skin, and the bones in the flesh, so are we, soul and body, clad and enclosed in the goodness of God. Yes, and more closely. . . . There is no created being who can know how much and how sweetly and how tenderly the Creator loves us." (*Julian of Norwich: Showings*, page 186)

Rituals in Our Lives

We have already discussed some symbols we use in our ordinary lives. Here are some other examples of symbol and ritual at work:

Happy Birthday! The ritual elements of a birthday celebration are almost unvarying: a birthday cake, candles, the singing of a song of good wishes. The eating of the cake (or variation thereof) is particularly important, because eating together is a symbol of sharing our lives. This symbol of sharing and solidarity is so meaningful that often pieces of cake are saved for those who cannot be present, or sent with others to bring to them. The message is: "You are one with us."

Walking rituals Some cultures and traditions, including our Catholic tradition, use walking as a ritual. Walking together is an expression of solidarity. It is a symbol of the journey of life and that we do not walk alone on this journey. Walking together is also meditative and prayerful. In a procession or a pilgrimage, there is a movement forward, but it is at a human pace, providing time for reflection and prayer along the way.

In our Catholic liturgy, we often use processions (walking together) to enter or leave our worship space, and to move around within it. For example, we may have a short procession before the reading of the Gospel and at the Presentation of the Gifts. We approach the receiving of Communion in procession. Processions have been a popular way for the community of faith to celebrate a feast or a saint and to pray together. Pilgrimages to holy places remain popular, though often the pilgrims ride in cars or on buses. The pilgrimage to the shrine of Saint James of Compostela, in Spain, has been famous since the ninth century. Serious pilgrims still make this journey across northern Spain on foot.

Article 7 Sacraments: Sign and Mystery

The Sacraments are signs of God's love. They are signs of his presence in our lives. They are rituals, instituted by Christ and handed down to us through Scripture and Tradition, by which God gives us his very life of grace. In order to appreciate their richness and to define the meaning of *Sacrament,* we need to define a few related terms.

© fstockfoto / Shutterstock.com

The first term is *sign.* In everyday language, *sign* has a definite and limited meaning. A red, eight-sided sign with the letters *S-T-O-P* written on it means "stop."

This command is its entire meaning. A sign pointing down a road to a nearby town says "To Riverdale." The sign gives you directions to Riverdale.

However, when we say that "a Sacrament is a sign of God's love," we mean that this sign, this Sacrament, is much more than a pointer or a command. The word *sign* in this instance means "symbol," a sign that points beyond itself, a sign that invites us to consider the deeper meaning present within it.

Explain the difference between this arrow as a sign and a Sacrament as a sign.

The words *sign* and *symbol* have shaped our understanding of the Sacraments for centuries. In the Gospel of John, the miracles of Jesus are called *signs,* not because they are commands or directions, but because they point to a deeper reality: that God is here among us. The Gospel account of the miracle at Cana, when Jesus turned water into wine, ends with, "Jesus did this as the beginning of his signs in Cana in Galilee and so revealed his glory, and his disciples began to believe in him" (John 2:11). Though the Sacraments are different from Jesus' miracles, they are signs because they call us to faith in a deeper reality: God is here among us. They are signs through which Christ acts sacramentally to bring about what they signify: They communicate to us the grace of Christ and bring us into deeper relationship with him.

Sacrament and Mystery

In the fifth century, when the New Testament was translated from its original Greek into the then-common language of Latin, the Greek word for *sign* was translated into *sacramentum.* It is from this word that we get our English word *Sacrament.* In the Eastern Catholic Churches, the Sacraments

How Do the Sacraments Work?

We have already seen that the Sacraments work because God—Father, Son, and Holy Spirit—is at work in them. Through the centuries, questions arose as to the validity of the Sacraments under various circumstances. Is it "better" to receive a Sacrament from a priest known to be holy? Are people really baptized or married if the priest is not as holy as he could be? What if the recipients are not known for their overall goodness—do the Sacraments still work for them? These kinds of questions were pondered by scholars and theologians until finally the Council of Trent, in 1547, declared that the Sacraments act *ex opere operato*—literally, "by the work worked," or, as the *Catechism of the Catholic Church* translates, "by the very fact of the action's being performed" (1128). In this the Council of Trent agreed with the statement of Saint Thomas Aquinas: "The sacrament is not wrought by the righteousness of either the celebrant or the recipient, but by the power of God" (*Summa Theologica* III, 68, 8).

None of us is in a position to judge another person's holiness or "righteousness" or closeness to God. The power of Christ and the Holy Spirit acts in the Sacraments independently of the personal holiness of the person administering the Sacrament. Grace can neither be seen nor quantified; each of the Sacraments works whether we feel it or not. However, the fruits (or effects) of the Sacrament do depend on the faith of the one who receives it.

At the words of consecration, bread and wine become the Body and Blood of Christ. This is the "mystery of faith" that we proclaim at every Eucharist.

© P Deliss / Godong / Corbis

are called mysteries. This puts focus on the Sacraments as the means by which we enter into the greatest mystery: the mystery of Christ. Through the Sacraments, or mysteries, we encounter Christ's life-giving presence in our lives.

The core of every Sacrament is the **Paschal Mystery** of Christ—his Passion, death, Resurrection, and Ascension into Heaven—and his promise to be with us always. (You may recall that *Paschal* refers to Passover, when the angel *passed over* the houses of the Israelites and spared their firstborn sons, and, centuries later, when Jesus, the Son of God, *passed over* from death to life, and spared us from eternal death.) The Paschal Mystery is most evident in the Eucharist, when we offer bread and wine and receive it back, by the words and actions of the priest and by the power of the Holy Spirit, as Christ's own Body and Blood, given up for us.

Yet in every Sacrament, we die with Christ by letting go of some of our "former selves" (the stubborn, sniping, or indifferent selves) and come to a new risen life with him by embracing in faith the life of grace and love he offers us. In every Sacrament, in every one of these signs of God's love, we enter into the mystery of Christ's death and Resurrection and then allow him to enter into our lives so that we may repeat this "trustworthy" saying of the early Christians:

> If we have died with him
>> we shall also live with him;
> if we persevere
>> we shall also reign with him.
>> (2 Timothy 2:11–12)

The Sacraments Are . . .

Understanding the meaning of *sign, symbol, sacrament,* and *mystery,* we can now approach the exact definition of a **Sacrament**:

> The sacraments are efficacious signs of grace, instituted by Christ and entrusted to the Church, by which divine life is dispensed to us. The visible rites by which the sacraments are celebrated signify and make present the graces proper to each sacrament. They bear fruit in those who receive them with the required dispositions. (*CCC,* 1131)

Let us break apart this definition. First, the Sacraments are *efficacious* signs. This means that they are *effective* and that they actually *work,* because Christ is at work in them. They are not empty words and gestures but words and ges- tures that carry with them the power of God.

The Sacraments are signs of *grace.* Grace is not a "thing" we get but a relationship with God that we are *in.* Grace is divine favor, the free and undeserved help that God gives us in order that we might become his adopted children and share his divine life.

The Sacraments were *instituted by Christ and entrusted to the Church.* The Sacraments originate in Christ. This does not mean that he dictated the particular words and gestures that are part of every Sacrament. But, as we look at Christ, we see him at work—healing, forgiving, giving of himself in the Eucharist. That work, by his will and power, has been entrusted to the Church in the Sacraments. Through the Sacraments, Christ works in his people today.

Paschal Mystery

The work of salvation accomplished by Jesus Christ mainly through his Passion, death, Resurrection, and Ascension.

Sacrament

An efficacious and visible sign of God's grace, instituted by Christ and entrusted to the Church, by which divine life is dispensed to us. The Seven Sacraments are Baptism, the Eucharist, Confirmation, Penance and Reconciliation, Anointing of the Sick, Matrimony, and Holy Orders.

sacramental economy

The communication or dispensation of the fruits of Christ's Paschal Mystery in the celebration of the Church's sacramental liturgy.

The visible rites (the symbols and rituals) by which the Sacraments are celebrated *signify (symbolize) and make present* the graces that belong to each Sacrament. We will take a closer look at the symbols and rituals as we study each individual Sacrament.

The Sacraments bear fruit in those who receive them with the *required dispositions.* A Sacrament gains us entry into the mystery of Christ, the life of grace and love. But we need to have the required disposition. That disposition is an attitude of faith. How much faith? Jesus said that faith the size of a mustard seed, the smallest of all seeds, is enough (see Luke 17:6). Jesus takes us as we are and brings us, with him, to where he wants us to be.

There are Seven Sacraments. The *Sacraments of Christian Initiation* are Baptism, Confirmation, and the Eucharist. The *Sacraments of Healing* are Penance and Reconciliation and Anointing of the Sick. The *Sacraments at the Service of Communion* are Holy Orders and Matrimony. ☩

Article 8 Sacraments: Signs of Christ

Did you ever think of Jesus Christ as a Sacrament? Jesus Christ, the Son of God, is the great sign of God's love for us and of how we are to love God. God sent his Son as the culmination of a long history of salvific events that have revealed his presence and actions. The sending of his Son into the world is his final Revelation and eternal intervention in human history. In "Eucharistic Prayer IV," this history (called *salvation history*) and its culmination in Jesus Christ is briefly outlined:

> We give you praise, Father most holy,
> for you are great
> and you have fashioned all your works
> in wisdom and love.
> You formed man in your own image . . .
> And when through disobedience he had lost your friendship,
> you did not abandon him to the domain of death. . . .
> And you so loved the world, Father most holy,
> that in the fullness of time
> you sent your Only Begotten Son to be our Savior.

> *(Roman Missal,* "Eucharistic Prayer IV*")*

In this article we review the meaning of this great gift of Jesus Christ and the ways he continues to save us today, especially through the Sacraments of the Church. For Jesus is the Father's final answer to our sin and suffering. When the Word became flesh and God became man, the world changed. Even those who kept the Old Law to the best of their ability would find new life in Jesus. As the Apostle John wrote: "While the law was given through Moses, grace and truth came through Jesus Christ. No one has ever seen God. The only Son, God, who is at the Father's side, has revealed him" (John 1:17–18). We sometimes call Jesus the Original Sacrament because he is the most basic way we encounter God and is the ultimate sign of God's love.

© Jon Perry/iStockphoto.com

In the Sacraments, we encounter the Risen Christ. Jesus enters our hearts and our lives, to heal us and to guide us. A Sacrament is a meeting with Jesus Christ himself.

The Sacramental Economy

Christ commissioned the Church to carry on his work, to carry on his very presence in the world, through the Sacraments. The Eucharist is the primary Sacrament through which Christ enters our lives, but all the Sacraments *signify and make present* the work of Christ in our lives, through grace. This is called the **sacramental economy**.

We are all familiar with the monetary system, the economy that runs on money. Through work (physical or intellectual), we make goods and services. We sell our goods and services to others. We get money, and then we spend our money on other goods and services that other people offer. This is how our economy works. We do not trade or barter. We receive and spend money as a substitute for trading and bartering. In this way we can provide ourselves and others with everything we need to live. Under ordinary circumstances, in order to eat, to clothe ourselves, to have shelter, to live, we must be in the flow of money. Without money, we are stuck. (It is said that money is a good servant but a terrible master.)

The sacramental economy runs on grace. Try to remember that grace is not a thing; rather, grace is a relationship with God and a participation in his life. So it is not *exactly*

sanctifying grace
The grace that heals our human nature wounded by sin and restores us to friendship with God by giving us a share in the divine life of the Trinity. It is a supernatural gift of God, infused into our souls by the Holy Spirit, that continues the work of making us holy.

actual graces
God's interventions and support for us in the everyday moments of our lives. Actual graces are important for conversion and for continuing growth in holiness.

like money. That being said, other comparisons work. In order to live, to share God's life, to participate in the mystery of Christ, we must be in the flow of grace. Without grace, without God's life, we are stuck.

Through the Sacrament of Baptism, we were adopted as God's sons and daughters, and we have been living "in grace" (as long as we have steered clear of mortal sin) since that moment. Grace has made us God's children and, in Christ, has brought us into the life of the Trinity.

What Is Grace?

Sanctifying grace is the free gift of God's life, first given to us at Baptism and renewed in us in all the Sacraments. Sanctifying grace orients us toward God. We might say it "tilts us" in his direction. It helps us to live according to his call. Through the Holy Spirit, sanctifying grace heals our souls of sin and makes us holy.

Sanctifying grace gives us a permanent disposition that enables us to live with God. This type of grace is distinct from *actual graces*, which are God's interventions in our lives. His initiative in the work of grace both prepares us to respond and demands that we respond, but it does not limit our freedom. Instead grace "responds to the deepest yearnings of human freedom, calls freedom to cooperate with it, and perfects freedom" (*CCC*, 2022).

Freedom

When we freely respond to and cooperate with God, we open ourselves to even more grace and more freedom. We sometimes imagine that sin will make us free or happy. "If I could only do *that*," we think, "I'd really feel good. I'd really be free and happy!" But this could not be further from the truth. True happiness and true freedom come from responding to grace.

For example, imagine you have a friend who struggles with math, but math comes fairly easily to you. You suggest that you could help. After only one tutoring session, your friend is beginning to get it and is so grateful for your help! You feel good. You feel happy. Whose idea was this to help your friend? God's. Who gave you "the gift of math" so that you *could* help your friend? God. Who helped you to say yes

Amazing Grace

The popular hymn "Amazing Grace" was written by an Englishman, a former sea captain and slave trader named John Newton (1725–1807). Newton wrote the song from personal experience. He was not a religious man, and his life was a series of misadventures. Eventually he became a sailor and then a slave trader. He was notorious for his profanity, his insubordination, his mockery of believers, and his denunciations of God. One night, a terrible storm battered his vessel. Exhausted, with the rest of the crew, from hours of bailing water, and expecting to be capsized, Newton called out, "Lord, have mercy upon us!" This was the beginning of his conversion. He began to think about his life and his relationship with God. A few years later, he quit the sea and began to study theology.

Ordained in the Church of England, Newton wrote the verses to "Amazing Grace" for a prayer meeting on New Year's Day in 1773. The song caught on in the United States, especially among African Americans. During the twentieth century, the song's popularity surged.

Here are the words of the first verse of the hymn:

> Amazing grace! How sweet the sound,
> That saved a wretch like me!
> I once was lost but now am found,
> Was blind, but now I see.

These words have been directly related to verses in the Parable of the Prodigal Son (see Luke 15:32) and in the healing of the man born blind (see John 9:25). For John Newton, as for all who are open to it, God's grace brings salvation and leads from darkness to light.

to the idea of helping? God. You responded to grace, and if you continue to respond to grace, you will freely choose to help your friends, and others, in the future.

Doorways to Life

Without this flow of God's life, grace, we are stuck. But we have hope because Christ founded the Church to be the ordinary channel of his grace, his life, for his followers. Christ wants to be accessible and available through the Church and the Sacraments, especially the Eucharist, in which he is really and substantially present. This was his plan of *salvation* for us. We need not be stuck in our sin. Through the Sacraments we were given a door, a way in, to the life of grace, the life of relationship with God. This life is what we are made for. It is only through God that we are able to live a fully human life and find true happiness.

The Church communicates the grace she signifies and so we can say that the Church is a sacrament. She is the sign and instrument of communion between God and human beings, and the means of bringing about that communion. Thus the Church in this world is the sacrament of salvation. All salvation comes from Christ through the Church.

The coming of Christ to live among us was not a one-time event. It is an all-time event that continues through the Church. Being a sacrament of the communion of human beings and God also means that the Church is the sign of unity among all people. As Jesus said, "This is how all will know that you are my disciples, if you have love for one another" (John 13:35). Jesus intended the Church, which includes all who are members of the Body of Christ, to be that sign of love. He intended the Sacraments to be those doorways to divine life, open to all people of all times and in all places. ☦

From the circle of Jesus and the Apostles, the Church has expanded to circle the world. Like a circle, it expands without losing its shape or its identity. It is the sacrament of God's love and salvation, welcoming all.

© Andresr / Shutterstock.com

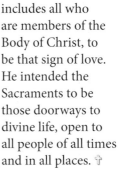

Article 9 Sacraments: Signs of Redemption

We do not often use the word *redeem* in ordinary life, but it has its moments. We *redeem* coupons at a store. We might say something like, "This old table was *redeemed* from the scrap heap," or "This afternoon I am going to the dry cleaner to *redeem* my shirts." What can we learn from these uses of the word *redeem*?

The Cross: Symbol of Redemption

In Roman times crucifixion was common. It was a cruel way of keeping order in the far-flung provinces of the Roman Empire. Basically, crucifixion was death by torture, a little at a time. It was a horrible way to die. Eventually, with the passage of time and with reflection upon the events of the Paschal Mystery, the cross, an instrument of death, became a sign of new life. Depictions of Jesus nailed to the cross, based on scriptural accounts, began to appear in Christian devotion and art.

This passage from the Gospel of John recounts that both blood and water flowed from the side of Christ as he died: "One soldier thrust his lance into his side, and immediately blood and water flowed out. An eyewitness has testified, and his testimony is true; he knows that he is speaking the truth, so that you also may [come to] believe" (19:34–35). The footnote in the New American Bible states that this emphasis may be John's way of showing the reality of Jesus' death, and that the blood and the water may be a symbolic reference to the Eucharist (blood) and Baptism (water).

What a graphic and beautiful way to show us that the Sacraments flow from the heart of Christ and that they put us in direct contact with his life and love!

redemption

From the Latin *redemptio,* meaning "a buying back"; referring, in the Old Testament, to Yahweh's deliverance of Israel and, in the New Testament, to Christ's deliverance of all Christians from the forces of sin.

Generally, we can say that *to redeem* something implies taking something from one state of being to another. A coupon is just another piece of paper until we *redeem* it and get some value in return. An old table is doomed until someone with a good eye *redeems* it and makes it useful and valuable again. Shirts will stay at the dry cleaner forever unless their owner comes and *redeems* them—gets them back to his closet, where they belong.

The word *redeem* comes from a Latin word meaning "to buy back" or "to purchase." Meanings for the word *redemption* include "deliverance" or "rescue." At the time of Jesus, this is exactly what the People of God were looking for. They were a conquered people, being ruled by the Romans. Their great faith in God, which had led them from slavery in Egypt to the Promised Land, was disintegrating, little by little, into a tissue of legalisms that were just as oppressive, in their own way, as the political oppression of the Romans. It was at this point in time that God chose to send his Son into the world as its rescuer, its deliverer, and its redeemer.

As Jesus himself said, he did not come to destroy the Old Law but to fulfill it. When people were tithing their harvests of herbs and spices to give one tenth to the Temple, as the Law directed, he did not object. He commended them. But he also warned them not to neglect the bigger things, like mercy and fidelity. Jesus accused the leaders of being blind guides who were straining out gnats but swallowing camels (see Matthew 23:23–24)!

The People of God at the time of Jesus definitely needed **redemption**. They needed to be brought back to the truth about God and about themselves. They needed to be brought back into a graced relationship with God and freed from the burden of the sin. So that was the mission of Jesus: to conquer sin and death, to redeem his People, to bring them back to God, in freedom and in truth.

So what about us? Are love and faithfulness gaining ground in our time, in our lives? Are we concentrating on the bigger things in our lives and in our world? Or are we straining out gnats and swallowing camels too? You may have heard the saying "Don't sweat the small stuff." Keep the bigger picture—what life is really about—in mind. How are you doing on that?

Fortunately for us, the teachings of Jesus and his work of redemption did not die in the tomb. His work of redemption reaches people of all times and all places.

The Paschal Mystery (the Passion, death, Resurrection, and Ascension of Jesus Christ) happened in history, but it transcends history because it never ends. When Christ rose from the dead, he destroyed death. He conquered sin. We could also say that he destroyed "time" as we know it because in his Resurrection he transcended time. Christ drew everything, including time, into his risen life.

In Christ, time became eternal. Christ is present in all time—the past, the present, and the future. He can meet us in our time, in the liturgy, especially in the Sacraments, because he lives forever in eternity. And that is not all. When we participate in the liturgy, we step into Christ's eternity. We share his eternal life. We are no longer time-bound to this day or this year. Our present and our future are safe with him, now and forever. We are brought back to God, in time and in eternity, where we belong. We are *redeemed*. ✝

Pray It!

The Jesus Prayer

The Jesus Prayer is an ancient way of praying that comes to us from the prayer practice of the Eastern Churches. The prayer itself is this: "Lord Jesus Christ, Son of the living God, have mercy on me, a sinner." The prayer honors the name of Jesus, asks his mercy, and reminds us that we must come before God in truth and in humility. We admit that we are not perfect human beings, but we want to try our best, and we trust that God forgives when we are sorry for our sins.

This prayer is rooted in the Gospels and echoes verses from three New Testament books: Philippians (2:6–11), Mark (10:46–52), and Luke (18:13). You might like to look up these verses and consider the Jesus Prayer in this wider Gospel context.

Take some time, perhaps once each day, to say the Jesus Prayer. You will be connecting with a long tradition of prayer, and you will be making room in your mind, your heart, and your life for Jesus Christ, Son of the living God.

Article 10 The Praying Church

Do you have a favorite place to pray? It need not be a physical place. It can be somewhere in your imagination. Take time to go there often.

If you have ever watched waves crash upon a beach and then recede, in a beautiful and mysterious rhythm, you have some idea of the reciprocal relationship of prayer. "Prayer unfolds throughout the whole history of salvation as a reciprocal call between God and man" (*CCC*, 2591). God is always calling each of us to this mysterious encounter with him. His call surges into our lives, sometimes like a wave's mighty crash or quiet ripple, and then recedes, giving us time and space to respond. When we do, prayer unfolds, in our lives and in the Church.

In this article we discuss the prayer of the Church, beginning with the official liturgical prayer of the Liturgy of the Hours. Then we explore both communal and private prayer, and the various forms that prayer may take in our lives. We end with the three major kinds of prayer: vocal prayer, meditation, and contemplation.

© Lynne Carpenter / Shutterstock.com

Liturgy of the Hours

Also known as the Divine Office, the official, public, daily prayer of the Catholic Church. The Divine Office provides standard prayers, Scripture readings, and reflections at regular hours throughout the day.

The Liturgy of the Hours

As we have learned, there is no greater prayer than the liturgy, the public prayer of the Church. In the liturgy we lift up our hearts to the Lord as we pray in the name of Jesus, in the power of the Holy Spirit. The Liturgy of the Hours, prayer designated for certain hours of the day, is part of the public prayer of the Church. The **Liturgy of the Hours** originated with the Jewish practice of meeting several times a day for prayer. The first Jewish Christians continued this practice as they met daily in the Temple (see Acts of the Apostles 2:46). This practice evolved into the basic structure of the Liturgy of the Hours we know today: an opening hymn, psalms, a reading from Scripture, the Lord's Prayer, and the prayer of the day from the liturgy.

The Liturgy of the Hours is the prayer of the whole people of God. It is prayed (or chanted in the ancient melodies of Gregorian chant) most completely by the contemplative orders of the Church. The ordained members of the Church are also obliged to pray the Liturgy of the Hours each day. Laypeople are also encouraged to pray on a regular basis and

to include at least the major hours (Morning and Evening Prayer) in their daily prayer. This is, of course, in addition to the celebration of the Sunday Eucharist and the feasts of the liturgical year. If there is a monastery or convent of monks or nuns near you, it would be worthwhile to visit them and pray with them. In the Liturgy of the Hours, the entire Church prays in the Holy Spirit and opens its heart to God.

Communal and Private Prayer

When we pray outside of liturgy, either alone or with others, our **prayer** is a small, quiet stream flowing into the great river of living waters, the liturgical prayer of the Church. When we raise our minds and hearts to God (see *CCC*, 2559), we do so as individuals, yet as members of Christ's Body. United with Christ in Baptism, we are heard as beloved children of God in Christ. United with others in prayer, we have been assured by Jesus himself that "where two or three are gathered together in my name, there am I in the midst of them" (Matthew 18:20). And when we pray alone, we are not really alone, because we are in communion with Christ and with the Church (see Ephesians 3:18–21).

Some ways we pray with others spring from particular cultures or local traditions. These expressions of faith are called "popular piety." *Piety* means religious reverence or devotion. These expressions are called "popular" because they are "of the people." They include customs like novenas (nine days of prayer) requesting the intercession of a saint; processions in honor of Our Lord, Our Lady, or particular saints; and the crowning of a statue of Our Lady during the month of May. Although these popular expressions of faith are not part of the official liturgy, the Church encourages them as long as they express the spirit of the Gospels and offer sound guidance in living a Christian life.

prayer
Lifting up of one's mind and heart to God or the requesting of good things from him. The five basic forms of prayer are blessing, praise, petition, thanksgiving, and intercession. In prayer we communicate with God in a relationship of love.

© François Guenet / Art Resource, NY

Thérèse was a young nun in a Carmelite monastery in France. After her death, her writings were circulated. Saint Thérèse (1873–1897), now recognized as a Doctor of the Church, taught "Do little things out of great love."

Prayer of the Heart

Since ancient times, Christians have practiced "the prayer of the heart." In the Semitic view, the heart is the center of the body. From the heart springs both good and evil *thinking*, as well as what we call feelings or emotions. Thus, according to the fathers and mothers of the desert (the first monks and nuns), if you can direct and control your thoughts, you can direct and control your heart, your desires, and your prayer.

In simplest terms, "the prayer of the heart" is repeating a phrase—a Scripture verse or a short prayer—over and over again, calmly and sincerely, until it becomes part of you. Some choose a different Scripture verse each day. Others may choose the Jesus Prayer: "Lord Jesus Christ, Son of the living God, have mercy on me, a sinner." Still others choose just one word: "God," "love," or "peace." This prayer becomes our foundation, something we fall back on amid the demands of our lives. For example, you can be listening in class or waiting in a checkout line or stopped at a stoplight, and your prayer word or phrase will come to mind. In this one simple word or phrase, God is reaching out to you and you are reaching out to him.

So try it. In your Scripture verse or prayer word, you will find that God is with you, every minute, every hour, every day of the week.

Personal prayer is a living relationship with God and is essential for a believer and a follower of Christ. No relationship can survive without communication, and that is what prayer is. It may not even need words. Sometimes deep thoughts and feelings are communicated in a glance, a gesture. It is the same with you and God. He knows you, loves you, and can read you like a book. Saint Thérèse of Lisieux, a young woman living an obscure life in a Carmelite monastery, described it this way: "For me, prayer is a surge of the heart; it is a simple look turned toward heaven, it is a cry of recognition and love, embracing both trial and joy."

Forms of Prayer

Through the inspiration of the Holy Spirit, various forms of prayer have arisen in the Church: blessing and adoration, petition, intercession, thanksgiving, and praise. The Holy Spirit continues to teach the Church, recalling all that Jesus has taught and helping her to pray, inspiring new expressions of these ancient forms.

In prayers of *blessing,* we bless God because he has first blessed us: "Blessed be the God and Father of Our Lord Jesus Christ, who has blessed us in Christ with every spiritual blessing in the heavens" (Ephesians 1:3). We *adore* God for his greatness, his power, and his holiness. We marvel at his creation, and wonder that he has made us as part of it. In prayers of *petition,* we pray for our needs, most especially our need for forgiveness. We also pray for the coming of the Kingdom, and for what we need to cooperate with the mission of Christ on earth. Through prayers of *intercession,* we pray for the needs of others. We ask on behalf of another, just as Jesus continually intercedes with the Father for us.

In prayers of *thanksgiving,* we acknowledge God as the Creator and thank him for his goodness. The Eucharist is our primary prayer of thanksgiving; from it flows thanksgiving for all of God's gifts, in every circumstance. Prayers of *praise* erupt in joy and express our love for God, recognizing above all that he is God. Praise "embraces the other forms of prayer" (*CCC,* 2639), for in it we acknowledge not only what God does but also Who he is—the source and goal of our lives, the One in whom "'we live and move and have our being'" (Acts of the Apostles 17:28).

Live It!

Desert Time

The earliest monks and nuns lived in the desert. They were following an inner call to seek God and to live the Gospel more closely. In your life, you too may need a "desert time" when you can seek God in prayer and reflection. Here are a few ideas:

1. Take a short time each day to read God's Word and to meditate on it. Look over the readings for the coming Sunday. Let the Word of God speak to you through them.
2. Use a short form of Morning or Evening Prayer from the Liturgy of the Hours, and pray with the Church.
3. Choose a Scripture verse for the day or the week.
4. Pray the Rosary.
5. Draw a peaceful scene. Mentally place yourself and Jesus within it. What is Jesus saying to you?
6. Start and keep a "prayer and life journal." Make up your own prayers.

Sacramentals

Sacramentals are sacred signs instituted by the Church rather than by Christ. They include blessings; actions, such as blessing ourselves with holy water while making the Sign of the Cross; and objects, such as blessed ashes or holy cards. Sacramentals occupy an important place in the life of the Church. They prepare us for the Sacraments and contribute to our holiness, our closeness to God, in varying circumstances of our lives.

Among all sacramentals, blessings come first. The Church blesses persons, meals, objects, and places. Every blessing includes praise of God for his works and gifts. Blessings also lift up the Church's intercessory prayer for us, that we may be able to use God's gifts in the spirit of the Gospel.

Because every baptized person is called both to be a "blessing" and to bless, the Church derives its power to bless from Baptism. In certain circumstances, laypeople can bless: Parents can bless their children, for example. When a blessing concerns Church and sacramental life, it is usually reserved for the ordained—bishops, priests, or deacons. Blessings of certain ministers in the Church, like lectors, altar servers, and catechists, are sacramentals.

Some blessings are consecrations to God, like the blessing of an abbot or an abbess or the rite of religious profession.

Some objects that can be blessed are familiar to us: a crucifix; rosary beads; palms; and holy cards with pictures of Jesus, Mary, or the saints. These objects are also sacramentals. We treat them with respect because they are part of our spiritual inheritance. They are not jewelry or magic. They have no power in themselves, but their power comes from the faith of the Church, which blesses them and offers them to us as helps and supports in our journey to God.

You might evaluate your relationship with God by thinking about these forms of prayer. Are you always petitioning for your needs and hardly ever praising or thanking? Do you bless God and praise him? Consider whether your relationship with God may benefit from a greater variety of prayer.

Three Expressions of Prayer

In the Christian tradition, three major expressions of the life of prayer have come down to us: vocal prayer, mental prayer and meditation, and contemplative prayer.

Vocal prayer uses words to speak to God. The words can be spoken aloud or silently, and we can pray them alone or in a group. Memorized prayers are one kind of vocal prayer. So are prayers you make up yourself. This kind of prayer is also sometimes called spontaneous prayer. You can always use your own words to tell God what you are thinking or feeling.

Meditation uses our thoughts, imagination, and emotions to get in touch with God. In meditation, we can use Scripture, the Rosary, pictures, or creation as ways to focus our minds and hearts on him.

Contemplation, sometimes defined as "resting in God," is a wordless prayer. It is another way of listening for God's movement in our lives. It is faith meeting his love in silence. By being silent and peaceful, we enter into union with God—Father, Son, and Holy Spirit.

We can be open to contemplation, but it is always a gift from God: Eye has not seen nor ear heard "what God has prepared for those who love him" (1 Corinthians 2:9). ✞

Part Review

1. How are a symbol and a ritual related?

2. What is a Sacrament?

3. What is the Paschal Mystery?

4. What do we mean by *sacramental economy?*

5. How do the Sacraments fulfill Christ's plan of redemption for us?

6. What is grace?

7. Explain the difference between sanctifying grace and actual grace.

8. Describe each of the three expressions of prayer: vocal prayer, meditation, and contemplation.

9. What is the Liturgy of the Hours?

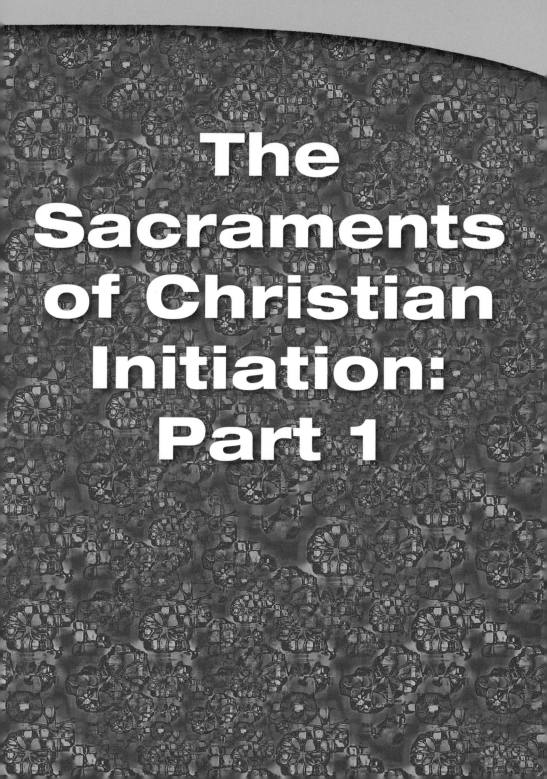

The Sacraments of Christian Initiation: Part 1

Part 1

Baptism

The Sacraments of Christian Initiation are the three Sacraments that initiate us into the life of Christ and the life of the Church: Baptism, Confirmation, and the Eucharist. These three Sacraments begin our lives as followers of Christ. In this section we explore the Sacraments of Baptism (part 1) and Confirmation (part 2). We discuss the Sacrament of the Eucharist, the "source and summit of the Christian life" (*Catechism of the Catholic Church [CCC],* 1324), separately in section 3.

This part's exploration of Baptism includes discussion of the Sacrament's scriptural roots and history and provides an overview of two rites the Church follows for Baptism: the Rite of Christian Initiation of Adults and the Rite of Baptism for Children. Along the way you will be encouraged to reflect on the meaning of Baptism in your own life: What does it mean to be baptized? to follow Jesus Christ? to belong to the Church?

The topics covered in this part are:

Article 11 Introduction to Baptism

The **Sacrament of Baptism**, the first Sacrament of Christian Initiation, is the basis of the entire Christian life. In Baptism we become members of Christ and of the Church, and we also become sharers in her mission to bring the Good News of Jesus Christ to the world.

The word *Baptism* comes from the Greek word *baptizein*, which means "to plunge." In Baptism we are plunged into the waters of death in order to rise to new life in Christ.

Baptism is also called "the bath of enlightenment," for through Baptism we are enlightened by the Word that is Christ and receive "the true light" (John 1:9) that enlightens every follower of Christ.

The next time you witness a Baptism, either in your own family or at a parish celebration, try to think about its meaning as plunging into death in order to rise into life, and as the bath of enlightenment.

> **Baptism, Sacrament of**
> The first of the Seven Sacraments and one of the three Sacraments of Christian Initiation (the others being Confirmation and the Eucharist) by which one becomes a member of the Church and a new creature in Christ.

© Khoroshunova Olga / Shutterstock.com

The Waters of Life: Creation

The Sacrament of Baptism finds its roots in the Old Testament, the Old Covenant with God, the Old Covenant that Jesus came "not to abolish but to fulfill" (Matthew 5:17). These roots begin in the Book of Genesis.

"Since the beginning of the world, water . . . has been the source of life" (*CCC*, 1218). At the beginning of creation, the Holy Spirit hovered over the waters, breathed on them, and brought life from them (see Genesis 1:1).

This is what the Church remembers at every Baptism: The Holy Spirit hovers over the possibility of every human life, and brings wonderful gifts to fruition in it. In Baptism a human being becomes a new creation in the Father, the Son, and the Holy Spirit.

The Great Flood

But water can be deadly. It is a fact that, among all the natural disasters possible in this world, human life is most frequently lost not through earthquakes, fires, or tornadoes, but through flooding. Again, we find in the Book of Genesis a

Consider your experiences with water, both positive and negative.

picture of that kind of flood. Human life had been overtaken by sin. In the account of Noah's ark, we are told that God was so disgusted with the human state of affairs that he wanted to start over. He wanted to save a remnant of his people and of his creation so that eventually all could be saved.

Noah's ark, and all the people and animals in it, survived the waters of the Flood. A dove (symbol of the Holy Spirit!) brought evidence that land (symbol of the Promised Land) was near. At every Baptism a human being is "buried" in water as a symbol of death and at the same time is brought through those same waters into new life, life in Jesus Christ and in his Church.

From Death to Life: The Exodus

The Israelites' passage through the Red Sea also gives us insight about Baptism. The People of God, with their leader Moses, were led from slavery to freedom, from certain death to new life, by passing through the waters of the Red Sea. At first Pharaoh agreed to let God's People leave peacefully, but then he changed his mind. He sent his chariots and charioteers to chase them down and bring them back. The Red Sea loomed ahead. They were caught! How would they cross? Moses lifted his rod, the waters parted in great walls to the left and to the right, and God's People marched through on dry land.

© Historical Picture Archive/CORBIS

The Church remembers all this at every Baptism. The waters of Baptism are the waters that part for *us*, so that we can be freed from sin and can continue our journey to the Promised Land of eternal life. The image of the Israelites' safe passage through the waters of death is an image of the freedom that is ours through Baptism.

At every Easter Vigil, the Israelites' passage through the Red Sea is proclaimed in the beautiful song of the Exsultet and in the third reading (Exodus 4:15—15:1). When you hear these proclamations, thank God for your Baptism.

The Waters of the Jordan

The River Jordan is a symbol of Baptism that leads us from the Old Testament to the New. In order to reach the Promised Land, God's People had one more river to cross: the Jordan River. When they did, they knew they were "home free." Centuries later, in the same River Jordan, John the Baptist offered a baptism of repentance to the people. He was offering them a chance to prepare themselves to recognize and follow the Messiah, the Anointed One, when he

Poor, Wayfaring Strangers

An old folk song illustrates one of the symbolic meanings of the River Jordan. The song goes like this:

> I'm just a poor, wayfaring stranger
> A-travelin' through this world of woe
> There is no sickness, no toil or danger
> In that fair land to which I go.

> I'm goin' home to see my mother
> I'm goin' home no more to roam
> I'm just a-goin' over Jordan
> I'm just a-goin' over home.

In the song, the wayfaring stranger is near death. He is going "over Jordan" to the Promised Land—that is, to Heaven. He is going to a land free from sickness, toil, and danger. He is going home.

But what if we see the River Jordan as a symbol of the waters of Baptism? Then going "over Jordan" would mean being baptized into Christ. The "fair land" is the Promised Land, here a symbol of the Church itself. In the Church, through the waters of Baptism, we poor, wayfaring strangers find our true home.

catechumen

An unbaptized person who is preparing for full initiation into the Catholic Church by engaging in formal study, reflection, and prayer.

should appear. Of course, we know that John was the first to recognize Jesus as this very Messiah. The writer of the Gospel of John, when recounting this important moment of recognition, notes carefully that "this happened in Bethany across the Jordan, where John was baptizing" (1:28). In this Messiah, in Jesus, is true freedom.

When the water is blessed for Baptism, these four great events of salvation history—creation, Noah's ark, the crossing of the Red Sea, and the crossing of the River Jordan—are commemorated. They prefigure the mystery of the Sacrament of Baptism. Because these events are part of the Church's memory and understanding of salvation, they illuminate our own understanding of what the Sacrament of Baptism does for us.

Fulfilled in Jesus Christ

All these events of salvation history are fulfilled in Jesus Christ. When Jesus was baptized in the waters of the River Jordan, the heavens opened. The Holy Spirit, who had hovered over the waters of creation, descended upon Jesus as "the firstborn among many" (Romans 8:29) and the beloved Son of the Father (see Mark 1:11). On the night before he died, Jesus celebrated the Passover, the passing over of the Jews from slavery into freedom. He spoke of his Passion as a "baptism" with which he was to be baptized (see Mark 10:38, Luke 12:50). When Jesus died and was raised from the dead, he passed from death to life and brought us out of the slavery of sin into the "glorious freedom of the children of God" (Romans 8:21). Jesus, then, is the true Ark in which we have been saved.

When the Jewish leader Nicodemus came to Jesus by night, Jesus told him, "No one can enter the kingdom of God without being born of water and Spirit" (John 3:5). After his Resurrection, Jesus entrusted this mission of baptizing all nations to his Apostles (see Matthew 28:12). In the Acts of the Apostles, we find that Peter is following Jesus' instructions, for in Peter's address to the crowd immediately after Pentecost, he tells them, "Repent and be baptized, every one of you, in the name of Jesus Christ for the forgiveness of your sins; and you will receive the gift of the holy Spirit" (Acts 2:38). The same promise holds true for us today. ☩

Article 12 Christian Initiation in the Early Centuries

© LE SEGRETAIN / CORBIS SYGMA

It is the third century in Rome. It is the night before Easter Sunday. It is early evening, just before dark. You are gathered with other men and women, some old, some young like yourself, near a gurgling stream that feeds into the Tiber River. You are a **catechumen**. You have been learning the Christian faith and living, as best you can, as a follower of Jesus for the past three years. Now, tonight, you will be baptized. Your catechist is here, and your sponsor (your companion in the faith, who offered your name as a candidate) is by your side. The priest is standing up to his knees in the waters, with the deacon at his side ready to help him and the catechumens during the ritual.

In Baptism, we are called from darkness into light. How can you, in Christ, be light for the world?

The men stand in one group, the women in the other. One by one, you are called by name. You strip off your robe and walk into the waters. You are immersed three times, in the name of the Father, and of the Son, and of the Holy Spirit. You come up dripping. You are anointed with Sacred Chrism, wrapped in a towel, dried off, and then given a new white garment. It is dark now, and a glowing candle is thrust into your hands as you and the others begin to walk toward the assembly. They have been gathered for some time, listening to the readings from the prophets and from the Apostles. They are waiting for you to join them, for the first time, in the Prayers of the Faithful.

The bishop greets you at the door, seals you in the Holy Spirit with the seal of Sacred Chrism, and leads you into the assembly. As the prayers begin, you realize that you can now pray with your brothers and sisters; no one has dismissed you, and soon you will receive the Eucharist, the Body and Blood of Christ. For this is the night of celebration of the Resurrection of Jesus Christ. This is the night of new life and new beginning. "Yes," you say to yourself, "this is the night of my resurrection too, my resurrection in Christ and my new beginning in him. Alleluia!"

Three Special Sacraments

The previous vignette presented a rough approximation of the receiving of a catechumen into the Church in the early centuries. In this vignette we can recognize the **Sacraments of Christian Initiation**: Baptism, Confirmation, and the Eucharist. These three Sacraments have been linked from the very beginning. Receiving all three of them at the Easter Vigil or at the Vigil of Pentecost was the usual way of becoming a Christian in the early Church.

The Sacraments of Christian Initiation involved much preparation. The vignette told us that this catechumen had been studying and learning for three years! The early Christians realized that change is not easy, and that a com-

The Baptism of Christ

Even though, as the Son of God, Jesus had no need to repent, he asked to be baptized. He wanted to show his solidarity with us. It was at this event that the Father's voice was heard, saying, "This is my beloved Son, with whom I am well pleased" (Matthew 3:17). At this baptism the Father acclaimed his Son. At our own Baptism, we are adopted as the Father's sons and daughters in Christ.

© Hisham Ibrahim/Corbis

At Jesus' baptism the Holy Spirit appeared in the form of a dove. The presence of the Holy Spirit prefigures the presence of the Holy Spirit at the Baptisms of the followers of Christ that were to come. John the Baptist himself compared his baptism with the Baptism to be brought about by Jesus: "The one who sent me to baptize with water told me, 'On whomever you see the Spirit come down and remain, he is the one who will baptize with the holy Spirit'" (John 1:33).

Did John realize that when he baptized Jesus, the heavens would open to reveal the presence of the Holy Trinity? Probably not. But ever since, whenever someone is baptized in the name of the Father, and of the Son, and of the Holy Spirit, the "heavens are opened" and the Holy Trinity is present.

mitment to a way of life requiring love, forgiveness, and service to others took time. This "learning" was not simply hearing information about Jesus and the truths of the faith; it involved active learning and practicing a new way of life in the midst of the Christian community—the Christian way of life. During the process of preparing, the catechumen was supported by the liturgy and by the personal involvement of the community and was provided with **catechesis**, or oral instruction, aimed at education and formation in the Christian life. ♱

Christian Initiation, Sacraments of
The three Sacraments—Baptism, Confirmation, and the Eucharist—through which we enter into full membership in the Church.

catechesis, catechists
Catechesis is the process by which Christians of all ages are taught the essentials of Christian doctrine and are formed as disciples of Christ. Catechists are the ministers of catechesis.

Article 13 The Rite of Christian Initiation of Adults I

Aspects of the catechumenal process followed in the early centuries of the Church eventually fell away as circumstances changed and Baptism was more commonly administered in infancy. However, throughout the centuries, the process of becoming a fully initiated member of the Church has always involved the following essential elements: the proclamation of the Word, acceptance of the Gospel and conversion to a new way of life, the profession of faith, Baptism, the outpouring of the Holy Spirit, and reception of the Eucharist (see *CCC*, 1229).

Rite of Christian Initiation of Adults
The process by which an unbaptized person, called a "catechumen," and those who were baptized in another Christian denomination, called "candidates for full communion," are prepared to become full members of the Church.

Today, as always, Baptism is the first Sacrament of Christian Initiation. We use two different but closely related rites when celebrating this Sacrament. We celebrate the Rite of Baptism for Children when baptizing children who have not reached the age of reason (seven years). Those baptized as young children usually complete their initiation (with the Sacraments of Confirmation and the Eucharist) later in childhood or during their teen years. When baptizing older children (seven and older) and adults, we celebrate the **Rite of Christian Initiation of Adults (RCIA)**. Those celebrating according to the RCIA are fully initiated during the same liturgy of their Baptism. Those adults who have already been baptized in another Christian faith community, as well as adult Catholics who have been baptized but never practiced their faith, participate in the RCIA but are not rebaptized. They are called candidates, and they prepare to receive the remaining two Sacraments of Christian Initiation, Confirmation and the Eucharist.

In articles 13–15, "The Rite of Christian Initiation of Adults I," "The Rite of Christian Initiation of Adults II," and "The Rite of Christian Initiation of Adults III," we explore the RCIA. In article 16, "The Rite of Baptism for Children," we look at the Rite of Baptism for Children. We devote three articles to the RCIA because, in its various elements, it outlines the essence of Christian discipleship. In these articles we focus on the rite primarily as it applies to those who are unbaptized.

The Restoration of the Catechumenate

The Second Vatican Council's *Constitution on the Sacred Liturgy* (*Sacrosanctum Concilium,* 1963) called for the restoration of the catechumenate, the process of initiation known and practiced in the early Church (see 64). This beautiful communal process was recovered and reestablished as the normative process for an adult (or a child who has reached the age of reason) to become a Catholic. In 1972 the *Rite of Christian Initiation of Adults (RCIA)* was published.

The Stages of the Rite of Christian Initiation of Adults

An unbaptized person who is thinking of becoming a Catholic has a wonderful and life-changing journey ahead. But it is not a journey that he or she will take alone. The Rite of Christian Initiation of Adults involves a journey within community. Certainly there will be times of solitary decision and individual reflection, but the process is in itself an introduction to life within the Church. The process involves the local parish and also the local diocese. As we examine the process, we will see how an individual person is welcomed, catechized, chosen (or "elected") for Baptism, and then admitted to the Sacraments of Baptism, Confirmation, and the Eucharist—all in the midst of, and with the help and support of, the local Church.

The process is structured to include seven stages—four distinct periods of time and three steps, as follows:

- Period of Inquiry (Period of Evangelization and Precatechumenate)
- First Step: Rite of Acceptance into the Order of Catechumens

Candidates for the Sacraments

The Rite of Christian Initiation of Adults is first of all intended for catechumens, those who have not been baptized. Those who have already been baptized do not participate in the baptismal rites of the RCIA, as they are already members of the community of the faith. The Rite of Christian Initiation of Adults can be adapted to those who have already been baptized but have not practiced the Christian faith. For example, if a person was baptized in a Protestant church, she or he would not be baptized again but would be a candidate for the Sacraments of Confirmation and the Eucharist. Someone who was baptized in the Catholic Church but never practiced the faith would not be baptized again but would also be a candidate for the Sacraments of Confirmation and the Eucharist. A Catholic who was never confirmed may also, in some instances, join the catechumens and other candidates in formation sessions while preparing for Confirmation.

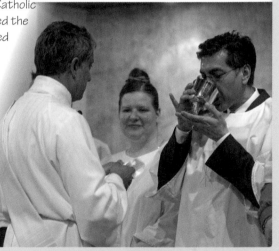

© Bill Wittman / www.wpwittman.com

- Period of the Catechumenate
- Second Step: Rite of Election or Enrollment of Names
- Period of Purification and Enlightenment
- Third Step: Celebration of the Sacraments of Initiation
- Period of Postbaptismal Catechesis or Mystagogy

You will notice that each step is preceded by a time, or period, of preparation. In this article and the next two, we discuss each period and step in detail.

evangelization

The proclamation of the Good News of Jesus Christ through word and witness.

Period of Inquiry

A person interested in being baptized in the Catholic Church begins by becoming an "inquirer." The official name for this time of inquiry is the period of **evangelization** and precatechumenate. *Evangelization* means "the proclamation of the Gospel of Jesus through word and witness." During this time the inquirer listens to the Good News, learns about the Catholic faith, and discerns a call to live the Gospel life as a Catholic. This process of evangelization unfolds through meetings with priests, deacons, the religious education or catechumenate director, catechists, and often other inquirers and parishioners. The duration of this inquiry time is flexible.

First Step: Acceptance into the Order of Catechumens

The Rite of Acceptance into the Order of Catechumens follows the period of the precatechumenate. In this rite the

© Bill Wittman / www.wpwittman.com

The priest welcomes the candidate with the Sign of the Cross marked on the forehead. From the beginning, the cross of Christ, the doorway to true and eternal life, is the sign of faith and the mark of the Christian.

inquirers publicly declare their intention to follow Christ and are accepted as catechumens. The celebrant greets them (preferably at the door of the Church) and asks:

> "What is your name?"
> The candidate gives his or her name.
> "What do you ask of God's Church?"
> The candidate answers: "Faith."
> Celebrant: "What does faith offer you?"
> Candidate: "Eternal life."
>
> (*RCIA*, 50)

The faith required for Baptism is a "beginning" faith, a faith that will develop within the community of believers, the Church. Sponsors must be ready to help the new believers on the road of Christian life, and the entire Church community is responsible to some extent for the development of the gift of faith given at Baptism.

The celebrant tells the candidates that because they have followed God's light, the way of the Gospel lies open before them. He encourages them to continue to walk in the light of Christ and to commit their lives each day to his care. The celebrant then asks the candidates if they are prepared to begin their journey. When they answer that they are, the celebrant asks the sponsors and the community if they are ready to "help these candidates find and follow Christ" (*RCIA,* 53). The assembly answers: "We are" (53).

The celebrant then signs the foreheads of the candidates with the Sign of the Cross. The celebrant may also sign other parts of the body (ears, eyes, lips, and so on). Then the candidate's sponsor does the same. The celebrant then prays a concluding prayer, asking for grace, protection, and perseverance for those who have been accepted into the order of catechumens.

The Rite of Acceptance always includes the Liturgy of the Word and often takes place during the Eucharist. Here, for the first time, the catechumens have assembled together and, in most cases, will be dismissed together after the homily.

Period of the Catechumenate

The catechumenate is a time of formation. During this time the catechumens are gradually introduced to the Catholic faith. They are also guided in the Christian way of living in love for God and neighbor and in gratitude for Christ's salvation. Catechumenal formation is carried out in these ways:

1. **Catechesis** Catechesis, gradual and complete, aims not only to help the catechumens understand the Church's teaching but also to introduce them to the mystery of Christ. This catechesis is generally coordinated with the liturgical year and incorporates celebrations of the Liturgy of the Word (see *RCIA,* 75, 1).

© Bill Wittman / www.wpwittman.com

A catechetical session is led by an experienced person of faith who can help the catechumens to integrate knowledge of Christ and the Church with a new way of thinking, loving, and living.

Rite of Election
The Rite, which takes place on the first Sunday of Lent, by which the Church elects or accepts the catechumens for the Sacraments of Christian Initiation at the Easter Vigil. The Rite of Election begins a period of purification and enlightenment.

elect
The title given to catechumens after the Rite of Election while they are in the final period of preparation for the Sacraments of Christian Initiation.

2. **Spiritual development** The spiritual life of the catechumens deepens through their participation in the life of the community. Gradually, their views and actions reflect more and more the Christian way of life. They learn to pray, to witness to the Gospel through words and actions, and to live rooted in the hope that Christ makes possible (see *RCIA*, 75, 2).

3. **Liturgy** The catechumens are supported by liturgical rites, especially celebrations of the Word, during Sunday Mass with the community and at other times when celebrations of the Word are planned for the catechumens, as well as blessings and anointings (see *RCIA*, 75, 3).

4. **Apostolic witness** The catechumens learn to work with others to share the Gospel and to build up the Church through the witness of their actions and their profession of faith (see *RCIA*, 75, 4).

We noted that the catechumen baptized in the early Church in Rome spent three years preparing for initiation. Today the duration of the catechumenate varies according to the faith development of the individual catechumen.

Catechumens are considered "part of the household of Christ" (*RCIA*, 47). Although not yet baptized, a catechumen who dies during the catechumenate is given a Christian burial. ✝

Article 14 The Rite of Christian Initiation of Adults II

The next step in the Rite of Christian Initiation of Adults is the **Rite of Election** or Enrollment of Names. The word *election* implies a choice. The Church has *elected* to accept the catechumens for the Sacraments of Christian Initiation. They are no longer called catechumens. They are given a new title: the **elect**.

Second Step: The Rite of Election or Enrollment of Names

The Rite of Election is usually held on the First Sunday of Lent. It is the bishop of the diocese, or his delegate, who admits the candidates to the Rite of Election and to the

Godparents

Sometime before the Rite of Election, those preparing for Baptism choose godparents. A godparent must be a practicing Catholic, over the age of eighteen, who can support this particular person in his or her faith journey—formally from the Rite of Election through reception into the Church and beyond. It is the responsibility of the godparent "to show the candidates how to practice the Gospel in personal and social life, to sustain the candidates in moments of hesitancy and anxiety, to bear witness, and to guide the candidates' progress in the baptismal life" (RCIA, 11). Godparents are chosen

for their good qualities, their example, and their friendship. This choice is made with the consent of the pastor or priest, and sometimes with the consultation of the catechists.

Sacraments. The rite takes place at the cathedral; however, in dioceses that cover vast distances, regional groupings of parishes often celebrate the Rite of Election together at a centrally located parish church.

Called and Chosen

The Rite of Election begins after the homily when the catechumens are presented. The godparents are asked to affirm that the catechumens are worthy and prepared to be admitted to the ranks of the elect and to look forward to receiving the Sacraments of Baptism, Confirmation, and the Eucharist at Easter.

The catechumens are asked if they wish to enter fully into the life of the Church through the Sacraments of Bap-

© Bill Wittman / www.wpwittman.com

A godparent takes on a special responsibility, beginning with the Rite of Election. They "stand up" or vouch for a catechumen's readiness for the Sacraments. Godparents are a living example of the Christian life.

tism, Confirmation, and the Eucharist. After they respond, "We do," they are asked to offer their names for enrollment (see *RCIA*, 132). As one option, they may inscribe their names, usually in a special book. After all have offered their names, the act of admission or election takes place. The bishop turns to the candidates and says:

> "I now declare you to be members of the elect, to be initiated into the sacred mysteries at the next Easter Vigil."
> The candidates respond, "Thanks be to God."
>
> (*RCIA*, 133)

After the act of election, the liturgy continues with intercessions for the elect. Then the bishop, with outstretched hands, prays a prayer over the elect, that they may be helped and strengthened in the coming days. After this, if the Eucharist is being celebrated, the elect are dismissed.

Period of Purification and Enlightenment

The Rite of Election begins a period of what the Church calls purification and enlightenment. This time is intended to purify and enlighten the minds and hearts of the elect. This

Live It!

Questions of Faith

In the Rite of Election, the godparents are asked to attest to the candidates' readiness for the Sacraments by answering the following questions:

- Have they faithfully listened to God's Word proclaimed by the Church?
- Have they responded to that Word and begun to walk in God's presence?
- Have they shared the company of their Christian brothers and sisters and joined with them in prayer?

These questions set out the basics of the Christian life: listening to God's Word, responding to that Word, and joining in Christian community with others. Those of us who have long been members of the Church may find these questions to be valuable guidelines on our journey with Christ. We might ask ourselves how well we have listened and responded to the Word of God this week, and how regularly we seek to pray with the members of our community of faith through liturgical prayer and devotions.

involves examination of conscience and doing penance as well as deepening one's knowledge of, and relationship with, Jesus Christ. The period customarily coincides with the season of Lent, which is a time of purification and enlightenment for the whole Church. The elect participate in reflection that helps them to prepare for Baptism while the others in the community reflect on the meaning of their Baptism.

During a scrutiny, the elect kneel while the priest, with hands outstretched, prays that the power of the Holy Spirit may come upon them. Godparents show support by placing their hands on the shoulders of the elect.

Scrutinies

During this period, the elect participate in three **scrutinies**, liturgical rites celebrated on the third, fourth, and fifth Sundays of Lent. These rites aid in self-examination and repentance, and have the spiritual purpose of healing any weakness or sin. These rites also strengthen what is good, and help the elect to "hold fast to Christ" (*RCIA*, 141).

The scrutiny takes place after the homily. As the elect stand with bowed heads or kneel, the assembly prays several petitions directly for them as they prepare to receive the Sacraments at Easter.

This is followed by an exorcism, a prayer that the elect may acknowledge their weaknesses and put their trust in God. If it can be done easily, the celebrant lays hands on each of the elect. Then, with hands outstretched over all of the elect, he prays that their hearts may be touched by the Holy Spirit. The laying on of hands and the outstretched hands of the celebrant are both signs of the presence of the Holy Spirit, who is called upon to purify the hearts of the elect and to prepare them for all the graces God is preparing for

scrutinies
Rites within the Rite of Christian Initiation of Adults that support and strengthen the elect through prayers of intercession and exorcism.

them. After the Liturgy of the Word, the elect are dismissed as usual.

The Creed and the Lord's Prayer

The period of purification and enlightenment also includes two presentations—the Apostles' Creed or the Nicene Creed, and the Lord's Prayer. The presentations take place on weekdays during the third week of Lent (Creed), and the fifth week of Lent (Lord's Prayer).

Ideally, the key elements of the Christian faith are not presented on paper. Instead, in each instance, the elect are asked to stand and *listen* as the Creed and the Our Father are recited for them. This represents the personal, spoken handing on of the faith. This kind of learning explains Saint Paul's words that we receive the Spirit from faith in what we hear (see Galatians 3:2). In handing over the Creed and the Lord's Prayer to the elect, the Church asks the elect not only to learn them by heart but to *live* them by heart. ✝

The Paschal Candle is a symbol of the Risen Christ, who overcomes all darkness, sin, and death. It remains lit for the entire Easter Season. It is also lit at Baptisms and at funerals, as a sign of new life in Christ.

Article 15 The Rite of Christian Initiation of Adults III

As the end of Lent nears, the elect, with the entire Church, are focused on the saving events of Holy Week and the Paschal Mystery of Jesus Christ, the mystery into which they will soon be immersed through the Sacraments of Baptism, Confirmation, and the Eucharist. For the elect, Holy Saturday is a special day of preparation, and they are urged to use it as a day of reflection in preparation for the Easter Vigil, when they will celebrate the Sacraments of Christian Initiation.

Third Step: Celebration of the Sacraments of Christian Initiation

Imagine this: It is the Easter Vigil. We are gathered in assembly, with the elect in our midst. The new fire has been lit. The Church is dark. Out of the darkness, a voice sings out, "Light of Christ!" We respond, "Thanks be to God!" We turn and see a flame marching slowly toward us, a flame at the top of a tall white candle. As smaller candles are lit from this flame, light slowly overcomes the darkness. Now it is your turn to light your small candle, and to pass it on.

The tall candle (the **Paschal candle**, the symbol of the Risen Christ in our midst) has reached the front of the church. All eyes are upon it as the deacon sings these ancient words excerpted from the Exsultet (named after its first word, *Exult!* or *Rejoice!*):

> These, then, are the feasts of Passover,
> > in which is slain the Lamb, the one true Lamb,
> > whose Blood anoints the doorposts of believers.
>
> This is the night,
> > when once you led our forebears, Israel's children,
> > from slavery in Egypt
> > and made them pass dry-shod through the Red Sea.
>
> This is the night
> > that with a pillar of fire
> > banished the darkness of sin.
>
> This is the night
> > that even now, throughout the world,
> > sets Christian believers apart from worldly vices
> > and from the gloom of sin,

Paschal candle
Also called the Easter candle, this is the large, tall candle lit at the Easter Vigil by a flame from the new fire; the symbol of the Risen Christ. It is lit in the sanctuary for Masses during the Easter season, and during the year is kept near the baptismal font. It is lit at Baptisms and at funeral services throughout the year as a sign of the presence of the Risen Christ among us.

Pray It!

Rejoice! Sing! Exult!

In the hustle and bustle of our lives, we tend to forget about Easter and its significance for our lives throughout the entire year. The Exsultet will help us to remember. Here is a short passage from that beautiful proclamation to help us remember that we are living risen lives with Jesus:

> Exult, let them exult, the hosts of heaven
> exult, let Angel ministers of God exult,
> let the trumpet of salvation
> sound aloud our mighty King's triumph!
>
> Be glad, let earth be glad, as glory floods her,
> ablaze with light from her eternal King,
> let all corners of the earth be glad,
> knowing an end to gloom and darkness.
>   (Roman Missal)

As you pray, may glory fill you, and may gloom and darkness come to an end!

leading them to grace
and joining them to his holy ones.

(Roman Missal)

Easter

The day on which Christians celebrate Jesus' Resurrection from the dead; considered the most holy of all days and the climax of the Church's liturgical year.

The Exsultet sets the context for the entire Easter Vigil. It prepares us for the Liturgy of the Word, which reacquaints us with the history of our salvation. It reminds us that this night is our passover feast, and, in a special way, is the passover feast of the elect, when they will pass through the waters of Baptism, will be washed clean of sin, and, with Christians everywhere, will be restored to grace and holiness. In Baptism, Confirmation, and the Eucharist, Christ will rise in them and will bring them "out of darkness into his wonderful light" (1 Peter 2:9). For all these reasons, the **Easter** Vigil is the most appropriate time for the Celebration of the Sacraments of Christian Initiation.

Baptism

As the elect come forward for Baptism, we pray for them in the Litany of the Saints. The water is then blessed. The blessing recalls the meaning of water as God's creation and its use in the Sacraments. It also recalls the wonderful works of God throughout the history of our salvation (see *RCIA*, 210). Near the end of the blessing, the Paschal candle is lowered into the water (either once or three times) as a sign that it is Christ himself who gives life and power to the waters of Baptism.

The water of Baptism is a sign of new life. Water can be poured three times over the head, or the entire body can be immersed three times in a pool of water.

© Bill Wittman / www.wpwittman.com

The Place of Baptism

The location for Baptism changed and developed through the centuries. At first the place of Baptism was a nearby river or stream with running waters. Later, as Roman bathing customs (anointing with oil, new clean clothing) began to be incorporated into the rite, the place of Baptism was moved to a baptistery, a building near the church in which a large pool or tub was installed. Eventually, when infant Baptisms became the norm, a smaller vessel or font replaced the larger pool. The baptistery was moved to a room to the side of the narthex (lobby) of the church. When the catechumenate was restored after Vatican Council II, Baptism by immersion became an option. Some newer churches are being built with baptisteries that include pools. In most parishes a temporary pool is installed for the Easter Vigil and remains a focus and reminder of new life during the Easter season.

The profession of faith, in the form of the baptismal promises, follows. The elect promise to reject sin and profess their belief in God the Father, God the Son, and God the Holy Spirit.

Then the elect come forward, one by one, to be buried with Christ in Baptism and to rise with him to new life. The celebrant may baptize the candidate either by immersion three times or by the pouring of water over the head three times, saying the following:

mystagogy
A period of catechesis following the reception of the Sacraments of Christian Initiation that aims to more fully initiate people into the mystery of Christ.

(Name), I baptize you in the name of the Father,
(The celebrant immerses or pours water the first time.)
and of the Son,
(The celebrant immerses or pours water the second time.)
and of the Holy Spirit.
(The celebrant immerses or pours water the third time.)
(*RCIA*, 226)

Saying these words and pouring the water, or immersing in water, are the essential elements of the Sacrament of Baptism.

White Garment Immediately after Baptism, the new Christian is given a new white garment. New life, new clothes! We all know the wonderful feeling of hopping out of the shower or bathtub and putting on fresh, clean clothing. For the new Christians, given a new white garment, it is the same thing, only multiplied eternal times. This garment symbolizes that the newly baptized have clothed themselves in Christ.

Lighted Candle The godparents of the newly baptized are called forward. They are given a candle, which they light from the Paschal candle and present to the newly baptized, who are urged to "keep the flame of faith alive in your hearts" (*RCIA*, 230).

Confirmation

In the absence of the bishop, the same priest who baptized the candidates is authorized to confirm the newly baptized. The Holy Spirit will strengthen them to be active members of the Church "and to build up the Body of Christ in faith and love" (*RCIA*, 233). (We discuss the meaning of the Sacrament of Confirmation in detail in part 2 of this section.)

After the Sacrament of Confirmation, the priest then leads the entire assembly in renewing their baptismal promises. After renouncing sin and affirming belief in God, the assembly is sprinkled with the newly blessed baptismal water. At Easter we are all new again. We all share in the wonderful gifts of Baptism and Confirmation.

And now we prepare for the Sacrament of the Eucharist, when the new Catholics in our midst (both those who have just been baptized and confirmed, and those who made a profession of faith and received Confirmation) will receive

Holy Oils for Anointing

Three different oils are used in the Church's liturgies. The *Oil of Catechumens* is blessed olive oil used to anoint those preparing for Baptism. This oil is a symbol of the candidates' need for God's help and strength to renounce sin as they prepare for Baptism. The *Sacred Chrism* is perfumed olive oil that has been consecrated by a bishop. It is a sign of the sweet fragrance of Christ and the good works of his Body, the Church. It is used in the Sacraments of Baptism, Confirmation, and Holy Orders. Sacred Chrism is also used to anoint and dedicate a new altar or church (or a newly renovated church) to the service of God. The *Oil of the Sick* is blessed olive oil used in the Sacrament of Anointing of the Sick. This oil strengthens those who are sick and prepares for death those who are dying. These holy oils are kept in the baptismal area of the church, in a small cabinet or niche in the wall called the ambry. Look for it the next time you are in church!

the Body and Blood of Christ for the first time. Thus their Christian initiation will be complete.

The Eucharist

The Liturgy of the Eucharist continues as usual. Before saying, "Behold the Lamb of God," the celebrant may have a few words to say to the newly baptized and confirmed. He may remind them that the Eucharist will complete their Christian initiation and that with Jesus in the Eucharist, they will continue their journey "from here to eternity."

Period of Postbaptismal Catechesis or Mystagogy

Mysta-what? Mystagogy! This is a Greek word meaning "study of the mysteries." Another term for this RCIA period is *Period of Postbaptismal Catechesis*—that is, catechesis after Baptism.

After the Easter Vigil, the newly initiated Catholics are called by the Greek term *neophytes,* meaning "beginners." The time of **mystagogy** is "a time for the community and the neophytes together to grow in deepening their grasp of the

Original Sin

From the Latin *origo*, meaning "beginning" or "birth." The term has two meanings: (1) the sin of the first human beings, who disobeyed God's command by choosing to follow their own will and thus lost their original holiness and became subject to death, (2) the fallen state of human nature that affects every person born into the world.

paschal mystery and in making it part of their lives through meditation on the Gospel, sharing in the eucharist, and doing the works of charity" (*RCIA*, 244). The neophytes' godparents, pastors, catechist, and entire parish community help them to do this.

During this time the neophytes are helped to reflect on their recent Celebration of the Sacraments of Christian Initiation and on their being incorporated into Christ and into the Church. Through this reflection and new understanding, they are able to perceive the faith more fully, and their vision of the Church and the world is renewed and expanded.

An appropriate celebration close to Pentecost Sunday, marking the end of the Easter season and the immediate postbaptismal catechesis, might be held for the neophytes. In some parishes, neophytes continue to gather monthly during the year for continued support and guidance in their new lives as Catholics.

We have completed our study of the Sacraments of Christian Initiation as they are prepared for and celebrated in the Rite of Christian Initiation of Adults. In the next part, we continue our study of Christian initiation as celebrated in the Rite of Baptism for Children and in the Sacrament of Confirmation. In section 3 we explore the Sacrament that completes Christian Initiation: the Eucharist. ✝

Article 16 The Rite of Baptism for Children

Baptizing infants and young children is an ancient tradition of the Church. As mentioned earlier, today when infants and young children are baptized, we celebrate the Rite of Baptism for Children. Baptisms celebrated according to this rite include the same elements as those celebrated according to the RCIA; however, the Rite of Baptism for Children compresses a number of elements into one liturgy. As the baptized child progresses in age and understanding, appropriate instruction and involvement in the Christian way of life is offered so that the life of faith nourished by the grace of Baptism can also grow.

Baptism in an Emergency

The ordinary ministers of Baptism are the bishop, the priest, and, in the Latin (Western) Church, the deacon. In case of necessity, anyone, even a non-baptized person, can baptize by using the Trinitarian formula. Life takes many strange turns, and one day you may be called upon to baptize someone who is at the point of death. In that case, follow these instructions:

1. Have in your heart the intention of baptizing the person as a follower of Christ and a member of his Body, the Church.

2. Pour water on the candidate's head while saying, "I baptize you in the name of the Father, and of the Son, and of the Holy Spirit" (*CCC,* 1284).

© Tetra Images / Corbis

These actions (the pouring of water or immersing in water, and invoking the Holy Trinity) are the essential elements of Baptism.

God's Life Is Pure Gift

God's life is a generous gift. It does not depend on our merits or how old we are. Thus, from the earliest times, Baptism, with its gifts of entry into Christian life and true freedom, has been administered to children. This is because Baptism, a grace and gift of God, does not depend on any human merit. By this the Church fulfills the words of Jesus, that "no one can enter the kingdom of God without being born of water and Spirit" (John 3:5). By bringing a child to the Sacrament of Baptism, parents and godparents share their most precious possession, their faith and the faith of the entire Church, with this child. In doing so they truly nurture this little one at the deepest level.

Baptism frees us from **Original Sin**—the sin of the first man and woman, who disobeyed God's command by choosing to follow their own will and so lost their original holiness and became subject to death, which is passed on to us. Because of this sin, the Church baptizes even those who haven't committed personal sin—infants and young children.

The gift of Baptism must be affirmed throughout life, in our everyday choices to live by faith, hope, and love. And even if we say no, God never gives up. He will always try to find us and bring us back to him. As we read in the Letter to the Romans:

> What will separate us from the love of Christ? Will anguish, or distress, or persecution, or famine, or nakedness, or peril, or the sword? . . . No, in all these things we conquer over- whelmingly through him who loved us. For I am convinced that neither death, nor life, nor angels, nor principalities, nor present things, nor future things, nor powers, nor height, nor depth, nor any other creature will be able to separate us from the love of God in Christ Jesus our Lord. (8:35,37–39)

Celebrating Baptism

Before the Baptism of a child, pastors have the responsibility of preparing parents for the celebration of Baptism with full understanding. Often parents of infants and young children are gathered in groups to be prepared by pastoral counsel and prayer for the coming celebration.

The Sacrament of Baptism is celebrated in the midst of the community simply because, in Baptism, the child becomes a child of God and a member of the community. The community will be the "village of faith" in which the child will be raised.

It is preferable that the Sacrament of Baptism be celebrated on a Sunday, the day of the Lord's Resurrection. Ideally, it is celebrated at the Mass, as this underlines the child's incorporation into the Body of Christ, the community of faith.

Whether celebrated within the Mass or not, the Rite of Baptism for Children begins with the reception of the child. First, the celebrant greets the family and asks for the child's name. He then asks the parents,

> "What do you ask of God's Church for [Name]?"
> Parents: "Baptism." (They may also say: *faith, the grace of Christ, entrance into the Church*, or *eternal life*)
> (*Rite of Baptism for Children*, 37)

Both parents and godparents agree to help the child grow up in the faith, loving God and neighbor. Just as the catechumens were welcomed into the order of catechumens, the priest then says to the child:

> N., the Christian community welcomes you with great joy. In its name I claim you for Christ our Savior by the sign of his cross. I now trace the cross on your forehead, and invite your parents (and godparents) to do the same. *(Rite of Baptism for Children,* 41)

The Liturgy of the Word follows. After the homily, the Prayer of the Faithful is offered for the child, the godparents, and the family. Then, as in the scrutinies of the Rite of Christian Initiation of Adults, the celebrant prays a prayer of exorcism. He prays that this child may be set free from Original Sin and that the Holy Spirit may dwell within this child.

The celebrant then anoints the child on the chest with the oil of the catechumens, "the oil of salvation," as a strengthening before Baptism. The family, with child, and celebrant go to the font. Following a brief prayer for the child, the celebrant blesses the water, if it is not already blessed. The parents and the godparents then renew their baptismal promises.

Baptism of Blood and Desire

We must remember that *"God has bound salvation to the sacrament of Baptism, but he himself is not bound by his sacraments"* (CCC, 1257).

Baptism, birth into new life in Christ, and the Church itself, which we enter through Baptism, are necessary for salvation and are the ordinary means to reach salvation. However, because God is not bound, there are some circumstances in which a person can be saved without having been baptized. Those who die because of their faith in Christ yet have not received the Sacrament of Baptism are baptized by that very death suffered in, with, and for Christ. This is the called the *Baptism of blood* (see CCC, 1258).

There are those who die without Baptism yet have lived good, truth-seeking lives. They may have been ignorant of the Gospel, but may have done God's will according to the best of their ability and understanding. It may be assumed that, had they known Baptism was necessary, they would have desired it explicitly. This is known as the *Baptism of desire* (see CCC, 1260). Catechumens who die while preparing to be baptized can also be saved.

For infants who die without Baptism, the Church entrusts them to the mercy of God and to the tenderness of Jesus, who said, "Let the children come to me; do not prevent them" (Mark 10:14).

This child is being baptized by immersion in a very large baptismal pool in the Cathedral of Our Lady of the Angels, in Los Angeles, California.

© CURAphotography / Shutterstock.com

In Water and the Holy Spirit

Finally, the celebrant asks the parents and godparents if it is their will that the child (and he says the name of the child) should be baptized in the faith of the Church. When they answer, "It is," the celebrant baptizes the child as follows:

> N., I baptize you in the name of the Father
> *(immerses child or pours water upon it)*
> and of the Son
> *(immerses child or pours water upon it)*
> and of the Holy Spirit
> *(immerses child or pours water upon it).*
> *(Rite of Baptism for Children, 60)*

After Baptism the child is anointed on the crown of the head with the chrism of salvation, **Sacred Chrism**. This newly baptized child is now a child of God, a priest (joining in worship), prophet (listening to and living God's Word), and king (responsible to serve) in Jesus Christ!

Symbols of New Life

Sacred Chrism
Perfumed olive oil consecrated by the bishop that is used for anointing in the Sacraments of Baptism, Confirmation, and Holy Orders.

The clothing in the white garment is next. This is the outward sign of Christian dignity, as the white color is the symbol that the new Christian has put on Christ and has risen with Christ. With the help of friends and family, the child is to bring this dignity "unstained into the everlasting life of heaven" *(Rite of Baptism for Children, 63)*.

The celebrant then gives the child a candle, saying, "Receive the light of Christ" *(Rite of Baptism for Children, 64.)* A parent or godparent carries and lights this candle for the child. This candle is brought home and can be lit on significant days in the child's life, such as a birthday or baptismal anniversary.

The garment and the candle carry the same significance as in the Rite of Christian Initiation of Adults. But, in the case of a child, the "light of Christ" is entrusted to the parents and godparents. It is their responsibility to keep the light of Christ burning brightly in the life of the newly baptized child (see *Rite of Baptism for Children*, 100.)

If Baptism is celebrated at the Eucharist, the Mass continues with the Preparation of the Altar and the Gifts. If Baptism is celebrated outside of the Mass, it continues with the Lord's Prayer and blessings of the mother, the father, and the assembly.

The rite ends with the following:

Celebrant: "Go in peace."
All: "Thanks be to God."
(*Rite of Baptism for Children*, 70) ✝

Holy Water

The holy water, blessed by a priest or bishop for use at Baptism and for private use as a sacramental, is a reminder of our Baptism.

We find a holy water font at the entrance of every church. It is customary to dip our fingers in the holy water and bless ourselves with the Sign of the Cross as we enter the church, as a reminder of our Baptism.

The entire assembly may be sprinkled with holy water at Sunday Mass. This is often done during the Easter season. This replaces the Penitential Act, and reminds us that we are a holy people, ready to worship God as we share in the priestly, kingly, and prophetic mission of Christ.

Many families keep a small bottle of holy water at home to use in small holy water fonts. Sometimes, following ancient custom, it is sprinkled through the house in the midst of storms or even in the midst of a family crisis. Parents may also bless the family with holy water before bedtime.

Holy water has been penetrated by the power of the Holy Spirit. It is no longer "ordinary water." It is a tangible sign that carries with it the presence of God.

Article 17 Baptism: The Source of Christian Living

All through our lives, the gifts of Baptism keep giving. However, it is up to us to open these gifts each and every day. The theological term for the gifts of Baptism is *effects*. The effects of Baptism are what Baptism does for us. These effects are:

- We die and rise with Christ.
- We are freed from Original Sin and all personal sins.
- We become adopted children of God.
- We become members of the Church and sharers in the priesthood of Christ.

A Question of Why

Ryan leaned into the doorway of the walk-in closet that his dad fondly called his "home office."

"Dad," he said.

"Hmm," said his father, staring intently at the computer screen.

"I have a question."

"Okay," his dad said, still staring at the screen. "Just a second." He jiggled the mouse and clicked a few times. "Come on," he urged the computer.

Ryan wondered why people talked to their electronics. It made no sense.

"Okay," his dad said, and twirled around in his chair to face his son. "What's this about?"

"It's a question for school," said Ryan. "Why did you have me baptized?"

"Oh. Well." His dad tipped back in his chair until his head almost touched the bookcase behind him. "Let's see. We wanted you to grow up Catholic, that's for sure."

"Okay," said Ryan. "Thanks."

"Wait," his dad said. "There's something else."

Ryan waited. His dad tipped forward, back again, closed his eyes, opened them, and looked at Ryan.

"We wanted," his dad said, "to give you the best we had: our faith in God."

"After that," he continued, as he gave his son a look that was a mixture, as usual, of love, pride, and concern, "we made a promise to God and to you—that we would help you to live that faith to the best of our ability—and yours."

- We receive a permanent or indelible sacramental character; therefore the Sacrament of Baptism can never be repeated.
- We are empowered by the Holy Spirit for discipleship.

In this article we look at each of these effects of Baptism.

Dying and Rising with Christ

At Baptism we are united with Christ and we share in his Paschal Mystery: the Passion, death, Resurrection, and Ascension of Jesus through which we are saved from sin and death. This dying and rising is what the waters of Baptism symbolize. Baptism holds the promise that, at our death, if we have been faithful to Christ, he will take us up into a new and resurrected life. This is the ultimate way we participate in the Paschal Mystery.

© Tran The Vuong / iStockphoto.com

Catholic Wisdom

Death to Life

Saint Paul's whole purpose in life was to urge and exhort the people of his time—and ours—to believe in the Lord Jesus Christ. Through his writings, God speaks to us today:

> Are you unaware that we who were baptized into Christ were baptized into his death? We were indeed buried with him through baptism into death, so that, just as Christ was raised from the dead by the glory of the Father, we too might live in newness of life. (Romans 6:3–4)

In the meantime, the dyings and risings that are part of our lives right now can help us to understand and participate in the Paschal Mystery more deeply. There are experiences we face in life in which we "die" a little: the loss of a friend, unfair treatment, an illness or other physical suffering, the hurt of a divorce. But because of Baptism, we face these little deaths in Christ, with Christ, and through Christ. And because of Christ, we can look beyond our earthly sufferings to resurrection in him.

Freedom from Original Sin

Picture yourself tied up in chains, weighed down by their iron weight. You cannot move. You are stuck. You have a feeling you will never get free. This is a picture of Original Sin. We inherit it as part of our human condition. But when we choose Christ (or when our parents choose Christ for us), our chains are broken. All sins—personal sin as well as Original Sin—are forgiven. We are free! We are graced! We are sons and daughters of God in Christ!

Of course, suffering, illness, and death remain, as well as certain inherent weaknesses of character and an inclination to sin, called *concupiscence*. But we have the strength, through grace, to resist temptations that arise from this inclination, and sin cannot harm us if we fight against it. Baptism requires an ongoing conversion, a continual turning toward God in the midst of our everyday lives. And we know that in Christ the final victory over sin, suffering, and death is ours.

Children of God

Our understanding of adoption by God can be deepened by looking briefly at the writings of Saint Paul. In Galatians, chapter 4, he describes the situation of an heir that is too young to make decisions about his inheritance, supervised by guardians, and "no different from a slave" (verse 1).

Saint Paul compares the heir's situation with our own before Christ came to redeem us: we were enslaved by sin and death. But after our redemption in Christ, Saint Paul explains, our situation changed radically: we were ransomed by Christ and adopted in him as children of God. Paul calls on the Holy Spirit, the fountain of prayer within us, as evidence of this adoption: "As proof that you are children,

God sent the Spirit of his Son into our hearts, crying out, 'Abba, Father!' So you are no longer a slave but a child, and if a child then also an heir, through God" (Galatians 4:6–7).

As children of God, we become members of Christ, partakers in the divine nature, and temples of the Holy Spirit. At Baptism we are given sanctifying grace, the grace that enables us to believe in God, to hope in him, and to love him. We are given the power to live and act under the inspiration of the Holy Spirit, and to use his gifts in our lives. We are also given the grace to grow in goodness and to turn away from sin and selfishness.

© Juice Images/Corbis

Friendship is one of God's greatest gifts. Sharing ourselves with others is part of belonging to the Body of Christ. Each friendship is unique and should always seek to include, not exclude, others.

Members of the Church

Baptism makes us members of the Church, the People of God, the Body of Christ. We are not alone anymore: "We are members one of another" (Ephesians 4:25). We have been baptized into one Spirit, and we share our spiritual gifts with one another, for "to each individual the manifestation of the Spirit is given for some benefit" (1 Corinthians 12:7). Paul is talking about spiritual gifts (like hospitality and preaching) and he emphasizes that, of all these gifts, the greatest gift is love (see 1 Corinthians, chapter 13.)

As members of the Church, we no longer belong to ourselves but to Christ. The rights and duties of a baptized person flow from belonging to Christ. As part of the Body of Christ, we find our places in the community of faith by serving others and by showing respect, love, and obedience to Church leaders. Participating in the spreading of the Gospel through apostolic and missionary work is also a duty of Baptism and an opportunity to share the great gifts we have received. In return we, as baptized persons, have certain rights: to receive the Sacraments, to be nourished with the Word of God, and to be guided by other spiritual helps the Church provides. Anointed as sharers in the priest-

common priest-hood of the faithful
The name for the priesthood shared by all who are baptized. The baptized share in the one priesthood of Jesus Christ by participating in his mission as priest, prophet, and king.

hood of Christ, we are called together to worship, especially on Sundays and holy days, and so to support one another in following Christ. For we are now included among those true worshippers who, as Jesus said, "will worship the Father in Spirit and in truth" (John 4:23).

Through Baptism we are also united with all who have been baptized, even if they were not baptized in the Catholic Church. These are our fellow Christians, and we see them as our brothers and sisters in Christ. Baptism is *"the sacra-mental bond of unity"*[1] (*CCC*, 1271) among all those who, through it, are reborn into Christ.

Sacramental Character of Baptism

In Baptism we receive an anointing with Sacred Chrism. This is a sign of the gift of the Holy Spirit. Eventually the holy oil disappears. Not so the indelible *character* of Baptism that comes with it! The character is an invisible mark on the soul. We are chosen and sealed for Christ, and consecrated for Christian worship. This invisible mark can never disap-pear, and Baptism can never be repeated.

The seal of Baptism both "enables and commits Chris-tians to serve God"[2] (*CCC*, 1273) by participating in the liturgy, living holy lives, and serving others in love. In the Eucharist we pray for those who have died "with the sign of faith" (*Roman Missal*, "Eucharistic Prayer I"). This sign of faith, the character of Baptism that we share with them, gives us hope that they live eternally and that we also will share eternal life with them one day.

Empowered for Discipleship

The word *Christ* means "anointed." In the Sacrament of Bap-tism, we are anointed and incorporated into Christ, as Priest, Prophet, and King. Our anointing empowers us to be dis-ciples, to be priests, prophets, and kings in Christ. As priests, we are empowered to worship. (See the sidebar on the next page, "The Common Priesthood of the Faithful," for a fuller explanation of this privilege.) As prophets we are empow-ered, as Jesus said, to "hear the word of God and act on it" (Luke 8:21). As kings we are to use our gifts in the service of others. We do not usually think of kings as servants. Jesus himself explained the nature of his kingship: "I am among you as the one who serves" (Luke 22:27). This is the pattern of discipleship we are to follow. ✝

The Common Priesthood of the Faithful

Baptism gives us a share in the priesthood of Christ. This is called the **common priesthood of the faithful**. The word *common* means "for all," as in for all those who are baptized. From this word we get the words *communal* and *community*. As we are incorporated into Christ, who is Priest, Prophet, and King, so we are given the gift of proclaiming the praises of God, "who called you out of darkness into his wonderful light" (1 Peter 2:9). "The faithful exercise their baptismal priesthood through their participation, each according to his own vocation, in Christ's mission as priest, prophet, and king" (*CCC*, 1546). This common priesthood is, of course, different from the ministerial priesthood, which we will look at in section 5, when we study the Sacrament of Holy Orders.

© Martin Gerten/epa/Corbis

Part Review

1. Name four events in salvation history associated with water that help us to understand the meaning of the Sacrament of Baptism.

2. What is the Rite of Christian Initiation of Adults (RCIA)?

3. What are the four periods and the three steps of the RCIA?

4. Describe the four aspects of formation presented in the catechumenate.

5. What are the essential elements in the Sacrament of Baptism?

6. What is mystagogy?

7. Who are the ordinary ministers of Baptism?

8. Describe how to baptize in an emergency.

9. Choose one of the six effects of Baptism and explain its meaning.

Part 2

Confirmation

The Holy Spirit is with us. As followers of Jesus and members of the Church, we know this.

Our study of the Sacrament of Confirmation gives us the opportunity to learn more about the Holy Spirit, the Third Person of the Trinity, who lives within the heart of the Church and within the heart of every Christian. We will learn about the work of the Holy Spirit, the origins of the Sacrament of Confirmation, and the effects of this Sacrament in our lives. The Holy Spirit is with us and in us, for "You are in the spirit, if only the Spirit of God dwells in you" (Romans 8:9).

The topics covered in this part are:

© Attila JÁNDI / Shutterstock.com

Article 18 The Holy Spirit among Us

The Prophet Ezekiel was one of the most influential prophets in the history of Israel and in the history of our salvation. When the Jews were exiled to Babylon, Ezekiel went with them and prophesied the fall of Jerusalem. Yet, in the midst of this great loss, Ezekiel prophesied a renewal of life and a new covenant with God that has only come about through Jesus Christ. One of Ezekiel's most profound visions was this:

The hand of the Lord led me out and set me in the center of a vast plain that was filled with dry bones in every direction. He made me walk among them, to see how very many they were. The Lord asked me, "Can these bones come to life?" I answered, "Lord God, you alone know that."

The Lord told me to prophesy to the bones, to tell them, "Dry bones, hear the word of the Lord!" And so I did.

The Lord told me to say, "See! I will bring my spirit into you, that you may come to life. I will cover you with skin, and put spirit into you so that you may come to life and know that I am the Lord." And so I did.

While I was prophesying, I heard a noise. It was a rattling, as the bones came together, bone joining bone. But there was no spirit in them.

Then the Lord told me to say, "From the four winds come, O spirit, and breathe into these slain that they may come to life." And so I did.

And the spirit came into them. They came alive and stood upright, a vast army. (Adapted from Ezekiel 37:1–11)

[The Lord] said to me: "Son of man, these bones are the whole house of Israel! They are saying, 'Our bones are dried up, our hope is lost, and we are cut off.' Therefore, prophesy and say to them: Thus says the Lord GOD: Look! I am going to open your graves; I will make you come up out of your graves, my people, and bring you back to the land of Israel. . . . You may come to life, and I will settle you in your land. Then you shall know that I am the LORD. I have spoken; I will do it—oracle of the LORD" (Ezekiel 37:11–14).

This is what the Holy Spirit does. Where death abounds, the Holy Spirit brings life. Where there is loss and confusion, the Holy Spirit guides and clarifies. Where despair settles in, the Holy Spirit brings hope—not a vain and empty hope, but a hope based on the sure promises of the Lord.

The Promise of a Messiah

Another significant prophet, the Prophet Isaiah, prophesied that from the family of David would come a Messiah upon whom the Spirit of God would rest:

> But a shoot shall sprout from the stump of Jesse,
>   and from his roots a bud shall blossom.
> The spirit of the LORD shall rest upon him:
>   a spirit of wisdom and of understanding,
> A spirit of counsel and of strength,
>   a spirit of knowledge and of fear of the LORD,
>   and his delight shall be the fear of the LORD.
>
>   (Isaiah 11:1–3)

Centuries passed. Then an angel, a messenger of God, visited a young woman, Mary of Nazareth, and told her she had been chosen to be the mother of the Messiah, the Son of the Most High God. The angel said: "The holy Spirit will come upon you, and the power of the Most High will overshadow you. Therefore the child to be born will be called holy, the Son of God" (Luke 1:35). Jesus was conceived of the Holy Spirit and was in total communion with the Holy Spirit throughout his entire life and mission.

In this Ethiopian manuscript, Jesus has his arms crossed over his chest in a traditional Christian posture of prayer. This form of reverence is still used in the Eastern Churches when receiving Holy Communion.

After the baptism of Jesus in the Jordan River, John the Baptist said of Jesus: "I saw the Spirit come down like a dove from the sky and remain upon him. I did not know him, but the one who sent me to baptize with water told me, 'On whomever you see the Spirit come down and remain, he is the one who will baptize with the holy Spirit.' Now I have seen and testified that he is the Son of God" (John 1:32–34).

John the Baptist knew the prophecies of Isaiah and Ezekiel. He recognized that Jesus was the Son of God and the hoped-for Messiah, because the Holy Spirit came down from the Father, rested upon Jesus, and remained upon Jesus. After Jesus' Resurrection, the Father and the Son would send the Holy Spirit, the Giver of Life, upon the Church.

The Promise of the Holy Spirit

At the Last Supper, Jesus prepared his Apostles for what was to come. He promised that he would not leave them orphans. Jesus said, "I will ask the Father, and he will give you another Advocate to be with you always, the Spirit of truth" (John 14:16). An *advocate*, Jesus' word for the Holy Spirit, is someone who speaks up for you, someone who is on your side in conflict, someone who is a trusted helper and advisor.

In the Gospel of Luke, immediately before the Ascension of Jesus, the disciples were gathered in Jerusalem. Jesus appeared among them, and told them, "And [behold] I am sending the promise of my Father upon you; but stay in the city until you are clothed with power from on high" (Luke 24:49). Here Jesus names the Holy Spirit in two ways: "the promise of my Father" and "the power from on high."

This promise and this power came upon the Apostles and disciples, with Mary, the Mother of the Lord, as they were gathered together in prayer on the fiftieth day after Passover, the day called Pentecost. (*Pente* is the Greek word for *fifty*.) There was the sound of a strong driving wind, filling the entire house. Tongues as of fire came to rest on each of them. And they were all filled with the Holy Spirit (see Acts of the Apostles 2:1–4.)

The Holy Spirit had an immediate effect upon the small group of believers. They left the house and began to proclaim the Good News in different tongues. Because Pentecost was a harvest festival, many Jews had come from many different areas to celebrate the feast in Jerusalem. Noticing this group of people that was speaking in tongues, they were "confused because each one heard them speaking in his own language" (Acts of the Apostles 2:6). Those who believed and were baptized received the same Holy Spirit that had been given to the Apostles.

The Charismatic Renewal

In the last half-century, a movement characterized by an openness to the *charisms*, or gifts, of the Holy Spirit documented in the New Testament has grown among Catholics. The most extraordinary of these are the gift of miracles and the gift of tongues (see *CCC*, 2003)—that is, the gift of praising God in a language unknown to the speaker. Other charismatic gifts are the interpretation of tongues, prophecy, discernment of spirits (knowing whether guidance is from a good spirit or an evil one), and healing.

Pope Benedict XVI, addressing international leaders of the Catholic Charismatic movement in 2008, spoke of charisms as "visible signs of the coming of the Holy Spirit" and noted that a positive element of the movement is its emphasis on the outpouring of the Spirit's gifts in the world today. Pope Benedict spoke also of the need for the authenticity of charisms to be discerned by pastors and for charismatic communities to safeguard their Catholic identities and remain closely bonded to the bishops and the Pope.

At a charismatic prayer meeting, you will find spontaneous prayer, readings from Scripture, prayer in tongues, and spontaneous song. Yet, the process of the meeting is free-flowing and orderly. Many find that charismatic prayer helps them to live their lives with more joy and peace.

The purpose of every gift of the Holy Spirit, including the charismatic gifts, is to build up the Church. We can be sure that the Holy Spirit works in each of us for a good purpose, no matter what our own particular gifts might be (see 1 Corinthians 12:7). And, as Saint Paul reminds us, of all the gifts, "the greatest of these is love" (13:13).

© Aldo Murillo / iStockphoto.com

Confirmation, Sacrament of

With Baptism and the Eucharist, one of the three Sacraments of Christian Initiation. Through an outpouring of the special Gifts of the Holy Spirit, Confirmation completes the grace of Baptism by confirming or "sealing" the baptized person's union with Christ and by equipping that person for active participation in the life of the Church.

Wind, fire, and "different tongues" are all signs of the presence of the Holy Spirit. Like wind, the presence of the Holy Spirit can be strong or gentle. Like wind, the Holy Spirit is not seen, but his effects can be powerful. Like fire, the Holy Spirit purifies us and leads us through darkness by his eternal light. Like ecstatic tongues of prayer, the Holy Spirit can be heard in many languages and in many ways. At Pentecost, the Holy Spirit led the Church, then a small band of believers, into the mission mandated by Jesus Christ: to bring the Good News of salvation to the entire world. ✟

Article 19 Confirmation: East and West

"The wind blows where it wills, and you can hear the sound it makes, but you do not know where it comes from or where it goes; so it is with everyone who is born of the Spirit" (John 3:8).

These words of Jesus, spoken to Nicodemus, a religious leader, sum up the way the Holy Spirit works. Under the influence of the Holy Spirit, the Church has grown and developed throughout history, influencing and transforming the complicated web of human cultures, and from within those diverse cultures, bringing humanity into a sacred encounter with Christ.

The history of the **Sacrament of Confirmation** reflects this involvement in different cultures that accounts for differing practices in the Eastern Churches and the Western (Latin) Church. You will recall that Christian initiation is accomplished in the three Sacraments of Christian Initiation (Baptism, Confirmation, and the Eucharist) together. Baptism begins new life, Confirmation strengthens that new life, and the Eucharist nourishes new Christian life through the transforming power of the Body and Blood of Christ.

In the first centuries of the Church, Confirmation was celebrated following Baptism in the same liturgy, and the bishop was the ordinary minister of Confirmation. Gradually, due to the increased number of infant Baptisms, the distance between parishes, and the growth of large dioceses, it became more and more difficult for the bishop to be present at every Baptism. The response to this situation differed in the East and the West. In the West, Confirmation ("the completion of Baptism," [*CCC*, 1290]) was delayed until the bishop could be present. This remains the usual practice today in the Latin Church. In the Churches of the East, the three Sacraments were never separated. Because the sacred oil used at Confirmation, called *myron*, which means "chrism," had been consecrated by the bishop, the link to the bishop was maintained. And so today, in the Eastern Churches, Confirmation immediately follows Baptism and is administered by the priest. Reception of the Eucharist follows (even for infants).

The Age of Confirmation

The Church mandates that a candidate for Confirmation must have reached the age of reason (at least seven years of age). In the United States, the age of Confirmation has been set by the United States Conference of Catholic Bishops as between the age of discretion (about seven) and about sixteen years of age. An individual bishop can set a specific age within this range for his diocese. Some dioceses have adopted the "restored order" of receiving the Sacraments: first Baptism, then Confirmation, and lastly, the Eucharist. In this order a baptized child who has reached the age of reason will receive Confirmation followed by First Communion in the same liturgy. Administering the Sacraments in this order emphasizes the Eucharist as the culmination of Christian initiation.

This child was baptized and chrismated (or confirmed) and is receiving the Eucharist. All communicants in the Eastern Churches receive the Body (a small piece) and Blood of Christ together from a spoon.

© Saint Elias Ukrainian Catholic Church, Brampton, Ontario, Canada / www.saintelias.com / Andrei Komar

The Bishop as Sign

Both the Western (Latin) Church and the Eastern Churches, in their practice of the Sacraments of Christian Initiation, reflect profound truths about the Church. The practice of the Eastern Churches emphasizes the unity of Baptism, Confirmation, and the Eucharist. The practice of reserving Confirmation to the bishop in the Latin Church emphasizes that the Sacrament strengthens the communion of the newly confirmed with the bishop and highlights the connection of the Sacrament with the apostolic origins of the Church. Why is this communion with the bishop so important? The bishop is a sign that the Church is truly one (unified), catholic (universal), and apostolic (descended from the Apostles). Every bishop was ordained by a bishop who was ordained by a bishop who was ordained by a bishop and so on. This line can be traced back to the Apostles, the ones whom Jesus chose to lead his Church at the beginning. This is called *Apostolic Succession*. **Apostolic Succession** is sacramental, handed on through the laying on of hands in the Sacrament of Holy Orders.

© KEITH BEDFORD / Reuters / Corbis

A bishop places the mitre, a symbol of the authority of the bishop, on the head of a newly ordained bishop.

The Minister of Confirmation

In the Latin Church, as we have seen, the Sacraments of Baptism and Confirmation became separated, as discussed in the previous part. With the restoration of the catechumenate, when adults and children who have reached the age of reason are baptized, Confirmation is administered immediately after Baptism, followed by reception of the Eucharist. In the Latin Church, the bishop is the ordinary minister of Confirmation; however, when the need arises, he may grant a priest permission to administer the Sacrament. This is often the case at the Easter Vigil. If someone is in danger of death, however, any priest can administer Confirmation: "Indeed the Church desires that none of her children, even the youngest, should depart this world without having been perfected by the Holy Spirit with the gift of Christ's fullness" (*CCC*, 1314). ✝

Apostolic Succession

The uninterrupted passing on of apostolic preaching and authority from the Apostles directly to all bishops. It is accomplished through the laying on of hands when a bishop is ordained in the Sacrament of Holy Orders as instituted by Christ. The office of bishop is permanent, because at ordination a bishop is marked with an indelible, sacred character.

Article 20 The Rite of Confirmation

In the Book of the Prophet Joel, we find a wonderful description of the work of the Holy Spirit:

> It shall come to pass
> I will pour out my spirit upon all flesh.
> Your sons and daughters will prophesy,
> your old men will dream dreams,
> your young men will see visions;
> Even upon your male and female servants,
> in those days, I will pour out my spirit.
> I will set signs in the heavens and on the earth.
>
> (Joel 3:1–3)

This prophecy, fulfilled at Pentecost, is again fulfilled at every Confirmation. The effects of the Holy Spirit, which we discuss in more detail in the next article, are not always dramatic. But they are real, for, as Jesus told his disciples, the Father in Heaven will always give the Holy Spirit to those who ask (see Luke 11:13).

Who, then, is eligible to receive the Sacrament of Confirmation? We have already discussed that a candidate for

Baptism must be within the required age range. The candidate must also do the following:

- profess the faith
- be in the state of grace
- desire to receive the Sacrament
- intend to live as a disciple of Christ and witness to the faith, both within the Church and in the world

This stained-glass window portraying the Holy Spirit is the window over the main altar at the Basilica of Saint Peter in Rome. Why do you think this window is appropriate for this papal basilica?

© P Deliss / Godong / Corbis

Preparing for Confirmation

Without Confirmation the initiation of a Christian is incomplete. Preparation for Confirmation aims at leading the Christian to a deeper relationship with Christ and a "lively familiarity" with the Holy Spirit (see *CCC*, 1309). This means that the candidate should know the Holy Spirit, recognize him at work in his actions and gifts, and be willing to follow his inspirations. In the world we live in, following Christ is not always easy. The Holy Spirit is there to help us with his gifts of grace, courage, and love.

Candidates for Confirmation also seek out a sponsor. To emphasize the unity of Baptism and Confirmation, it is appropriate that this sponsor be one of the candidate's godparents.

Of course, just as the Apostles and the Mother of God prepared for the coming of the Holy Spirit with intense prayer, so must the candidate prepare for the Sacrament of Confirmation with heartfelt prayer.

Celebrating the Rite

In a sense, the Rite of Confirmation begins before the actual celebration of the Sacrament. At the Chrism Mass celebrated during Holy Week, the bishop consecrates the Sacred Chrism and shares it with all the parishes in his diocese. This is in itself a significant action that is, in a certain way, a part of the Sacrament of Confirmation.

The celebration of the actual Rite of Confirmation "takes place as a rule within Mass in order that the fundamental connection of this sacrament with all of Christian initiation may stand out in clearer light" (*Rite of Confirmation*, 13). The celebration includes the following elements.

Introductory Rites

As does every other liturgy, the Sacrament of Confirmation begins with the gathering of the assembly. Candidates, sponsors, families, and other members of the community gather in the designated church. Candidates often process into the church with the bishop, the parish priests, and the other liturgical ministers.

The Liturgy of the Word

The explanatory notes for the Rite of Confirmation inform us that the celebration of the Word should be given a lot of emphasis because it is through the Word of God that the Holy Spirit flows out upon the Church and upon each one of the baptized and confirmed (*Rite of Confirmation*, 13). Through the hearing of God's Word, we learn his will for us, and in the Holy Spirit, we are strengthened to carry it out.

Presentation of the Candidates

The pastor, deacon, or catechist presents the candidates to the bishop, usually by the calling of names. Each candidate stands, or, if possible, comes individually to the sanctuary. (If the candidates are children, they are accompanied by one of their sponsors or parents.)

Homily or Instruction

The bishop gives a brief homily. The rite suggests that the following ideas, among others, be included in these remarks:

> You have already been baptized into Christ and now you will
> receive the power of his Spirit and the sign of the cross on
> your forehead. You must be witnesses to all the world to his

suffering, death, and resurrection; your way of life should at all times reflect the goodness of Christ. Christ gives varied gifts to his Church, and the Spirit distributes them among the members of Christ's body to build up the holy people of God in unity and love. (*Rite of Confirmation,* 22)

Renewal of Baptismal Promises

When Confirmation is celebrated separately from Baptism (which is usually the case in the Latin Church), the liturgy includes the Renewal of Baptismal Promises. In these promises the candidates renounce Satan and sin and profess their faith in God. This renewal helps to express the close relationship between Confirmation and Baptism. The Renewal of Baptismal Promises ends this way:

> Bishop: "This is our faith. This is the faith of the Church. We are proud to profess it in Christ Jesus our Lord."
>
> The entire assembly responds: "Amen."
>
> (*Rite of Confirmation,* 23)

The Laying On of Hands

The laying on of hands has been a sign of the descent of the Holy Spirit since the time of the Apostles. This laying on of hands communicates the grace of Pentecost in the Church. The bishop extends his hands over the candidates. The bishop alone sings or says a prayer, asking the Father to send the Holy Spirit upon the candidates to be their guide and helper. He prays: "Give them the spirit of wisdom and understanding, the spirit of right judgment and courage, the spirit of knowledge and reverence. Fill them with the spirit of wonder and awe in your presence" (*Rite of Confirmation,* 25).

© Bill Wittman / www.wpwittman.com

Several priests join the bishop in the laying on of hands, but only the bishop sings or says the accompanying prayer. The laying on of hands is an ancient symbol of prayer for the coming of the Holy Spirit.

Renunciation of Sin

In the early ages of the Church, adult candidates for Baptism renounced their old way of life and their old allegiances to Satan and to sin. As a sign of conversion, the candidates faced west (associated with darkness and the devil) to renounce sin, and then faced east (associated with the rising sun and the light of the Risen Christ) to affirm their Christian beliefs.

In our Renewal of Baptismal Promises, we are asked if we reject Satan, his works, and his empty promises. What does it mean to respond, "I do"?

Renouncing "Satan and all his works and all his empty promises" (*Rite of Confirmation*, 23) means rejecting sin. Like the early Christians, we promise to turn away from the darkness of sin and to turn toward the light—the light of Christ. This decision must be affirmed on a daily basis because the opportunities—temptations—to cooperate with Satan, his works, and his empty promises are endless.

For example, all people naturally tend to seek love, respect, and the approval of others. However, we can get caught up in seeking approval or "people pleasing" through harmful choices, such as using alcohol, tobacco, drugs, and other substances. It can also lead us to value things that don't really matter over those that do. For example, the desire for approval might make us choose to be friends with certain people at school, even if fitting in with these people is likely to lead to risky or sinful choices, or even damage our relationships with important people in our lives, such as our parents, or with God. Naturally, seeking respect and approval is not wrong, but the sinful choices we might make to feel accepted and win approval are. A misguided search for love and approval is one path toward darkness and the misery of sin we might encounter in everyday life.

Rejecting Satan does not mean we will never sin, but it does mean that each day we must make an effort to live as a disciple of Christ. With the help of God's love and grace, we will realize when we are heading into the darkness and turn around once again to walk in the light of Christ.

This laying on of hands is very important, even though it is not the action by which Confirmation is conferred. It is a vital expression of the Church's prayer. It also makes the Rite of Confirmation more complete and contributes to a deeper understanding of the Sacrament (see *Rite of Confirmation*, 9).

The Anointing with Sacred Chrism

Very early in the development of the Sacrament of Confirmation, the anointing with Sacred Chrism was added to the laying on of hands. You may remember that the title Christ means "anointed one." So does the derivative title that we bear, Christian.

In the East, with the anointing, the formula for the words is, "The seal of the gift of the Holy Spirit." The Sacrament is called, from the name of this anointing, Chrismation.

In the West the formula for the words is: "Be sealed with the Gift of the Holy Spirit." The Western term, *Confirmation*, defines this Sacrament as confirming and strengthening baptismal grace. Thus "the essential rite of Confirmation is anointing the forehead with sacred chrism (in the East, other sense-organs as well), together with the laying on of the minister's hand and the words" (*CCC*, 1320).

In the celebration of the Sacrament, the candidate stands before the bishop. The sponsor of the candidate stands near, with his or her right hand on the candidate's shoulder. Either the candidate or the sponsor says the name of the candidate. The bishop dips his right thumb into the Sacred Chrism and makes the Sign of the Cross on the forehead of the one to be confirmed. The celebration then continues as follows:

> The bishop says: "N., be sealed with the Gift of the Holy Spirit."
> The newly confirmed responds: "Amen."
> The bishop says: "Peace be with you."
> The newly confirmed responds: "And also with you."
>
> (*Rite of Confirmation*, 27)

Anointing in the Early Church

In the early centuries, a "double-anointing" after Baptism was the custom in the Roman Church. The priest who baptized also anointed the neophyte upon coming out of the baptismal pool; this anointing was followed by a second anointing from the bishop. The first anointing with Sacred Chrism, by the priest, is still part of the Rite of Baptism for Children. This anointing is the sign of the participation of the newly baptized in the prophetic, priestly, and kingly office of Christ. Today when an adult is baptized and confirmed, the first anointing is omitted and the only postbaptismal anointing, that of Confirmation, is performed (see *CCC*, 1291).

The Holy Spirit is poured out, with all his gifts, once again.

The Prayer of the Faithful

After all have been confirmed, the Prayer of the Faithful follows. In this prayer, we pray for the newly confirmed, for their parents and godparents, for the Church, for all people of every race and nation, and that the work of the Holy Spirit, begun in the Church at Pentecost, be continued in the hearts of all who believe (see *Rite of Confirmation*, 30).

The Liturgy of the Eucharist

When the Sacrament of Confirmation is celebrated within the Mass, the celebration continues with the Liturgy of the Eucharist. The Profession of Faith (the Creed) is omitted, as this profession was made in the Renewal of Baptismal Promises. Some of the newly confirmed may be asked to join in bringing the gifts of bread and wine to the altar.

Great importance is attached to the saying of the Lord's Prayer, "because it is the Spirit who prays in us and in the Spirit the Christian says, 'Abba, Father'" (*Rite of Confirmation*, 13).

Celebrating the Sacrament of Confirmation within the Mass links Confirmation to Christian initiation as a whole, which "reaches its culmination in the communion of the body and blood of Christ" (*Rite of Confirmation*, 13). At the end of the Eucharistic celebration, a special blessing is prayed over the people, asking the Father, the Son, and the

The Character of Confirmation: Marked for Life

Like Baptism, the Sacrament of Confirmation imprints a spiritual mark, an indelible character, on the soul. This means that this Sacrament is so unique that, like Baptism, it can be received only once in a lifetime. This character is permanent.

Another term for this mark or character is *seal of the Holy Spirit*. A seal is an identifier. It is like a brand mark, like a seal on a letterhead or diploma, or like the embossed seal you find on documents that have been certified by a notary public. These seals show that the documents are real and authentic. The seal of the Holy Spirit marks the newly confirmed person as belonging to Christ, as an authentic and fully initiated Christian. The Sacred Chrism is the sign of this seal.

Holy Spirit to give special gifts of love, courage, and faith to the newly confirmed and to the entire assembly. The bishop then blesses the entire assembly. ✝

Article 21 Life in the Holy Spirit

The Prophet Elijah was afraid for his life. He had spoken out against the false god Baal, and the prophets of that god were seeking to kill him. He hid in a cave on Mount Horeb, where the Lord found him and said, "Go outside and stand on the mountain before the LORD; the LORD will be passing by." The account continues:

> There was a strong and violent wind rending the mountains and crushing rocks before the LORD—but the LORD was not in the wind; after the wind, an earthquake—but the LORD was not in the earthquake; after the earthquake, fire—but the LORD was not in the fire; after the fire, a light silent sound.
> When he heard this, Elijah hid his face in his cloak and went and stood at the entrance of the cave. (1 Kings 19:11–13)

Elijah recognized the Lord in "a tiny whispering sound." Yes, the Holy Spirit can come in wind and earthquake and fire—but most of the time, we can recognize the Holy Spirit in the tiny whisperings of our hearts, in the inspirations for good that come to us and will not let us rest until we act on them. The Holy Spirit is with us, as baptized and confirmed Christians, as we strive to be "imitators of God, as beloved children, and live in love, as Christ loved us" (Ephesians 5:1–2).

The Prophet Elijah brings down fire from Heaven. (see 1 Kings 18:38). This mural is found in the Elijah Chapel in the Church of the Transfiguration in Israel. There is also a Moses Chapel in this church. Do you know why?

Gifts and Responsibilities

The greatest and overarching effect of Confirmation is "the special outpouring of the Holy Spirit as once granted to the Apostles on the day of Pentecost" (*CCC*, 1302). At Confirmation, we gather in prayer, with the Apostles; with Mary, the Mother of God; and with all the angels and saints. In answer to that prayer, the Holy Spirit comes to us in the anointing, the laying on of hands, and the words of the bishop. The Sacrament of Confirmation strengthens and confirms the graces and Gifts of the Holy Spirit received in Baptism. And with the Sacrament come its effects and responsibilities, which will last the rest of our lives. What are these effects and responsibilities? The Sacrament of Confirmation does the following for us:

- It gives the Holy Spirit in order to root us more deeply in the divine filiation—that is, in our adoption as sons and daughters of God. The Holy Spirit will lead and guide us: "For those who are led by the Spirit of God are children of God. For you did not receive a spirit of slavery to fall back into fear, but you received a spirit of adoption, through which we cry, '*Abba, Father!*'"(Romans 8:14–15).
- It unites us more firmly to Christ.
- It increases the Gifts of the Holy Spirit in us.
- It strengthens our relationship with the Church.
- It involves us more deeply in the Church's mission of bringing the Good News of salvation to all people.
- It helps us to bear witness to our faith through our words and actions.

(See *CCC*, 1303)

Gifts and Fruits of the Holy Spirit

All of the Sacraments of Christian Initiation are great gifts and carry great responsibilities. Saint Paul asks us, "Do you not know that your body is a temple of the holy Spirit within you, whom you have from God, and that you are not your own?" (1 Corinthians 6:19). We are not to be sponges, simply absorbing all the graces and blessings of the Sacraments; we are to be fountains, spreading the gift of life we have received—in service to others, and ready to give an answer

The Pentecost Sequence

A sequence (a poetic hymn following the Second Reading at the Mass) is sung or recited on Pentecost Sunday in honor of the Holy Spirit. We do not use this particular translation in the liturgy, but it can be used for our private prayer.

Come, Holy Spirit,
And send out from Heaven
Your radiant light.

Come, father of the poor,
Come, giver of gifts,
Come, light of our hearts.

Best consoler,
Sweet guest of the soul,
Sweetness of cool refreshment.

Rest in labor,
Relief in heat,
Consolation in weeping.

O most blessed light,
Fill the center of the hearts
Of your faithful.

Without your divine power,
There is nothing in humans,
Nothing is innocent.

Wash what is soiled,
Water what is dry,
Heal what is wounded.

Bend what is rigid,
Warm what is chilled,
Guide what is astray.

Give to your faithful,
Who trust in you,
The seven sacred gifts.

Give the reward of virtue,
Give the goal of salvation,
Give eternal joy.

Amen. Alleluia.

© Bill Wittman / www.wpwittman.com

in defense or explanation of our faith (always gently) when that is asked of us.

But we always have the help of the Holy Spirit. Throughout our lives we are sustained by the Seven Gifts of the Holy Spirit: wisdom, understanding, right judgment (counsel), courage (fortitude), knowledge, reverence (piety), and wonder and awe (fear of the Lord). These are messianic gifts that Christ has in all their fullness, and, in the Holy Spirit, they are shared with us (see Isaiah 11:1–2.) These gifts are not to be kept unopened on a shelf; instead, they are to be opened and used every day, in every need and every situation that affects ourselves or others.

When we "live by the Spirit" (Galatians 5:16), the fruits of the Holy Spirit begin to show up in our lives. These fruits are: charity, joy, peace, patience, kindness, goodness, generosity, gentleness, faithfulness, modesty, self-control, and chastity. These qualities or characteristics are called fruits because they are results of growth in Christ, the results of following the Holy Spirit's "tiny whispering sound" each day. They are also called fruits because they are the "firstfruits" of eternal life: They are a small taste of what Heaven will be like, and as such, they give us a bit of Heaven on earth.

When these fruits grow in us, they also nourish others. In cooperating with the grace of the Holy Spirit, you might find yourself being more joyful, more peaceful, or more patient with others. Because you are taking time to pray a little more sincerely, you might be surprised when your kindness helps someone else through a rough moment. Asking the help of the Holy Spirit might mean you grow in controlling your temper, and you may discover that a little self-control on your part can keep a situation from escalating or getting out of hand. Little by little, with the grace of the Holy Spirit, you are being transformed. You are becoming more true to yourself. You are becoming all that God meant you to be. And he will say of you:

© Kevin Dodge / Corbis

Kindness and gentleness are not always popular in our society. Does it sometimes take courage to be kind? Why? When?

> See, I am doing something new!
> Now it springs forth, do you not perceive it?
> In the wilderness I make a way,
> in the wasteland, rivers.
>
> (Isaiah 43:19)

Walk, therefore, in newness of life! ✝

22 Discernment of God's Will

Article

All through life, we *discern* (or find) the will of God for us. We want to know his will in big things, such as our choice of a vocation in life, and in smaller things too, such as whether to allow a friendship to grow, which part-time job to take, or whether to try out for a sports team or the school play or something else altogether. But first let's stop and ask: Does God really care?

Of course God cares. He created you with gifts and talents, and he wants you to use them. God wants you to be happy in this life, as well as in the next. Often you may find that the way is clear. You are able to go from one decision to another in peace and with no regrets. At other times, however, things can get cloudy. You may feel stuck and not know what to do in a particular situation. At those times especially, the help of the Holy Spirit can clear a path for you and help you to see your way to the right decision— one that is right for your life and for your relationship with God.

As we seek to discern what is right for our lives, the Church offers us certain helps, or guiding principles, to lead us. If we use these principles, or practices, we are more likely to find the right path, to "walk in the Holy Spirit," and to discover God's will for us. Let's explore four of these practices:

© Myth Photography / Shutterstock.com

What decisions are you discerning, if not now, then in the immediate future? Who can help you sort out the possibilities you will meet on the road ahead?

1. Know and pray with the Sacred Scriptures. One of the best ways to learn Scripture is to listen carefully during the liturgy. The liturgy is a scriptural treasury, and anyone who listens well at the Mass and at the other Sacraments, to the readings and the homily, will find that their knowledge of the Word of God will grow, with the help of the Holy Spirit. As you listen, try to catch a few words or phrases you can take with you. Saint Jerome, one of the Fathers and Doctors of the Church, once wrote, "Ignorance of the Scriptures is ignorance of Christ." In other words, the more we know Scripture, the more confident we can be that we are following the way of Christ.

2. Live the Sacraments. Participate regularly in the Eucharist and in the Sacrament of Penance and Reconcilia-

Your Call

An old American spiritual called "That Lonesome Valley" uses the example of Jesus to remind us that we are responsible for our choices.

> Jesus walked that lonesome valley.
> He had to walk it by himself.
> Nobody else could walk it for him.
> He had to walk it by himself.
>
> You must walk that lonesome valley.
> You've got to walk it by yourself.
> Nobody else can walk it for you.
> You've got to walk it by yourself.

During his Passion, Jesus walked that lonesome valley. One of his chosen friends had betrayed him. In the agony in the garden, he was, humanly speaking, alone. On the cross he cried out his agonized question, "My God, my God, why have you forsaken me?" (Matthew 27:46). Yet near his cross were four people who were literally standing by him: his mother Mary; Mary, the wife of Cleopas; Mary of Magdala; and John the Apostle.

At times being true to the call in life that reflects your unique relationship with God will lead you through a lonesome valley. Your friends may desert you; some may deny knowing you. Yet even in the midst of all that, you will find people who will stand by you. Those people may not be able to take away the pain you might experience, but they will be with you through it.

And most of all, you will find that God—Father, Son, and Holy Spirit—is with you. The Father will not forsake you. The Holy Spirit will strengthen you. And Jesus, who walked the lonesome valley before you, will walk it again—this time, by your side.

tion in a conscious and active way. Your involvement in the liturgy will lead to renewed life in the Holy Spirit, fuller participation in the mission of the Church, and more dedicated service to all in a spirit of unity and love.

3. Love the Catholic Church, the Church that Christ began. In his Letter to the Ephesians, Saint Paul urges husbands to love their wives "even as Christ loved the church and handed himself over for her to sanctify her, cleansing her by the bath of water with the word, that he might present to himself the church in splendor, without spot or wrinkle or any such thing, that she might be holy and without blemish" (5:25–27). The Church is Christ's own Body, the Temple of the Holy Spirit, and God's People, of which we are all members. Loving the Church does not mean excusing the sins

Live It!

Following the Holy Spirit

"If we live in the Spirit, let us also follow the Spirit" (Galatians 5:25). To help you follow the Spirit, here are a few ideas, based on Scripture and the letters spelling *HOLY SPIRIT*. With each idea is a Scripture verse. Try looking up one each day, asking how you can follow this verse in your life.

H elpfulness. The Holy Spirit is our Advocate, or *helper*. Psalm 54:6 and Isaiah 49:8–10. How can you trust the Holy Spirit to help you live according to God's will?

O penness to God. Isaiah 50:4. How can you open your life to God today?

L ove, the self-giving kind. See 1 Corinthians, chapter 13. Which kind of love can you live today?

Y outh, energetic and active. 1 Timothy 4:12. How can your life be an example for others to follow?

S criptures. Romans 15:4. Find a Scripture passage that gives you hope. Write it down and put it where you will see it often.

P rayer and praise. Psalm 150. Pray this psalm. Try setting it to music!

I ndwelling. Romans 8:11,14–17. Be open to the leading of the Holy Spirit today.

R ighteousness, justice. Micah 6:8. What does the Lord ask of you today?

I ntercession. Romans 8:26–27. What is your need today?

T ruth. John 16:12–15 and 2 John, verses 1–6. What truth can you live by today?

of its members, but it does mean helping to heal the consequences of those sins. Loving the Church means loving its members, from the Pope in Rome to the parishioner in the next pew, and working to help the Church grow throughout the world to bring salvation to all people.

    4. Pray to the Holy Spirit to know God's will and to follow Christ. Our greatest prayer is the liturgy, in which we participate in Christ's own prayer to the Father in the Holy Spirit. Even when we pray in private, we are participating in the great prayer of Christ's Body, the Church. Whenever we take the opportunity to pray, we are praying "in the Spirit," for it is the Holy Spirit who prays within us: "In the same way, the Spirit too comes to the aid of our weakness; for we do not know how to pray as we ought, but the Spirit itself intercedes with inexpressible groanings" (Romans 8:26). We may not know what God's will is; we may not even know what to pray for. But the Holy Spirit knows, and he prays within us for all that we need, whether or not we know how to name our need.

The Body of Christ

As members of the Body of Christ, we have access to the counsel of others as we seek the right path. In addition to following the guiding principles just listed, it is always a good idea, when seeking God's will and making any important decision, to seek the advice of someone who, as a follower of Christ, also seeks to be faithful to the inspirations of the Holy Spirit. That person could be a parent, a teacher, a school counselor, a priest or religious, or a catechist.

Pray It!

A Prayer to the Holy Spirit

This Prayer to the Holy Spirit is from the Eastern Churches. You might like to add it to your prayer repertoire:

> Heavenly King, Consoler Spirit, Spirit of Truth, present everywhere and filling all things, treasure of all good and source of all life, come dwell in us, cleanse and save us, you who are All-Good.[3]

(CCC, 2671)

As the Holy Spirit leads us, one step at a time, along our Christian journey, we are not alone. We travel as part of the Church, as members of the Body of Christ, each one sharing our gifts with one another, "living the truth in love" (Ephesians 4:15). Therefore we can rely on the guidance of other faithful followers of Christ to help us to discern God's will for our lives, whether it is in the big questions in life, such as knowing what vocation God is calling us to, or the smaller but still important ones, such as whether to continue a particular relationship or which service project to take part in. ✝

Catholic Wisdom

God Knows and Cares

Psalm 139 celebrates God's loving and personal knowledge of each one of us. The psalmist addresses God and asks:

Where can I go from your spirit?
From your presence, where can I flee?

. . . .

If I take the wings of dawn
        and dwell beyond the sea,
Even there your hand guides me,
        your right hand holds me fast.
                (Psalm 139:7,9–10)

You might like to look up this psalm and read it in its entirety.

Part Review

1. Name two prophets of the Old Testament who prophesied about the Holy Spirit.

2. Who was the New Testament prophet who recognized Jesus as the Messiah and Son of God?

3. What were the signs of the presence of the Holy Spirit on Pentecost?

4. Name two differences in the Sacrament of Confirmation as administered in the Eastern Churches compared to the Western (Latin) Church.

5. What is Apostolic Succession?

6. Who is eligible for the Sacrament of Confirmation?

7. What is the meaning of the Renewal of Baptismal Promises in Confirmation?

8. What is the essential Rite of Confirmation?

9. What is the relationship between Baptism and Confirmation?

The Sacraments of Christian Initiation: Part 2

Part 1

The Eucharist: Culmination of Christian Initiation

The three Sacraments of Christian Initiation—Baptism, Confirmation, and the Eucharist—are in reality one movement, inserting us into the Paschal Mystery of Christ, into his **Passion**, death, Resurrection, and Ascension. Through the Sacraments of Christian Initiation, we begin the fullness of life in Christ.

The Eucharist is the culminating initiation Sacrament and the "source and summit"[1] (*CCC*, 1324) of our life in Christ. In the Eucharist, Christ brings the Church and all of us, members of his Body, into his own sacrifice of thanksgiving and praise, offered to his Father once and for all on the cross. By this sacrifice (or offering), he pours out the graces of salvation upon his Body, the Church.

The Eucharist is the sign and cause of our union with Christ. As he did at the Last Supper, Christ gives us himself in the Eucharistic elements—his Body and Blood. As Christ becomes one with us, we become one with him. Our lives are caught up in the resurrected life of Christ.

In this first part of section 3, we discuss central aspects of the theology of the Eucharist, the Eucharist in Scripture, and the place of the Eucharist in the history of our salvation.

The topics covered in this part are:

23 What Is the Eucharist?

Passion
The sufferings of Jesus during his final days in this life: his agony in the garden at Gethsemane, his trial, and his Crucifixion.

Logos
A Greek word meaning "word." *Logos* is a title of Jesus Christ found in the Gospel of John that illuminates the relationship between the Three Persons of the Holy Trinity (see John 1:1,14).

In the Gospel of John, Jesus is introduced to us as the *Logos*, the Word, who is God and who existed before all time yet chose to take on a human nature, to become flesh for our sake: "And the Word became flesh / and made his dwelling among us" (1:14). The Word of God became one of us, in everything except sin, and even accepted death, death on a cross (see Philippians 2:7–8) to save us from sin and to bring us new life, now and forever.

But the Word of God who became flesh, who lived among us and loved us, who died for us and is now risen in glory, did not leave us orphans. The disciples of Emmaus begged him, "Stay with us" (Luke 24:29), and Jesus did exactly that—in the Eucharist. When Jesus said, "This is my body. . . . This is my blood" (Matthew 26:26–27), he said it for all time and for all people. For us today the Word of God, the Risen Christ, is given to us in the Eucharist. In this Eucharist the Word of God dwells among us.

The Eucharist is the Sacrament that makes present in the Mass the death and Resurrection of Christ. The Eucharist is "a sacrament of love, a sign of unity, a bond of charity, a Paschal banquet 'in which Christ is consumed, the mind is filled with grace, and a pledge of future glory is given to us'"[2] (*CCC*, 1323).

Understanding the Eucharist

The theology of **the Eucharist** includes many dimensions that help us to understand the meaning and significance of this Sacrament. This article explores the following:

- the signs of bread and wine
- the institution of the Eucharist
- Jesus' command to "Do this in memory of me"
- giving thanksgiving and praise to the Father
- the sacrificial memorial of Christ
- the sacrifice and memorial of the Church

© Saint Mary's Press / Brian Singer-Towns

This icon of Christ is found in the dome of the Church of the Holy Sepulchre in Jerusalem, the church built on Calvary, the site of the Crucifixion.

The Signs of Bread and Wine

At Mass, during the Preparation of the Gifts, we offer bread and wine. We give thanks to the Creator for these gifts, the fruits of the earth as well as of human hands, not only because these gifts will soon become the Body and Blood of Christ but also because they are symbolic of all the gifts God has given to us.

Bread and wine have been significant throughout salvation history. In the Old Covenant, bread and wine were offered in thanksgiving to God as symbols of all of his gifts. The offering of bread and wine of the priest Melchizedek (see Genesis 14:18) prefigures our own offering of bread and wine at the Eucharist (see *Roman Missal*, "Eucharistic Prayer I"). Bread, as a gift of God, took on a new meaning during the events of the Exodus. When fleeing from Egypt, the only bread the Jews could take with them was unleavened bread. Eating unleavened bread at the Passover became a symbol of God's faithfulness and their freedom. And later, when the people had nothing to eat in the desert, God sent bread from Heaven, called manna, to sustain them. Again, bread was a tangible sign of God's faithfulness and love.

Wine also had significant meaning in the Old Covenant. The drinking of wine, especially at "the cup of blessing," was a sharing of joyful anticipation of the coming of the Messiah in a new Jerusalem.

In the New Testament, Jesus' multiplication of the loaves and fishes prefigures the Eucharist and also looks back to the manna of the desert. The people who were listening to Jesus were in a deserted place, with no markets nearby. Yet Jesus, the Son of God, gave his people bread—the miracle of loaves, like manna in the desert.

In the wedding at Cana, Jesus used the miracle of the water turned wine to announce his presence among his people. In this sign he announced his saving presence. The wedding

Eucharist, the

Also called the Mass or Lord's Supper, and based on a word for "thanksgiving," it is the central Christian liturgical celebration, established by Jesus at the Last Supper. In the Eucharist the sacrificial death and Resurrection of Jesus are both remembered and renewed. The term sometimes refers specifically to the consecrated bread and wine that have become the Body and Blood of Christ.

© Magdalena Kucova / iStockphoto.com

at Cana is a sign of the heavenly wedding feast to come: Jesus himself is the Bridegroom, the Church is the Bride, and the members of the Church will drink new wine, the Blood of Christ.

In instituting the Eucharist, Jesus gave new meaning to the traditional Passover blessing of the bread and of the cup. He made the Passover bread and wine his own Body and Blood. Jesus made himself our Pasch, our Passover from the slavery of sin into the freedom of his risen life. When Jesus took up this cup, he looked forward to the Kingdom of God that he himself would initiate through his death and Resurrection.

In the Eucharist today, the bread and wine that become the Body and Blood of Christ (by the words of the priest and the invocation of the Holy Spirit) remain at the heart of the Eucharist.

The Institution of the Eucharist

Jesus' love is infinite. He showed that love throughout his earthly ministry, especially through the gift of himself so that we might be saved. In "Eucharistic Prayer IV," the priest, addressing God the Father, speaks of the love of Jesus and this gift of himself to us:

> For when the hour had come
> for him to be glorified by you, Father most holy,
> having loved his own who were in the world,
> he loved them to the end.
>
> *(Roman Missal)*

Jesus' institution of the Eucharist is a sign of his love. Jesus, in his own Body and Blood, left to his chosen companions a pledge of his deep love. And he asked his Apostles to share in, and to celebrate, this memorial of his death and Resurrection until he would come again in glory.

Significantly, it was at **Passover** time that Jesus chose to show that his love was a sacrificial love. As the Passover lamb was killed and eaten to sustain the life of God's People, so Jesus, the Lamb of God, would suffer, die, and be buried. Yet, this Lamb would triumph. This resurrected Lamb would share his sustenance with his people, would share his Body and Blood, not as an empty remembrance but as a living reality.

This Passover of Jesus fulfilled the hopes of the Passover of the Old Covenant. The Eucharist is the new Passover. In it we celebrate the passing over of Jesus from death to Resurrection. In every Eucharist we share in the Passover of Jesus and celebrate the hope of our own Passover from death to life in the glory of God's Kingdom. In the Body and Blood of Christ, we share even now in that glory.

"Do This in Memory of Me"

Jesus' words "Do this in memory of me" have a particular meaning for the Church. The memory the Church has of Jesus' words and actions at the Last Supper is not the kind of memory we might have of a special day or of a special event. When we say, "I will remember this moment for the rest of my life," that moment stays in the past. The "memory," or memorial, of the Eucharist is different; it is a living memory. The Church not only remembers Jesus and all he did for the sake of our salvation but also makes it present. We call this kind of memory by the Greek term **anamnesis**. This term also describes a particular part of the Eucharistic Prayer, which we will study later in this article.

In one sense, the Last Supper was really the "First Supper"—the first of many celebrations of the Eucharist that the Risen Jesus would share with his followers. After Jesus' return to his Father in Heaven, the memorial of the Last Supper continued through the work of the Apostles, who, like Jesus, took bread, broke it, blessed it, and gave it. Ever since the Last Supper, the Church has continually celebrated the memorial of the Eucharist in this same fundamental structure.

When we celebrate the Eucharist today, we share in and proclaim the Paschal Mystery of Jesus until he comes again, when we will all be brought together at the table of the Lord in the heavenly Kingdom. The Eucharist, as our making present of the Paschal Mystery of Christ, is both our strength for today's journey and our promise for the unending "tomorrows" of eternity.

Giving Thanks and Praise

The Eucharist is a sacrifice of praise and thanksgiving for the saving work of Christ on the cross and for the entire work of creation. In the Eucharist all of creation is offered to the Father through the death and Resurrection of his Son, Jesus Christ. The word *Eucharist* itself comes from a Greek word meaning "thanksgiving." In the Eucharist we thank God for all that is good, holy, beautiful, and just in our world and in our lives, and we thank him in a special way for the gift of his Son, Jesus. Not only did God create us, he also redeemed us and sanctified us, and made us worthy to be called his children. For these reasons, in the Eucharist, we sing his glory through Christ.

In the Eucharist, Jesus Christ unites us to himself, to his own praise of the Father, and to his intercessions for us. Jesus, as our High Priest, approaches God the Father on our behalf. He "is always able to save those who approach God through him, since he lives forever to make intercession for them" (Hebrews 7:25). In every Eucharist, Jesus himself prays for you!

Sacrifice and Memorial of Christ

In every Eucharist, after the words of institution, we find a prayer called the memorial, or, in Greek, the *anamnesis* (meaning "memory"):

> Therefore, O Lord,
> as we celebrate the memorial of the blessed Passion,
> the Resurrection from the dead,
> and the glorious Ascension into heaven
> of Christ, your Son, our Lord . . .

> (*Roman Missal,* "Eucharistic Prayer I")

But, like the word *memory* in the words of institution, this word *anamnesis* means more than just remembering Jesus or recalling a past event. In the Eucharist, when we remember Christ's Passion, death, Resurrection, and Ascension, we

Catholic Wisdom

In the Eucharist, because we are made one with Jesus, our prayer is united with his prayer. Saint Augustine sums up the prayer of Jesus in this way: "He prays for us as our priest; prays in us as our Head, and is prayed to by us as our God. Therefore let us acknowledge our voice in him and his in us"[3] (*CCC*, 2616).

are remembering, yes, but we are primarily proclaiming the mighty works of God that are made present in our midst.

For God and his works are not limited to the past. They are present now, and they will be present in the future: "We proclaim your Death, O Lord, and profess your Resurrection until you come again" *(Roman Missal)*.

Christ died once and for all on the cross, but his sacrifice remains ever present to us in the Eucharist. As the memorial of the Paschal Mystery, the liturgical action of the Eucharist *makes present* the work of salvation accomplished by Jesus Christ mainly by his Passion, death, Resurrection, and Ascension. In the Eucharist, Christ's Body, the body he gave up on the cross, and Christ's Blood, the blood he poured out for our salvation, is given to us. Every Eucharist is *our participation* in that one single sacrifice. In the Eucharist, we, as members of the Church, the Body of Christ, participate in Christ's sacrifice. Our prayers, our praise, our sufferings, our work, are united with him and are given priceless value.

Sacrifice and Memorial of the Church

In every Eucharist, the whole Church is united with the offering of Christ and with his intercession for us. We celebrate every Eucharist in union with the Pope because his is the ministry of Peter, the first of the Apostles, in the Church and is the sign of unity for the entire Church around the world. We also celebrate with, and name in prayer, our local bishop, who is responsible for every Eucharist celebrated in his diocese. At every Eucharist we pray for the Pope, our bishop, and all priests and deacons who minister at the Eucharist.

Every Eucharist brings us into unity with the members of the Church on earth as well as those in Heaven. We celebrate the Eucharist in union with the Blessed Virgin Mary and all the angels and saints. We also offer the Eucharist for the faithful departed, those who have "gone before us with the sign of faith" (*Roman Missal*, "Eucharistic Prayer I").

When Christ offers himself to the Father, he brings the members of his Body, the Church, with him. His Paschal Mystery is made present to us, that we might enter into it, offering our entire selves to God—in Christ, with Christ, and through Christ.

These six dimensions help us to understand the reality of the Eucharist. As we continue to grow in our awareness of the meaning of Christ's gift of himself in the Eucharist, in a deep and personal way, we will exclaim with Saint Paul, "Thanks be to God for his indescribable gift!" (2 Corinthians 9:15). ☩

The Cosmic Eucharist

Shortly before his death, the late Pope John Paul II wrote "The Eucharistic Church" (*"Ecclesia de Eucharistia"*). In this encyclical the Pope explains the Eucharist as bringing about a "oneness in time" between the Triduum (the three days of Christ's suffering, death, and Resurrection) and our own time. This is the "making present" of the Paschal Mystery in every Eucharist ("The Eucharistic Church," 5).

He also recounts his own experiences:

I have been able to celebrate Holy Mass in chapels built along mountain paths, on lakeshores and seacoasts; I have celebrated it on altars built in stadiums and in city squares. . . . This varied scenario of celebrations of the Eucharist has given me a powerful experience of its universal and, so to speak, cosmic character. Yes, cosmic! Because even when it is celebrated on the humble altar of a country church, the Eucharist is always in some way celebrated *on the altar of the world.* It unites heaven and earth. It embraces and permeates all creation. . . . Truly this is the *mysterium fidei* [mystery of faith] which is accomplished in the Eucharist: the world which came forth from the hands of God the Creator now returns to him redeemed by Christ. (8)

^{Article}

24 The Eucharist in the Scriptures

In this article we explore important Old Testament references to the Eucharist: the manna in the desert and its connection to the Bread of Life discourse in the Gospel of John; the unleavened bread of the Passover; and the priest Melchizedek, whose offering of bread and wine prefigures the presentation of the bread and wine in the Eucharist. We also consider the New Testament accounts: the multiplication of the loaves and the Last Supper accounts. We note how each of these references and events contributes to the meaning and significance of the Sacrament of the Eucharist.

© Zvonimir Atletic / Shutterstock.com

Bread and wine are ordinary gifts, but at the Eucharist they are transformed into something extraordinary. What ordinary gifts do you have? Will you give them to God to transform into something extraordinary?

The Manna and the Bread of Life

After the Israelites escaped from Egypt, they were led into a vast desert. The land was barren, and they could find no food. They complained to Moses and Aaron, saying that they would rather have died in Egypt, where they had their fill of bread, but "you have led us into this wilderness to make this whole assembly die of famine!" (Exodus 16:3). To answer their complaint, the Lord told Moses, "I am going to rain down bread from heaven for you" (16:4). This was manna, which appeared as fine flakes on the ground. It had to be gathered each day (except on the Sabbath; a double portion was gathered the day before), and it tasted like "wafers made with honey" (16:31). Such was the loving care God showered on his people.

Centuries later, Jesus explained the meaning of this manna, and of himself as the true Bread, in an incident recorded in the Gospel of John. One day Jesus was teaching in the synagogue at Capernaum. Jesus had just multiplied the loaves and fishes for the people. Then he walked on water. Now, as he taught, he engaged the crowd in discussion. The crowd asked him: "What sign can you do, that we may see and believe in you? What can you do? Our ancestors ate manna in the desert, as it is written: 'He gave them bread from heaven to eat'" (John 6:30–31).

Jesus eventually told them plainly: "I am the bread of life. Your ancestors ate the manna in the desert, but they died; this is the bread that comes down from heaven so that one may eat it and not die. I am the living bread that came down from heaven; whoever eats this bread will live forever; and the bread that I will give is my flesh for the life of the world" (John 6:48–51).

When God gave manna in the desert, it was to sustain life in this world; the bread that Jesus Christ, his Son, gave is a pledge of eternal life. We say that the manna from Heaven *prefigured* the Eucharist; it was a glimpse of the true Bread from Heaven, the life-giving Bread: Jesus himself.

Unleavened Bread

The Old Testament Passover event, when the Lord passed over the houses of the Israelites and spared the firstborn sons from death, prefigured the passing over of Jesus from death to life. In that Passover event, the Israelites ate unleavened bread, because they did not have time to wait for bread with yeast in it to rise before leaving Egypt in haste. They took the dough "as is," without yeast, and baked it into unleavened loaves (see Exodus 12:37–39.) To this day, the Jewish people celebrate the Passover with unleavened bread. And, in the Western Church, our Eucharistic bread is also unleavened, just as was the Passover bread that Jesus took, blessed, broke, and gave to his disciples.

The Jewish Passover supper begins with the youngest child asking this question: "What makes this night different from all other nights?" Then the story of the Passover is told and celebrated.

© Roger Ressmeyer / CORBIS

Melchizedek

The very first prefiguring of the Eucharist in the Old Testament was in the Book of Genesis (see 14:18–19), when the King of Salem and priest of God, Melchizedek, brought out bread and wine to greet Abram, later to be called Abraham, the father of the Jewish nation. In the Old Testament, Melchizedek offered the gifts of God's creation to Abraham; in the New Covenant, we offer our gifts of bread and wine to Christ, who makes them a perfect offering to the Father. Both Abraham and Melchizedek are named in "Eucharistic Prayer I," in which, after the consecration, the priest prays to the Father to accept our offerings:

> . . . as once you were pleased to accept
> the gifts of your servant Abel the just,
> the sacrifice of Abraham, our father in faith,
> and the offering of your high priest Melchizedek,
> a holy sacrifice, a spotless victim.
>
> *(Roman Missal)*

The Feeding of the Five Thousand

Now we turn to the New Testament, and to the multiplication of the loaves and fishes. This is also a prefiguring of the Eucharist, even though it is a New Testament event. As we know, the synoptic Gospels (Matthew, Mark, and Luke) are fairly similar in their accounts. They all start with five loaves and two fish, and end with twelve wicker baskets full of fragments. Only in the Gospel of John do we find the detail of the young boy who offered to share his five loaves and two fish with the Apostles, who gave them to Jesus, who then gave them back in abundance to the crowd.

In all the accounts, the actions of Jesus remind us of his actions at the Last Supper: in Mark, for example, he "said the blessing, broke the loaves, and gave them to [his] disciples" (Mark 6:41) to share with the people. The language of Matthew and Luke is similar. In John, however, Jesus "took the loaves, gave thanks, and distributed them" (John 6:11) to the people directly. Later in this chapter, in what is called "The Bread of Life Discourse," the teaching of Jesus about himself as the Bread of Life is revealed. (We discussed this discourse when we discussed the manna in the desert.) The miracle of the loaves had always been a sign of the Eucharist;

in the Gospel of John, the sign is deepened by the teachings of Jesus. You may want to find these accounts and read them for yourself: Matthew 14:13–21, Mark 6:30–33, Luke 9:10–17, and John 6:1–15.

The Last Supper

The Gospel accounts that have been most influential in our celebration of the Eucharist are, of course, the accounts of the Last Supper and their recording of the words and actions of Jesus when he broke the bread and gave it to his disciples, saying: "Take and eat; this is my body." Then he took the cup, gave thanks, and gave it to them, saying, "Drink from it, all of you, for this is my blood of the covenant" (Matthew 26:27–28). These Gospel accounts are Matthew 26:26–29, Mark 14:22–25, and Luke 22:14–20. (You may want to find these accounts yourself and note their similarities and differences.) The words given in the Gospel of Matthew are the words we pray in our liturgy.

The Apostle Paul and the Eucharist

As we know, the Apostle Paul was not with Jesus and the other Apostles and disciples at the Last Supper. Among the Jews he was called Saul, and he was not yet a follower of Christ. After the Resurrection, when the followers of Jesus were gathering together in prayer and in the breaking of the bread, Saul was actively persecuting them. He would have probably continued this indefinitely, had not Jesus intervened (see Acts of the Apostles 9:1–18). In time Saul became known by his Gentile name, Paul, and he became one of the pillars, with Peter, of the Church that Jesus founded.

Paul was not present at the Last Supper, yet his is the earliest written account of the institution of the Lord's Supper in the New Testament. How did he know what Jesus said and did? He knew because Jesus told him. Paul wrote, "For I received from the Lord what I also handed on to you. . . ." (1 Corinthians 11:23). ☦

The Eucharist in the Gospel of John

In the Gospel of John, there is no Last Supper account of the words of institution. However, we have already seen that the Gospel of John is very much concerned with the teachings of Jesus and the meaning of his statement, "I am the bread of life" (John 6:48). In the Last Supper account in John, Jesus is again teaching, by his actions, when he washes the feet of his disciples; and by his words, when he assures his disciples that he will prepare a place for them, that the Holy Spirit will come to help them, and that his life-giving love will remain with them. Chapters 14 and 15 of John's Gospel open the heart of Jesus to us and are among the most beautiful in the New Testament. These teachings reveal to us the inner meaning of the Eucharist.

The Gospel of John also records the wedding at Cana, and names it "the beginning" (2:11) of Jesus' signs. The wine has run out, and Jesus reveals his power by changing water into wine. It is such good wine that the headwaiter tells the bridegroom, "You have kept the good wine until now" (2:10). This miracle prefigures the events of the Last Supper, when Jesus transforms the bread and wine into his Body and Blood, given up for our salvation.

© The Gallery Collection / Corbis

Article 25 The Eucharist: Then and Now

In every age, since the beginnings of the Church, the Eucharist has been "the source and summit of the Christian life"[4] (CCC, 1324). Everything else the Church is and does—in all the other Sacraments, in the various ministries of the

Church, and in every apostolic work—finds its life-giving source in the Eucharist, for in the Eucharist we encounter Christ himself.

© P Deliss / Godong / Corbis

In the Eucharist, God acts to make us holy. In cooperation with his grace, our action consists in the worship and praise of Christ, and through him, of the Father, in the unity of the Holy Spirit. The Eucharist takes up into this praise and thanksgiving our own lives now, as they are, and unites us to heavenly liturgy, the worship and praise of the angels and saints in Heaven. In the Eucharist, we also have a pledge of future glory, for the Body and Blood of Christ is a sign of "the new and everlasting covenant" that Christ initiated at the Last Supper. The Eucharist is thus "the sum and summary of our faith" (*CCC*, 1327).

The Names of the Eucharist

Throughout the centuries the Eucharist has come to be called by many different names. Each name reveals something more of the rich depths of this Sacrament and invites us to see it from another aspect. Let us consider some of these names.

Eucharist

The word *eucharist* comes from the Greek word *eucharistein*, meaning "thanksgiving." The Greek prefix *eu* means "good." The word *charistein* comes from the Greek word *charisma*, meaning "grace." Together they came to mean "thanksgiving," just as the "grace" we say at table is a thanksgiving for our food.

The word *blessing* is also related to the Eucharist, for "Jesus took bread, said the blessing, broke it" (Matthew 26:26), and gave it to his disciples. This aspect of the Eucharist as blessing comes from the Jewish custom of the *berakah*, or prayer of blessing, which has overtones of thanks and praise, integral to the celebration of the Eucharist. As the Gospel expanded into the Greek world, so did the language of the liturgy. The Greek word *eulogein* literally means "good word" (*eu* combined with *logos,* meaning "word"). Thus it came to mean "a blessing." In the early writings of the

Church, it sometimes means the Eucharist itself, as in
1 Corinthians 10:16: "the cup of blessing."

The Lord's Supper

This recalls the meal that Jesus shared with his disciples
before his Passion and is also an anticipation of "the supper
of the Lamb" we will share with Jesus in the Kingdom
of Heaven (see 1 Corinthians 11:20, Revelation 19:9).

The Breaking of the Bread

It was the duty of the host at a Jewish
meal to break the bread and distribute it. We have seen Jesus do this at
the feeding of the five thousand. At
the Last Supper, it has special significance, for here Jesus distributes his
Body to the Apostles and from them
to the entire Church. This is the name
by which the Eucharist was known
among the early Christians, and it is
the action by which the disciples who
met Jesus on the road to Emmaus
recognized that it was truly Jesus
who had spoken to them and was
even now sharing himself with them:
"Their eyes were opened and they
recognized him" (Luke 24:31). The breaking of the bread
signifies that, even though the Bread is broken to share with
all, it is the one Christ that we share in his one Body (see
1 Corinthians 10:16–17).

© Geoffrey Clements / CORBIS

This painting is *The
Supper at Emmaus,*
by Diego Rodriguez
de Silva y Velazquez.
Read Luke 24:13–35.
How has the artist
captured the mood
of this account?
Then picture yourself
at the table. What
is your reaction to
Jesus?

The Eucharistic Assembly

The Greek word for assembly is *synaxis.* The Greek prefix
syn means "together." The word *axis* means "the central
point around which something turns." The etymology of
synaxis can give us insight about the Eucharist. The Eucharist is our *synaxis* because our entire lives turn around it.

The life of the early Christians in Jerusalem was cen-
tered around the Eucharist: "They devoted themselves to
the teaching of the apostles and to the communal life, to
the breaking of the bread and to the prayers" (Acts of the
Apostles 2:42). Sunday, the day of Resurrection, was the day

of assembly (see 20:7). As it was then, the Eucharist today is, and always will be, at the heart of the Church's life.

Because Sunday was the day on which Christ rose from the dead, it is the most significant day to celebrate the Eucharist. It is the day around which the entire liturgical year is built. Sunday is called "the Lord's Day" and should be a day of joy. We honor it by resting from work and by spending time with family and friends. Those who must work on

The Eucharist in the Early Church

In the second century, Saint Justin Martyr wrote a letter to the pagan emperor Antoninus Pius (138–161), explaining to him the Christian celebration of the Eucharist. In the following excerpt, notice the continuity between this celebration and the celebration of the Eucharist today:

On the day we call the day of the sun, all who dwell in the city or country gather in the same place.

The memoirs of the apostles and the writings of the prophets are read, as much as time permits.

When the reader has finished, he who presides over those gathered admonishes and challenges them to imitate these beautiful things.

Then we all rise together and offer prayers* for ourselves . . . and for all others, wherever they may be. . . .

When the prayers are concluded we exchange the kiss.

Then someone brings bread and a cup of water and wine mixed together to him who presides over the brethren.

He takes them and offers praise and glory to the Father of the universe, through the name of the Son and of the Holy Spirit and for a considerable time he gives thanks (in Greek: *eucharistian*) that we have been judged worthy of these gifts.

When he has concluded the prayers and thanksgivings, all present give voice to an acclamation by saying: "Amen."

When he who presides has given thanks and the people have responded, those whom we call deacons give to those present the "eucharisted" bread, wine and water and take them to those who are absent.[5]

(*CCC*, 1345)

Sunday are urged to spend time in leisure at another time during the week (see *CCC,* 2187).

The Holy Sacrifice

Similar names include the Holy Sacrifice of the Mass, the "sacrifice of praise," the spiritual sacrifice, the pure and holy sacrifice. All of these refer to the Eucharist as the sacrifice of Christ made present to us in the liturgy. This sacrifice of Christ, as the sacrifice of the New Covenant, surpasses all the other sacrifices offered to God throughout the history of salvation.

The Holy and Divine Liturgy

The Eucharist is sometimes referred to as the holy and divine liturgy, a term that seems to refer to the Church's liturgy in general rather than one Sacrament, because the Eucharist is the source and summit of the lives of Christians. For the same reason, this Sacrament is sometimes called the Sacred Mysteries. Another name for the Eucharist, Most Blessed Sacrament, also captures the centrality of the Eucharist. "It is the Sacrament of sacraments" (*CCC,* 1330).

Live It!

Eucharistic Living

*O*ne way to participate more fully in the Eucharist is to spend time reflecting on what the celebration means. Give some prayerful thought to the insights listed here. Write a couple of them down so you can carry them with you and read them before or after Mass next Sunday.

> Jesus said to them, "I am the bread of life; whoever comes to me will never be hungry, and whoever believes in me will never thirst." (John 6:35)

> God has no body now on earth but yours; no eyes but yours; no feet but yours; no hands but yours. Yours are the eyes through which the compassion of Christ must look out on the world. Yours are the feet with which he is to go about doing good. Yours are the hands with which he is to bless his people. (Saint Teresa of Ávila)

> This holy Mass, this Eucharist is clearly an act of faith. . . . This body broken and this blood shed for human begins encourage us to give our body and blood up to suffering and pain, as Christ did—not for self, but to bring justice and peace to our people. (Oscar Romero)

Holy Communion and Holy Mass

In the Eucharist we are united to Christ, and so we share with him and with the entire Church, as a single body, in a "holy communion." The Body and Blood of Christ are also called *holy things*, and, in the Eastern Churches, after the consecration, the Body and Blood of Christ are raised on high, and the priest sings out: "Holy things for the holy!" The Eucharist is also known as the bread of angels, bread from Heaven, medicine of immortality, and viaticum. The word *viaticum* means "with you on the way" and is the Eucharist given to the dying as they make their way toward eternal life. *Holy Mass* refers to the entire Eucharistic celebration but takes its name from *missa*, a Latin word for dismissal. The term *Mass* underlines the importance of the dismissal, which is a sending forth of the assembly to accomplish God's will in the world. ✝

Pray It!

Jesus, Living Among Us

On the Sunday after Trinity Sunday, we celebrate the Solemnity of the Body and Blood of Christ (*Corpus Christi*). But we can honor the Eucharist at any time of the year. This prayer is one that can be prayed before or after receiving Holy Communion:

Lord Jesus Christ,
we worship you living among us
in the sacrament of your body and blood.

May we offer to our Father in heaven
a solemn pledge of undivided love.
May we offer to our brothers and sisters
a life poured out in loving service of that kingdom
where you live with the Father and the Holy Spirit,
one God, forever and ever.
Amen.

(*Roman Missal,* Second Edition)

Part Review

1. What is the Paschal Mystery?

2. What does *anamnesis* mean in relation to the Eucharist?

3. How are the Passover, the Last Supper, and the Eucharist connected?

4. Name three Old Testament references that prefigure the Eucharist.

5. How do the words of Jesus in John 6:48–51 help us to understand the meaning of the Eucharist?

6. What is Saint Paul the Apostle's connection to the words and actions of Jesus at the Last Supper?

7. Name at least six significant names by which the Eucharist is known.

Part 2

The Celebration of the Eucharist

Some years ago, people who had set their alarm clock radios to "wake to radio" heard as their Sunday morning greeting a loud sputtering of automobile engines whizzing around a track and a booming voice announcing: "It's Sunday! Come on down to the raceway!"

We might imitate this enthusiasm: "It's Sunday! Come on down to the parish church!" Sunday is the Lord's Day, the quintessential day for the celebration of the Eucharist. The Eucharist is celebrated on the other days of the week, but the Sunday Eucharist is the Eucharist at which the entire community gathers. Sunday is the day we respond to our baptismal call to worship God together in the dignity of our common priesthood; to hear the Word of God proclaimed together and to be sent out to act on it prophetically in our everyday lives; and, through receiving the Body and Blood of Christ, to pledge our lives in service to all, as God's kingly people.

In the articles that follow, we learn more about the Eucharist. We explore the gathering of the assembly, the Liturgy of the Word, the Liturgy of the Eucharist, and the liturgical ministries involved in the Eucharist.

The topics covered in this part are:

Article 26 Gather Faithfully Together

In second-century Syria, a bishop compiled a book of instructions for his fellow bishops. One of the topics was the Sunday assembly. The bishop wrote: "Exhort the people to be faithful to the assembly of the Church. Let them not fail to attend, but let them gather faithfully together. Let no one deprive the Church by staying away; if they do, they deprive the Body of Christ of one of its members!" (*Didascalia*, chapter 13).

From those early days until our own, Christians have assembled for worship and praise, particularly on Sunday. The first Christians were Jews, and when they assembled they were following in the great Jewish tradition of coming together as a people to worship God. As believers in Jesus Christ, the Messiah, they continued to live and worship as Jews, adding "the breaking of the Bread" to their usual worship, as Jesus had instructed them. In fact, in the Acts of the Apostles, we read that the first Christians did this every day: "They devoted themselves to the teaching of the apostles and to the communal life, to the breaking of the bread and to the prayers. . . . Every day they devoted themselves to meeting together in the temple area and to breaking bread in their homes" (2:42–46).

Enter the Gentiles

With the apostolic efforts of the Apostle Paul and others, more and more Gentiles from various places in the Roman Empire became Christian. They gathered together, like the Jewish Christians, to read from the writings of the prophets and the letters of Paul and others, to pray together, and to celebrate the Eucharist together. The day chosen for this gathering was Sunday, the day of Christ's Resurrection. Not having synagogues or other special buildings available for worship, they gathered in private homes for the entire celebration. (More about the meaning of Sunday as a day of worship and rest can be found in article 32, "The Power of the Eucharist.")

Fortunately, many Middle Eastern and Roman homes were built around a central large room (sometimes a courtyard or _atrium_, as the Romans called it, open to the sky)

© DeA Picture Library / Art Resource, NY

A Roman atrium, with a shallow pool.

Church

The term *Church* has three inseparable meanings: (1) the entire People of God throughout the world; (2) the diocese, which is also known as the local Church; (3) the assembly of believers gathered for the celebration of the liturgy, especially the Eucharist. In the Nicene Creed, the Church is recognized as One, Holy, Catholic, and Apostolic—traits that together are referred to as "marks of the Church."

and could accommodate large groups. Thus, in the letters of Saint Paul, we find references to these gatherings: "Greet Prisca and Aquila, my co-workers in Christ Jesus. . . . Greet also the church at their house" (Romans 16:3,5). A reference to *Chloe's people* in 1 Corinthians 1:11 means "the people who meet at Chloe's house." These "house churches" were dynamic, small Christian communities of love and service.

What's in a Name?

The name **church**, given to the gatherings of Christians, has an extensive history and significant meaning. You may recall some of this from your previous studies, but let us briefly review this history and meaning as background for considering the meaning of our own Sunday gatherings today.

The word *church* comes from the Greek word *ekklesia*, meaning "an assembly." *Ekklesia* translates the Hebrew *qahal*, which means a divine call summoning to a gathering. It also means those who respond to that summons. Our English word *church* comes from the German translation of the Greek *ekklesia*, which is *kirke*. As we use and understand it, *Church* means those who are called as "'a chosen race, a royal priesthood, a holy nation, a people of [God's] own, so that you may announce the praises' of him who called you out of darkness into his wonderful light" (1 Peter 2:9). *Church* has three inseparable meanings: (1) the entire People of God throughout the world; (2) the diocese, which is also known as the local Church; (3) the assembly of believers gathered for the celebration of the liturgy, especially the Eucharist. "'The Church' is the People that God gathers in the whole world. She exists in local communities and is made real as a liturgical, above all a Eucharistic, assembly" (*CCC*, 752).

In Baptism we are called by God to be priests (worshippers), prophets (hearers and doers of the Word of God), and kings (servants of all, especially the poor and afflicted). In Baptism we are incorporated into the Church, which is One, Holy, Catholic, and Apostolic. Then, little by little, by our response to God's call in Baptism, and by participation in the liturgy of the Church, especially the Eucharist, we become more and more closely united with Christ and the Church. When we gather and celebrate with other members of the Church, we become more and more God's People, temples of the Holy Spirit, and members of the one Body of Christ.

The Music of the Church

Gregorian chant has "pride of place" in the Church because of its historic roots and because it is "specially suited to the Roman liturgy" (*Constitution on the Sacred Liturgy* [*Sacrosanctum Concilium*, 1963], 116). It is named after Pope Gregory I (540–604), who organized and simplified the cataloging of the various chants assigned to Church celebrations.

Another name for this chant is plainchant, because it is not meant to be sung in harmony but in one continuous melodic line. The French phrase *plein chant* means "full singing." However, in the late Middle Ages, other voices were added to this melodic line. This led to polyphony, or the singing in harmony, in Western music. The Church, however, continued to prefer plainchant, because the words of the Mass and of Scripture remained clear and unobscured. Gregorian chant is still sung in monasteries by monks and nuns who pray and sing the Divine Office several times a day.

Today there is a wide variety of musical expression allowed and encouraged in the liturgy. People from around the world are free to include their indigenous music in liturgical celebrations when it is compatible with the Catholic faith, giving witness to diversity within the unity and universality of the Church. But, in the local assemblies, Gregorian chant has not been lost. Its simple beauty continues to be appreciated, and, in both cathedral and parish churches, it is often interspersed with other styles of music.

The Gathering of the Assembly

In every Sacrament, and at every Eucharist, we begin with the gathering of the assembly. The **assembly** is the gathering of the baptized, and the Head of this assembly is Christ himself. He is the invisible presider over every Eucharist. The bishop or priest represents him and acts *"in the person of Christ the head"* (*CCC*, 1348) as he presides over the assembly, gives the homily, accepts the offerings, and prays the Eucharistic Prayer. The assembly and other ministers (lectors, those who bring up offerings, and those who distribute Communion) have active roles as well, which we will discuss in the last article in this part.

The Doors! The Doors!

In the early Church, the profession of faith and the Liturgy of the Eucharist were guarded carefully. It was feared that visitors would misunderstand or misinterpret what they heard and saw, to the detriment of the Church and of Christians. To this day, in the Eastern Churches, just before the Creed is proclaimed, the deacon chants: "The doors! The doors! In wisdom, let us attend!" In the early Eastern Churches, this was a warning for all unbelievers to leave the assembly so that only baptized members of the Body of Christ remained for the profession of faith and the sacred mysteries. The doors were then shut and no one was allowed to enter from that point. Today this chant alerts the assembly to prepare for the profession of the Creed.

© Saint Elias Ukrainian Catholic Church, Brampton, Ontario, Canada / www.saintelias.com / Andrei Komar

Introductory Rites

The Introductory Rites of the Mass bring us together as a worshipping community and prepare us for listening to the Word of God and for the celebration of the Eucharist.

After the Entrance Chant or gathering song, the assembly makes the Sign of the Cross, the sign in which we begin all of our prayers. The priest then greets the assembly by saying something like, "The grace of our Lord Jesus Christ, and the love of God, and the communion of the Holy Spirit be with you all," and the people answer, "And with your spirit" *(Roman Missal).*

Next the priest, deacon, or other minister may provide a brief introduction to the Mass.

Unless the Rite for the Blessing and Sprinkling of Water is done, the Penitential Act follows. The Penitential Act provides a moment for repentance of sin in silence. Ideally we have come to Mass having already prepared ourselves by examining our conscience. In the Penitential Act, Christ's role in salvation is recalled and our venial sin is forgiven. We do not want lingering sin to interfere with the message of God to us or our becoming more closely united to Christ. We want to give the Holy Spirit an assembly of clean hearts in which to dwell.

The Gloria follows—on Sundays (outside of Advent and Lent), on solemnities and feasts, and in solemn local celebrations. The Gloria expresses our joy in the Lord. It praises God for being who he is, and who he is to us: heavenly King, God, Father; Jesus Christ, Son of the Father, Lord God, Lamb of God, Holy One, Most High; "with the Holy Spirit, in the glory of God the Father. Amen."

At the invitation of the priest, "Let us pray," we pull ourselves together for a short time of silence. Then the priest prays the Collect or Opening Prayer. This prayer (pronounced COL-lect) sets our hearts and spirits "in sync" with the Church, with the readings of the day, and in anticipation of the celebration of the Eucharist to come. While praying the Collect, the priest extends his hands, as if gathering, or collecting, all of our own unspoken yearnings. We respond, "Amen."

We have been welcomed. We have proclaimed God's goodness in Christ. We have expressed sorrow for sin and hope in the Lord's mercy. We have expressed joy in the living God. We, as members of the Body of Christ with the rest of the universal Church, have responded to the Collect that helps us to speak our hopes and our needs. Now we are ready to listen to the Word of God. ✝

assembly

Also known as a congregation, a community of believers gathered for worship as the Body of Christ.

Article 27 The Liturgy of the Word

When Jesus, the Son of God, was tempted by the devil to use his power to turn stones into bread, Jesus replied:

> It is written,
> "One does not live by bread alone,
>> but by every word that comes forth from
>> the mouth of God."
>
>> (Matthew 4:4)

When Jesus says, "It is written," he is introducing a quote from the Book of Deuteronomy, the book of Jewish laws given to the people by Moses. That quotation refers to the manna God gave to his people: "[God] therefore let you be afflicted with hunger, and then fed you with manna, a food unknown to you and your ancestors, so you might know that it is not by bread alone that people live, but by all that comes forth from the mouth of the LORD" (Deuteronomy 8:3).

The manna we eat in the Eucharist is the New Manna, the New Bread from Heaven. The Word we hear in the Liturgy of the Word is the new and living Word of God, directed to us, in our time, and in our lives. The Word of God is not confined to the pages of the Holy Scriptures. It is ever "living and effective, sharper than any two-edged sword, penetrating even between soul and spirit, joints and marrow, and able to discern reflections and thoughts of the heart" (Hebrews 4:12).

Through the work of the Holy Spirit, the Word proclaimed supports and sustains our entire celebration of the liturgy. If we are attentive to the Word, the Holy Spirit plants that Word deep in our hearts, so that what we hear influences us on the deepest level. The Word becomes the root and foundation not only of our participation in the Eucharist but of the whole of our lives. In the liturgy the Spirit is also at work bringing us, as the Body of Christ, into greater unity and nurturing the development of our unique and diverse spiritual gifts (see *Lectionary for Mass*, introduction, 9).

Elements of the Liturgy of the Word

The main part of the Liturgy of the Word consists of three readings from the Sacred Scriptures (on Sundays) as well

Overview: The Celebration of the Eucharist

The Eucharistic celebration is one single act of worship, which always includes the following:
- the proclamation of the Word of God
- thanksgiving to God the Father for all his gifts, above all the gift of his Son
- the consecration of the bread and wine
- participation in the liturgical meal by receiving the Body and Blood of Christ

The celebration of the Eucharist follows a structure that has been handed down through the centuries. The Eucharistic celebration consists of two main parts, the Liturgy of the Word and the Liturgy of the Eucharist. This is an outline of a Sunday celebration:

1. Introductory Rites
   - Gathering of the Assembly (usually with an Entrance Chant or a song)
   - Penitential Act
   - *Kyrie* (Lord, Have Mercy)
   - *Gloria* (Glory to God)
   - Collect (Opening Prayer)

2. Liturgy of the Word
   - First Reading (usually from the Old Testament)
   - Responsorial Psalm (usually sung)
   - Second Reading (usually from the New Testament Letters)
   - Gospel Acclamation (Alleluia)
   - Gospel Reading
   - Homily
   - Profession of Faith (Nicene Creed)
   - Prayer of the Faithful

3. Liturgy of the Eucharist
   - Presentation and Preparation of the Gifts
   - Eucharistic Prayer
   - Communion

4. Concluding Rites
   - Greeting, Solemn Blessing, or Prayer over the People
   - Dismissal (usually with a closing song)

as psalms, canticles, and other Scripture verses between the readings. Following these are the homily, the Profession of Faith, and the Prayer of the Faithful.

Each Sunday Mass has three readings. The first is usually from the Old Testament, the second is from one of the Epistles, and the third is from one of the Gospels. This arrangement highlights the unity of the Old and New Testaments, for each one recounts a facet of the history of our salvation and looks to Christ and all he has done for us and our salvation as central to that history.

The First Reading

The First Reading draws us into the roots of our faith. Saint Paul called the Gentiles "the branch grafted onto the ancient tree" (see Romans 11:17), and, as the graft, we take our nourishment from the tree itself. As "Eucharistic Prayer I" notes, the father of the Jewish people, Abraham, is also our father in faith. The events of the Old Testament record the joys and sorrows, the tribulations and triumphs, of our brothers and sisters, those who have gone before us and have handed down their faith in God to us. They are the ancestors of Jesus, and their response to God prepared the world for the Messiah. The readings proclaimed at Sunday Masses were selected because of their relationship to the chosen Gospel readings and so the assembly would hear many of the most significant Old Testament passages (see *Lectionary for Mass*, introduction, 106.)

A leader of song helps the assembly to sing hymns, songs, and acclamations at appropriate times during the Eucharist. The Responsorial Psalm is sung as a response to the First Reading.

© Bill Wittman / www.wpwittman.com

The Responsorial Psalm

The Responsorial Psalm is a response to the first reading. On Sundays it is usually sung. This psalm gives us an opportunity to meditate on the Word of God. The custom of reading passages and singing psalms from the Old Testament reflects customs in Jewish worship that have been continued in the liturgy of the New Covenant.

The Second Reading

The Second Reading is usually from one of the Letters of Saint Paul or from the writings of the other Apostles. In these letters we can find many similarities to our life of faith today: the assemblies, the description of the Eucharist, the joy of sharing in a community of faith, the human problems involved in such a community—all are reflected in these letters from the founders of the earliest communities. But we do not read them because they are historical accounts; we read them because they are the Word of God and through them God speaks to our lives today.

© Bill Wittman / www.wpwittman.com

The reader plays an important role during the Eucharist, for the Word of God must be heard by all in order to be received and acted upon.

The Gospel Acclamation

The proclamation of the Gospel is preceded by an acclamation, which consists of the Alleluia and a Scripture verse. In Lent the Alleluia is omitted and is replaced by "Glory and praise to you, Lord Jesus Christ" *(Roman Missal)*. The assembly stands for this acclamation, which signifies readiness to hear God's Word through the Gospel proclamation.

The Gospel Reading

The Gospels occupy a central place in the liturgy and in the life of the Church because they have Jesus Christ as their center. Because the proclamation of the Gospel is the high point of the Liturgy of the Word, it is often accompanied by special elements. For example, it is proclaimed by the priest or deacon, and the assembly stands while listening. Before the proclamation the priest or deacon carries the Book of the Gospels to the *ambo* (the reading stand) and is sometimes accompanied by servers with candles and incense. Another special element is the threefold Sign of the Cross that everyone makes on their foreheads, lips, and chests before the proclamation of the Gospel.

The Homily

In the homily we are helped to discover the meaning of the Word of God for us today. At this point in the Eucharist, the Word of God has been poured over us like a deluge of riches. We have listened to the Word in two readings, a psalm, and an acclamation. Then we heard God's Word in the Gospel proclamation. What can we make of all this? What can we take with us to help shape our lives in the image of Christ? What can we do to respond to the Word of God that we hear? The homily helps us to answer these questions: "By means of the homily the mysteries of the faith and the guiding principles of Christian life are expounded from the sacred text during the course of the liturgical year" (*Constitution on the Sacred Liturgy*, 52). The homily must always lead the assembly to active participation in the Liturgy of the Eucharist: "Through the readings and homily Christ's paschal mystery is proclaimed; through the sacrifice of the Mass it becomes present" (*Lectionary for Mass*, introduction, 24).

Profession of Faith

When we say the Nicene Creed together, we respond with faith to the Word of God proclaimed in the readings and in the homily. Proclaiming the Creed (our profession of faith) reminds us of the truths of our faith and so prepares us to celebrate the Eucharist.

The Prayer of the Faithful

The Prayer of the Faithful is also called the Universal Prayer. In this prayer we pray for worldwide, national, and local needs; we pray for our government officials and our Church leaders; we pray for our parish, for neighbors and friends in need, and for those among us who have died. In his Second Letter to Timothy, Saint Paul urges that "supplications, prayers, petitions, and thanksgivings be offered for everyone, for kings and for all in authority, that we may lead a quiet and tranquil life in all devotion and dignity. This is good and pleasing to God our savior, who wills everyone to be saved and to come to knowledge of the truth" (1 Timothy 2:1–4).

The Readings of the Liturgical Calendar

Catholic churches all over the world read the same readings every day of the year. These readings are organized by the Church according to a set order. The readings are arranged in two cycles, one for Sundays and one for weekdays.

The Sunday and Weekday Cycles

The Sunday cycle is divided into three years: Year A, Year B, and Year C. In Year A we read mostly from the Gospel of Matthew. In Year B we read mostly from the Gospel of Mark. In Year C we read mostly from the Gospel of Luke. We read from the Gospel of John during the Easter season of all three years.

The weekday cycle is divided into two years: Year I and Year II. We read Year I in odd-numbered years (2011, 2013, 2015, and so on). We read Year II in even-numbered years. The Gospels are the same for both Year I and Year II. Each year begins with the Gospel of Mark, followed by Matthew, and then Luke. We read the Gospel of John during the Easter season. For the Seasons of Advent, Christmas, Lent, and Easter, for Sundays and weekdays, we read selections that are appropriate to the season.

Before the revision of the cycle of readings, which was mandated by Vatican Council II (1962–1965), we read only one New Testament reading and the Gospel on Sundays. We read the Old Testament on weekdays and certain solemnities only. Back then, the cycle of readings was just one year. If you went to the Mass every Sunday for a year, you would read 1 percent of the Old Testament and 17 percent of the New Testament. Our current *Lectionary for Mass,* over the course of its full Sunday and weekday cycles, includes 14 percent of the Old Testament and 71 percent of the New Testament (see United States Conference of Catholic Bishops [USCCB] Committee on the Liturgy, *Newsletter*, volume 43).

Celebrating the Word of God

The Liturgy of the Word is an essential element in every Sacrament. But did you know that the Liturgy of the Word can be celebrated on its own? Perhaps you have celebrated the Liturgy of the Word when gathered for a special prayer service. In this case a blessing and a dismissal usually follow the general intercessions. A celebration of the Liturgy of the Word is a beautiful way to begin or end a youth-group session or a day of retreat. It is also a wonderful way to pray when gathered at times of special joy or of crisis.

© Bill Wittman / www.wpwittman.com

The USCCB Web site provides the Mass readings for each day of the year. This can help you to prepare for the Sunday or weekday liturgy, or to pray and meditate on the Mass readings. ✞

28 The Liturgy of the Eucharist

As you will remember, the Eucharist is the memorial of Christ's Passover, his Paschal Mystery, his work of salvation accomplished mainly through his Passion, death, Resurrection, and Ascension. In the Eucharist this work is made present for us so that we might enter into it.

In the Liturgy of the Eucharist, the second main part of the Eucharistic celebration, we enter into Christ's Paschal Mystery in the most direct way possible. It is no wonder that the Eucharist is called "the Sacrament of sacraments" (*CCC*, 1211).

In this Sacrament, Christ is present in many ways. He is present in the priest. For it is Jesus Christ, our eternal High Priest, acting through the ministry of the priest, who offers the Eucharistic sacrifice. Only a validly ordained priest, acting in the name of Christ, can preside at the Eucharist and consecrate the bread and wine so they become the Body and Blood of the Lord (see *CCC*, 1411).

Christ is also present in the proclamation of the Word of God, and in the assembly, for he has assured us, "Where two or three are gathered together in my name, there am I in the midst of them" (Matthew 18:20). Whenever we gather in the Eucharistic assembly, we gather as the Body of Christ, and he is present in us and with us. But Christ is most especially present in the Eucharist in his Body and Blood.

The Real Presence of Christ in the Eucharist

The mode of Christ's presence under the Eucharistic elements is unique. Christ is present in his Body and Blood in the fullest sense: "It is a *substantial* presence by which Christ, God and man, makes himself wholly and entirely present"[6] (*CCC*, 1374). This presence is called the Real Presence of Christ.

The Responses of the Assembly

The responses of the assembly are usually very short: "Amen" is the most common. But they are very important. They are the ordinary means of our participation in the celebration of the Eucharist. Not everyone can sing in the choir, or read from Scripture as a lector, or take up the collection, or lead people to their places in the pews. But each one of us is a member of the one Body of Christ, and we are all called to participate in the celebration of the Eucharist by responding in prayer and raising our voices in song with the assembly.

We all know what it feels like to be part of an assembly in which many of the people seem willing to be "dead weight." They allow others to do their responding for them, and they stay silent during the singing of hymns. Charitably, we can say that they do not realize they are missed. Yes, the Mass will go on without their "Amen" and "Alleluia," but, just as it is rude to ignore a question or comment made by someone conversing with you, it is rude to ignore the invitations of the liturgy to affirm and to help carry out the action of Christ in our midst.

The solution? Saint John of the Cross once wrote, "If you want love, put love, and you will find love." It is the same with the Eucharist: If you want enthusiasm (*enthusiasm* literally means "having God inside you"), then give enthusiasm, and you will find enthusiasm. As an assembly, we need the respectful and attentive enthusiasm of each person present.

In the Sacrament of the Eucharist, we become more closely united to Christ and we are strengthened for our life as his disciples. As Saint Augustine, pointing to the Eucharist on the altar, said, "Be what you see, and receive what you are" (*Sermon,* 272). That is, be the Body of Christ and receive the Body of Christ. Christ becomes one with us so that we can become one with him, so that we can *become him,* as the Body of Christ in the world.

The Eucharist for You

The remainder of this article explores the Presentation and Preparation of the Gifts and considers the meaning of the prayers in this part of the Mass. In the next article, we study the Eucharistic Prayer, the heart of the Eucharist, in detail. As we do so, keep in mind that the liturgy is the work of the

Receiving the Eucharist

Saint Justin Martyr, an early Church apologist (someone who explains and defends the faith), offered these criteria for the reception of the Eucharist:

> Because this bread and wine have been made Eucharist ("eucharisted" according to an ancient expression), "we call this food *Eucharist*, and no one may take part in it unless he believes that what we teach is true, has received baptism for the forgiveness of sins and new birth, and lives in keeping with what Christ taught."[7] (*CCC*, 1355)

In these criteria we can easily see that receiving the Eucharist encompasses our entire lives of faith: membership in the Church, belief in the teachings of the Church, including the real presence of Christ in the Eucharist through **Transubstantiation**, and life lived according to the teachings of Christ. This is a goal toward which we strive, making progress little by little. A recipient of the Eucharist must also be in the state of grace and thus free from grave sin. This means that the recipient must be absolved from mortal sin in the Sacrament of Penance and Reconciliation before approaching the Sacrament of the Eucharist.

In addition, we also prepare for the Eucharist by fasting. This is a bodily reminder that the Eucharist is not ordinary food and drink. It also reminds us that, as we fast from food (for one hour in the Western Church, and usually from midnight in the Eastern Churches), we must also fast from thoughts and actions that would be unworthy of a follower of Christ, so soon to receive the Body and Blood of the Lord.

Our outward appearance and behavior should reflect our inward respect and seriousness. "Dressing up" for Sunday Mass is perhaps no longer the norm in many places, but being neat, clean, and modest in dress when attending the Mass is always "in style"! Clothing that may be appropriate for going to the movies or hanging out with friends may not be suitable for Mass. If you're not sure what's okay to wear and what isn't, choose something that covers more of you, not less, something a little dressier than what you'd wear on every other day of the week, something that communicates a respect and dignity appropriate for celebrating the "Sacrament of sacraments" (*CCC*, 1211).

Father; his Son, Jesus Christ; and the Holy Spirit; right now, today. God does not do this work for an anonymous crowd somewhere "out there." No one is anonymous to him. In the Eucharist, God's work of salvation is intended for the good of each one of us.

Presentation and Preparation of the Gifts

The celebration of the Eucharist began with a bare altar except for possibly a crucifix (if there is not one placed near the altar) and two candles (if they are not on separate stands next to the altar). Other necessary items are brought to the altar while an offertory hymn is being sung. These include:

- **the corporal** This is a square white linen cloth upon which all the sacred vessels are placed during the celebration of the Mass. The word *corporal* comes from the Latin word for "body," which is related to Body of Christ (*Corpus Christi*).

- **the purificator** This is a small piece of white linen, folded in three layers, much like a napkin, marked with a cross in the center. It is used by the priest to purify (clean) his fingers, the chalice, and the paten (the round dish used to hold the Host).

- **the chalice** This is the vessel into which the wine will be poured.

- **the *Roman Missal*** (or *Sacramentary*)

The gifts of bread and wine are then brought to the altar, on Sundays usually by members of the assembly in procession. In every parish, money is collected for the support of the parish and for the poor. In some parishes this collection is brought up with the gifts of bread and wine. Some parishes present food for the poor as well. Offerings for the support of the local parish and for the poor have been traditional in the Church from its very beginning.

In the offering of the gifts, you might remember the offering of the bread and the wine of the priest Melchizedek, whom we learned about in article 23, "What Is the Eucharist?" In this offering we ourselves are like Melchizedek, but we give our gifts of bread and wine into the hands of Christ, who will bring our gifts to perfection by changing them, by the words and actions of the

Transubstantiation
In the Sacrament of the Eucharist, this is the name given to the action of changing the bread and wine into the Body and Blood of Jesus Christ.

The bread that we offer becomes, through the words and actions of the priest and the work of the Holy Spirit, the Body of Christ. The Bread of Life is then broken and shared by all.

© The Crosiers / Gene Plaisted, OSC

How Often Do We Receive the Eucharist?

The Eucharist is our lifeline to Christ. Frequent reception of Holy Communion, especially when participating in the Eucharistic celebration, is warmly recommended by the Church. This is the most perfect form of participation in the celebration of the Eucharist. In fact, every Catholic is obliged to receive the Eucharist at least during the Easter season.

It is obligatory to take part in the Eucharistic celebration on Sundays and holy days of obligation. On those days, receiving the Body and Blood of Christ at the Eucharist is recommended highly. In addition, daily reception is encouraged. In fact, some spiritual writers of the early Church believed that the petition of Jesus in the Lord's Prayer, "Give us this day our daily bread," referred to not only the bread we need for our sustenance but also the Holy Eucharist. In fact, we are permitted to receive the Eucharist twice in one day if special circumstances call for it. For example, suppose you receive the Eucharist at a weekday morning Mass. Later you recall that in the evening your parish's fiftieth-jubilee Mass will be celebrated by the bishop. Can you receive Communion at the Jubilee Mass? Of course—as long as you participate in the entire Eucharistic celebration.

© Ocean / Corbis

priest and the work of the Holy Spirit, into his own Body and Blood.

After the priest has accepted the gifts, he raises the Host slightly and thanks God for the gift of this bread, which will "become for us the bread of life." The assembly responds: "Blessed be God forever" *(Roman Missal).* (If there is music or singing, the priest prays inaudibly and the assembly does not respond.)

The priest then pours wine into the chalice. But before he says the blessing, he adds a little water to the wine. This gesture has great significance, as it reminds us of the whole reason for Christ's coming to us in the flesh, and of what will soon be taking place for us in the reception of Holy Communion. The priest says, "By the mystery of this water and wine may we come to share in the divinity of Christ who humbled himself to share in our humanity" *(Roman Missal)*. The priest prays that we will become intermingled with Christ, as intermingled as the water is with the wine!

Then the priest raises the chalice slightly and thanks God for the gift of wine, which will "become our spiritual drink." The assembly responds, "Blessed be God forever" *(Roman Missal)*.

You may remember learning about a Jewish blessing prayer, called *berakah*, in article 25, "The Eucharist: Then and Now." The offering of the gifts of bread and wine are set in this ancient form of blessing and thanksgiving.

After washing his hands (see article 1, "What Is Liturgy?"), the priest concludes the Preparation of the Gifts by facing the people, extending his hands, and praying:

> Pray, brethren (brothers and sisters),
> that my sacrifice and yours
> may be acceptable to God,
> the almighty Father.
>
> > *(Roman Missal)*

Note that this is *our* sacrifice, not the priest's alone. The assembly concurs with the priest's prayer and says:

> "May the Lord accept the sacrifice at your hands
> for the praise and glory of his name,
> for our good
> and the good of all his holy Church."
> The priest then prays the Prayer over the Offerings, and the assembly affirms the prayer with "Amen."
>
> > *(Roman Missal)*

In the offering of our gifts, which will be transformed into the Body and Blood of Christ, we also offer ourselves. In the Eucharist, through the Body and Blood of Christ, we ourselves will be transformed. ✞

The Eucharist as Banquet and Sacrifice

"The Mass is at the same time, and inseparably, the sacrificial memorial in which the sacrifice of the cross is perpetuated and the sacred banquet of communion with the Lord's body and blood" (*CCC*, 1382). The Eucharist is a banquet because we receive Christ as food.

The Eucharist is also a sacrifice because it is a memorial, an *anamnesis*, of the sacrifice of Christ on the cross and his Resurrection. As a sacrifice the Eucharist is offered to make up for the sins of both the living and the dead, and to receive blessings from God for our spiritual or material needs.

© Godong / Robert Harding World Imagery / Corbis

_{Article} 29 The Liturgy of the Eucharist: The Eucharistic Prayer and Communion Rite

The Liturgy of the Eucharist continues with the Eucharistic Prayer, the high point of the Mass. The Eucharistic Prayer includes the following elements:

- the Preface and Preface Acclamation (Holy, Holy, Holy)
- thanksgiving to the Father for all his benefits, especially the gift of his Son
- the *epiclesis,* the institution narrative, the *anamnesis,* the offering, the intercessions, the Concluding Doxology and Amen

In this article we also discuss the Communion Rite, which is the final part of the Liturgy of the Eucharist.

At the Preface Dialogue, the priest invites us to join with him in the Eucharistic Prayer.

© Ocean / Corbis

The Preface and Acclamation

The Eucharistic Prayer is sometimes called by its Greek term, *anaphora.* Its literal meaning in Greek is "carrying up" or "offering." In the Eucharistic Prayer, which is the prayer of thanksgiving and consecration, we offer the bread and wine to be transformed into the Body and Blood of Christ.

The Eucharistic Prayer begins with the Preface Dialogue between the priest and the assembly. The priest greets the people with "The Lord be with you," and the people respond, "And with your spirit." The priest continues, "Lift up your hearts." The people respond, "We lift them up to the Lord." Here let us note that in the *anaphora*, with the bread and wine, we are also offering our hearts to the Lord.

The priest then introduces the theme of the entire Eucharistic Prayer: "Let us give thanks to the Lord our God" *(Roman Missal).* The people speak their agreement and say, "It is right and just" *(Roman Missal).*

The Preface follows immediately. "In the *preface,* the Church gives thanks to the Father, through Christ, in the Holy Spirit, for all his works: creation, redemption, and sanctification" (*CCC*, 1352). The Preface of the Eucharistic Prayer introduces us to the meaning of the Eucharist for us on this particular day. There are many prefaces, and they are quite beautiful. For example, in Preface I of the Nativity of the Lord, we hear:

> So that, as we recognize in him [Christ] God made visible,
> we may be caught up through him in love of things invisible.
>
> *(Roman Missal)*

At the end of the preface, as usual, the priest invites us to join with all the angels and saints in a hymn of praise, sometimes called the Preface Acclamation: "Holy, holy, holy . . ." We are never alone at the Eucharist. We are one with the entire Church on earth and in Heaven, and are surrounded by a cloud of heavenly witnesses.

Epiclesis

As we thank the Father for all his gifts, especially the gift of his Son, we include prayers for the living and the dead. We realize that we are in union with the entire Church.

Then the priest stretches both hands out over the offerings. This is the traditional

At the *epiclesis,* the priest stretches both his hands over the offering, invoking the Holy Spirit to come upon these gifts, to make them holy, that they might become the Body and Blood of Christ.

© Ocean / Corbis

gesture signifying the invocation of the Holy Spirit. In this prayer, called the *epiclesis* (meaning "invocation" in Greek), the priest asks the Father to send the Holy Spirit upon these offerings:

Make holy, therefore, these gifts, we pray,

by sending down your Spirit upon them like the dewfall,

so that they may become for us

the Body and **+** Blood of our Lord Jesus Christ.

(*Roman Missal*, "Eucharistic Prayer II")

(The cross is a signal that the priest should make a Sign of the Cross over the bread and the wine.)

The Institution Narrative and Consecration

At this point in the Eucharistic Prayer, we approach the consecration of the essential signs of the Sacrament of the Eucharist, the bread and wine. The Holy Spirit has been invoked upon these gifts, and so the priest pronounces the words of the Lord which he gave to his Church at the Last Supper: "This is my Body, which will be given up for you. . . . This is the chalice of my Blood. . . ." *(Roman Missal).*

This part of the Eucharistic Prayer is called the institution narrative, as it records the institution of the Holy Eucharist by Jesus. By these words, the action of Christ, and the power of the Holy Spirit, the Body and Blood of Christ is made sacramentally present, together with the sacrifice of Christ offered for all on the cross. By this consecration the Transubstantiation of the bread and wine is brought about. The word *transubstantiation* means "a change of substance." The "accidents" of bread and wine (how they look, taste, and feel) remain the same; but the substance (what the bread and

Catholic Wisdom

The Power of God's Word

Saint John Chrysostom was a great preacher. The following is Saint John's declaration of Christ's presence in the Eucharist:

It is not man that causes the things offered to become the Body and Blood of Christ, but he who was crucified for us, Christ himself. The priest, in the role of Christ, pronounces these words, but their power and grace are God's. This is my body, he says. This word transforms the things offered.[8] (*CCC*, 1375)

wine essentially *are*) has been changed. The Eucharist is not merely a symbol of Christ's presence; rather, Christ himself, living and glorious, is truly present in his Body and Blood, with his soul and his divinity, under the appearance of bread and wine.

The Elements of the Eucharist

The essential elements of the Eucharist are bread and wine. The Eucharistic bread is unleavened (without yeast), made of wheat. (In the Eastern Churches, the bread is leavened.) The wine is made from grapes. The bread and wine must be consecrated together, not separately, and they both must be consecrated in the Eucharistic celebration.

In the Mass, Christ is present "most *especially in the Eucharistic species*"[9] (*CCC*, 1373). He is present as the whole Christ—Body, Blood, soul, and divinity. How long does this real presence of Christ last? It begins at the moment of consecration and lasts as long as the Eucharistic species is present. It is important to note that, when the Host is broken into parts, Christ himself is not divided into parts. Christ remains whole and entire in each part.

The *Anamnesis,* Offering, and Intercessions

The *anamnesis* ("remembering" and making present) begins with the Mystery of Faith (or Memorial Acclamation), in which we proclaim the Paschal Mystery of Christ and what it means to us. This is one example:

> Save us, Savior of the world,
> for by your Cross and Resurrection
> you have set us free.
>
> *(Roman Missal)*

We then recall all that Christ has done for us, and we offer his sacrifice to the Father:

> Therefore, as we celebrate
> the memorial of his Death and Resurrection,
> we offer you, Lord,
> the Bread of life and the Chalice of salvation.
>
> *(Roman Missal,* "Eucharistic Prayer II")

This is followed by another *epiclesis*, still addressing the Father and calling on the Holy Spirit to make us one in Christ:

> Humbly we pray
> that, partaking of the Body and Blood of Christ,
> we may be gathered into one by the Holy Spirit.
>
> (*Roman Missal,* "Eucharistic Prayer II")

Intercessions for the entire Church follow, signifying that this Eucharist is celebrated in communion with the whole Church, the living and the dead, and with the pastors of the Church—the Pope, the local bishop, his priests and deacons, and all the bishops of the entire world.

The Amen

The Eucharistic Prayer ends with a Concluding Doxology, literally "words of praise," beginning with "Through him, and with him, and in him . . ." *(Roman Missal).* In Christ's Body and Blood, we have been made one. To the Doxology, in the unity of the Holy Spirit, the assembly responds with "Amen." This Amen assents to the very greatest prayer, the prayer in which we become one with Christ in his Paschal Mystery.

At the consecration, the priest says, "This is my Body. . . ." and "This is my Blood. . . ." thus following the instructions of Jesus to do this in his memory. Jesus is once again among us in his Body and Blood.

© Bill Wittman / www.wpwittman.com

The Communion Rite

The Liturgy of the Eucharist concludes with the Communion Rite. This part of the Mass begins with the praying of the Lord's Prayer, the Our Father. In this prayer we pray as one Body of Christ, asking for forgiveness of our trespasses "as we forgive those who trespass against us" *(Roman Missal)*.

The priest extends this prayer by continuing, "Deliver us, Lord, we pray, from every evil." We pray for freedom from sin and anxiety as we await and blessed hope and the coming of our Savior, Jesus Christ" *(Roman Missal)*. Although we hope for his coming at the end of time, we also joyfully prepare ourselves for his coming to us personally in this very Eucharist.

The assembly ends this prayer with the acclamation: "For the kingdom, the power and the glory are yours now and for ever" *(Roman Missal)*.

The priest or deacon invites us to share a sign of Christ's peace with one another. In the Eucharist, Christ gives us his own peace. We share a sign not only of our own goodwill but of the very gift of peace that Christ has given us.

While the priest prepares the Eucharist for the people by breaking the large Host into pieces (this part of the Communion Rite is called the Breaking of Bread or the Fraction),

Live It!

Be Part of the Miracle

One well-known Jesuit retreat director and writer on spirituality once commented as follows on Matthew 14:19, the miracle of the loaves:

> Christ breaks the loaves and works the miracle, but he distributes it through [us]. Normally Christ's miracles will reach [all people] only in this way. The light of God's lamp burns with the oil of our lives. This is the aspect of apostolic activity which raises it immediately into the realm of prayer. God needs us just as he needs the grain of wheat for the Eucharist. We too are to be broken, to be distributed, to be eaten. In this way we become part of the miracle; it is worked through us—but then, we have to be broken and distributed. (Peter G. van Breemen, *Called by Name*, page 168)

How will you share your time and talents with your school or your parish? How will you be broken and distributed among those who need your help? How will you be part of the miracle?

the "Lamb of God" is said or sung. The priest takes a small piece of the Host and places it into the chalice, saying inaudibly, "May this mingling of the Body and Blood of our Lord Jesus Christ bring eternal life to us who receive it" *(Roman Missal).*

Before Holy Communion is offered, the priest takes the Host, raises it slightly over the paten, and says, "Behold the Lamb of God" *(Roman Missal)*. This is our invitation to "the supper of the Lamb." Together with the priest, the entire assembly prays:

> Lord, I am not worthy
> that you should enter under my roof,
> but only say the word
> and my soul shall be healed.

> *(Roman Missal)*

This is a reference to the centurion who asked Jesus to heal his servant. He had such faith that he would not allow Jesus to make the journey to his home: "Only say the word and my servant will be healed" (Matthew 8:8). With this kind of faith in Jesus, we approach the reception of the Eucharist, the Bread of Heaven and the Cup of Salvation, the Body and Blood of Christ.

Pray It!

Anima Christi (Soul of Christ)

This prayer is an appropriate one to pray before or after receiving Holy Communion. You may want to choose a few favorite lines to pray.

Soul of Christ, sanctify me.
Body of Christ, heal me . . .
Passion of Christ, strengthen me.

Good Jesus, hear me.

In your wounds shelter me.
From turning away keep me.
From the evil one protect me.
At the hour of my death call me.
Into your presence lead me,
to praise you with all your saints
for ever and ever.
Amen.

After Holy Communion, a short period of silence is observed, or a song of praise may be sung. Then all stand for the Prayer after Communion. This prayer asks that the Sacrament of the Eucharist may take effect in our lives. The assembly responds: "Amen." Yes! It is true! ✝

Article 30 Ministries at Mass

In the last few articles, we explored the Liturgy of the Word and the Liturgy of the Eucharist. Now we turn our attention to the ministries involved in the celebration of the Eucharist.

The word *ministry* means "service." Those who help with the celebration of the Eucharist are often referred to as ministers. There are various roles of service to be carried out by both ordained and lay ministers in the celebration of the Eucharist. Before we begin discussing these, we must point out that the greatest minister of all, the greatest "servant of all," as he described himself (see Luke 22:27), is Jesus Christ.

In his visit to the British Isles in 2010, Pope Benedict XVI met with the Catholic bishops of England in the city of Birmingham. On the same day, he beatified John Henry Cardinal Newman, a former Anglican priest.

© ANTHONY DEVLIN / POOL/epa/Corbis

The Role of the Ordained

In every Eucharist we are united with the entire Church. The liturgy is God's work, in which the whole People of God participate. Every liturgy affects the entire Church, as well as the individual members of the Church. In the liturgy each member of the Church has a role, in accordance with that member's particular vocation, office, ministry, or participation in the Eucharist. The liturgy is ordered so that each person should carry out to the full his or her own role, without taking on the role of another.

The Pope and Bishops

In every Eucharist we are particularly united with the Pope as a sign of unity. We offer every Eucharist for the entire Church, and we pray for the Pope and for our local bishop by name. We name the bishop because he is responsible for the celebration of the Eucharist in our diocese, even if a priest offers that Eucharist. Even though the bishop is not physically present at every Eucharist in his diocese, he is present in spirit, for every Eucharist is the celebration of a local church gathered around its bishop. As Saint Ignatius of Antioch wrote in the early centuries of the Church: "Let only that Eucharist be regarded as legitimate, which is celebrated under [the presidency of] the bishop or him to whom he has entrusted it"[10] (*CCC*, 1369). Bishops, priests, and deacons are ordained ministers of the Church. They have all received the Sacrament of Holy Orders in varying degrees. (For more information, see section 5, part 1, "The Sacrament of Holy Orders.")

Priests

In the Eucharist the priest follows the command of Jesus and makes present the offering of Jesus himself to the Father. He, in the person of Christ, thus unites us, the Body of Christ, to our Head, Christ himself, in the very Body and Blood of the Lord. His entire ministry, to preach the Good News of Christ, draws its strength from the Eucharist. In the liturgy the priest stands at the head of the people, presides over their prayer, proclaims to them the Word of God, includes them with him in the offering of the Body and Blood of Christ to the Father in the Holy Spirit, and gives them the Bread of Life and the Cup of Salvation.

Deacons

The deacons of the Church assist the bishop and the priests in the celebration of the Sacraments, especially of the Eucharist. In their role of service at the liturgy, deacons, because of their ordination, are given first place. In the Eucharist they may proclaim the Gospel, preach the homily, announce the Prayer of the Faithful, direct the people as needed, pour the water into the chalice of wine at the Preparation of the Gifts, announce the Sign of Peace, assist in the distribution of Holy Communion, prepare the people for the Solemn Blessing ("Bow down . . ."), and dismiss the assembly.

The Role of the Assembly

The assembly as a whole has a role in the liturgy. Together with the priest, we offer Christ to the Father, and through Christ, we offer ourselves. As children of the Father, we are

The role of reader is one of the roles a layperson may fulfill.

© Bill Wittman / www.wpwittman.com

to make every effort to be a sign of unity to one another as brothers and sisters, and should not allow any individual preference, however devout, to detract from this unity. Whatever we do in the liturgy, we do as one body, whether that be listening to the Word of God, joining in the prayers, singing, or receiving Holy Communion. There is a beauty in the unity of liturgical gestures and postures (standing, sitting, or kneeling as appropriate), which is a sign of the beautiful unity of the Body of Christ (see *General Instruction on the Roman Missal*, 95–96.)

Particular Ministries for Laity

At the Eucharist the ordained ministers of the Church are, as needed, assisted by lay ministers. You may be familiar with the following lay ministries: altar server, lector, and extraordinary minister of Holy Communion.

Being an altar server is a privilege. Although most altar servers are young, many older people serve in this role as well. Altar servers must always be alert to the needs of the priest and deacon at the altar, and must assist in the liturgy in a dignified way.

The role of lector, or reader, is another ministry that can be filled by laypeople. Being a lector requires preparation and even some training. In order to read Scripture with meaning, the lector must first understand the Scripture passage he or she is assigned. Lectors are encouraged to practice their reading several times aloud at home, and even a few times in church, before reading it to the assembly. In public reading it is easy to stumble over words we know quite well, much less unfamiliar words that we have never before tried to pronounce! Everything in the liturgy deserves our best effort, and that certainly includes the readings, by which the Holy Spirit guides our lives.

The extraordinary ministers of Holy Communion assist at the Eucharistic celebration by distributing the Body and Blood of Christ. They also are privileged to take Holy Communion to those who are sick or homebound and unable to participate in the Mass. This ministry is an ancient one in the Church. Those who are vulnerable due to illness or advanced age require sensitive and reliable ministers. Thus this ministry requires preparation and prayerful dedication.

Several other ministries are ordinarily filled by laypeople. The *psalmist* (the singer of the responsorial psalm), the *schola cantorum* or *choir,* and the *cantor* or *choir director* are laypeople. Musicians are also vital to the celebration. Other ministries fulfilled by laypeople also help with the Eucharistic celebration: the sacristan (who arranges the liturgical books, vestments, and other things necessary for the celebration), the commentator (who may introduce the celebration and occasionally, with brief remarks, help the assembly understand the liturgical action better), and greeters and ushers (who greet the worshippers at the doors of the church, offer songbooks, help worshippers find seats, take up the collection, and sometimes direct processions). In larger churches and cathedrals, often a master of ceremonies is needed to help plan and carry out the liturgy with proper order and devotion.

You may already have taken on one or more of these ministries in your parish church or at your school. If so, you may have found that taking an active part in the liturgy gives you a unique perspective on "the work of God" in your parish. Ministers at the Eucharist are ordinary people, our neighbors and friends, who assist with something extraordinary: the great gift to us of the Body and Blood of Christ. ✝

Christ, Our High Priest

The title of high priest is taken from the Jewish liturgy. In that liturgy, once a year on the Day of Atonement, the high priest, after sacrificing a lamb or goat, entered the Holy of Holies, the inner sanctuary of the Temple, and offered the blood of the sacrificed animal in atonement for his sin and the

sins of the people. Jesus is the Eternal High Priest because he is both the high priest who offers the sacrifice and the victim (the new Paschal Lamb) who is sacrificed. Jesus sacrificed himself, once for all, during his Passion and death. But, in the Eucharist, in offering himself to the Father and giving himself to us in his Body and Blood, he unites us with him. We become part of his sacrifice, his Paschal Mystery—his Passion, death, Resurrection, and Ascension.

The epistle to the Hebrews describes Jesus as a compassionate High Priest who has been tested by temptation, as we are, but who never sinned. Now that he is victorious, he can help us, who are still struggling:

> Therefore, since we have a great high priest who has passed through the heavens, Jesus, the Son of God, let us hold fast to our confession. For we do not have a high priest who is unable to sympathize with our weaknesses, but one who has similarly been tested in every way, yet without sin. So let us confidently approach the throne of grace to receive mercy and to find grace for timely help. (Hebrews 4:14–16)

Part Review

1. Describe the worship of the first Christians. What common elements does it share with our worship today?

2. In the Eucharist what is the purpose of the Introductory Rites?

3. What is the purpose of the Penitential Act in the Eucharist?

4. In what ways is Christ present in the celebration of the Eucharist?

5. How is the Holy Spirit at work in the celebration of the Eucharist?

6. In what ways do the Liturgy of the Word and the Profession of Faith prepare us to celebrate the Liturgy of the Eucharist?

7. What is the Eucharistic Prayer and why is it the high point of the Eucharist?

8. How is Christ's Paschal Mystery proclaimed and made present in the Eucharist?

9. Describe the role of the assembly in the celebration of the Eucharist.

Part 3

The Eucharist in Daily Life

In his poem "East Coker," T. S. Eliot wrote, "In my end is my beginning." This is certainly true of the ending of the Eucharistic celebration. The Concluding Rites, as we will discuss in this part, both end the Mass and begin anew our Christian discipleship in prayer and action.

This is because the Eucharist is not something we receive just for ourselves. We are reminded of this in "Eucharistic Prayer IV":

> And that we might live no longer for ourselves
> but for him who died and rose again for us,
> he sent the Holy Spirit from you, Father,
> as the first fruits for those who believe,
> so that, bringing to perfection his work in the world,
> he might sanctify creation to the full.
>
> *(Roman Missal)*

This prayer reminds us of the work of the Holy Spirit in our lives. As we explored in earlier articles, the Holy Spirit, if we allow him, works through us to bring us to full life in Jesus Christ and to bring that fullness of life to others. The Holy Spirit helps us to be more and more what we have received in the Eucharist—the Body of Christ.

The topics covered in this part are:

- Article 31: The Concluding Rites: To Love and Serve (page 166)

- Article 32: The Power of the Eucharist (page 171)

- Article 33: Living the Eucharist (page 175)

Article 31 The Concluding Rites: To Love and Serve

The parish is a community, and every community has details to communicate when members are gathered: announcements of meetings, invitations to join in the coffee hour after the Mass, and announcements of the upcoming reception of Sacraments by members of the community. These announcements are appropriately made at the beginning of the Concluding Rites. Then the particular elements of the Concluding Rites unfold: the greeting, the Final Blessing, and the Dismissal.

The Greeting

The Concluding Rites begin with the greeting by the priest, "The Lord be with you," and the assembly's response, "And with your spirit" *(Roman Missal)*. This particular greeting functions as a good-bye. In fact, our English word *good-bye* is a shortened form of the phrase "God be with you." The priest—the president of our assembly, our presider, and our minister of the Eucharist—has brought us to Christ and Christ to us, and our last greeting to him is a greeting of good-bye, and also of thanks.

The final blessing sends us forth to glorify the Lord with our lives and to bring Christ's Good News and peace to all. We are the disciples of Jesus in the world today.

The Blessing

Following the greeting, the priest blesses the assembly. He may choose the Simple Blessing, the Solemn Blessing, or the Prayer over the People.

© Bill Wittman / www.wpwittman.com

The Simple Blessing

The blessing that follows the greeting is often this simple form:

> May almighty God bless you,
> the Father, and the Son, ✚ and the Holy
> Spirit.
> The assembly responds: Amen.
>
> *(Roman Missal)*

Symbols of the Eucharist

As you look around your cathedral or parish church, you may see, portrayed in stained glass or set into other art media, various symbols of the Eucharist. Here are a few of them to look for:

- **Chalice and Host** With the Chalice and Host, often grapes and bread, or grapes and sheaves of wheat are portrayed. Sometimes the Host is initialed with the letters *IHS* or *IHC*. These are the first three letters of *Ihsus* or *Ihcus*, Jesus' name in Greek.

- **INRI** These letters represent the Latin words *Iesus* (Jesus) *Nazarenus* (of Nazareth) *Rex* (King) *Iudaeorum* (of the Jews). This was the sign Pontius Pilate ordered to be written on the cross of Christ. These letters also may be found written on or above the Host, linking the sacrifice of the cross to the Eucharist.

- **The pelican** According to legend, the pelican has such great love for its offspring that it pierces its own breast to feed them with its blood. Thus the pelican became a symbol of Christ, whose love for us led to his sacrifice of himself on the cross and his feeding us with his own Body and Blood. The pelican is sometimes shown nesting on top of the cross.

- **The Lamb of God** The Lamb of God is both a symbol of the Resurrection of Christ (the victorious Lamb of God is a prominent symbol in the Book of Revelation) and a symbol of the Eucharist, for Christ is the sacrificial Lamb of God who died for us, rose again, and is now our Paschal Sacrifice. The Lamb of God is often shown carrying a banner of victory. Sometimes the banner is inscribed with the Greek word *NIKA*, which means "conqueror." When *NIKA* is preceded by *IC* (the Greek initials for Jesus Christ) and *XC* (the first and last letters for Christ in the Greek alphabet), the phrase "Jesus Christ Conqueror" is formed.

The Solemn Blessing

Some days in the liturgical year call for a solemn blessing. The priest (or deacon if present) addresses the assembly: "Bow down for the blessing" *(Roman Missal)*. The solemn blessing consists of three petitions (to which the assembly responds each time, "Amen") and concludes with:

> And may the blessing of almighty God,
> the Father, and the Son, + and the Holy Spirit,
> come down on you and remain with you for ever.
> All respond, "Amen."

The Prayer over the People

A third option for the blessing is the prayer over the people. After the invitation to bow for the blessing, the priest extends his hands over the people while he says or sings the prayer. The prayer has only one petition, and ends with the priest saying, "Through Christ our Lord," or a similar phrase, with the people responding, "Amen." After the prayer the priest then adds the ending formula of the solemn blessing.

Showing Love in Everyday Ways

We do not have to go far to find brothers and sisters to love—our family and friends, our relatives, our neighbors, and the people we meet in school and in stores, along the street, on public transportation, and at special events. The kind of love we offer each person is appropriate to that person. Showing love does not mean hugging everyone in sight, but it does mean respecting each person and recognizing that each person we meet is an individual human being, made in the image of God. It means not treating a person (a clerk in a store, a librarian, an usher in a theater) as if he or she were a machine dispensing services, to whom we can act with an "attitude" if all does not go exactly as we want. When dealing with our fellow human beings with love, we say "please" and "thank you"; we greet friends or anyone else we meet with pleasant hellos and good-byes; we extend a cheerful smile, even in the midst of a trying situation. Love means that we treat others with kindness and with a generous heart. As followers of Christ, we are called to show love to all people.

The Dismissal

Next the priest or deacon dismisses the assembly. He uses one of the following four options:

"Go in peace, glorifying the Lord by your life." *(Roman Missal)*

The message here is that now that you have received Christ, remain in him and remain in his peace. Let this Eucharist be the rock and the stronghold of your life. Remember the words of the Risen Christ to his disciples: "Peace be with you" (John 20:19). The implication is that if you are steady in the peace of Christ, you will be able to offer that peace to others, bringing glory to God.

"Go forth, the Mass is ended." *(Roman Missal)*

This option reflects the traditional Latin dismissal, *"Ite Missa est,"* or "Go, the Mass is ended." In this phrase the word *Missa* has given us the very word we use often for the celebration of the Eucharist: Mass. In another sense it is related to the Latin word *missio,* meaning "mission." So the sense of this dismissal is, "Go, you are sent on a mission for Christ." This dismissal reminds us that we are sent into the world by Christ to do his work and to follow his way.

Pray It!

Surrender to God's Will

This prayer is attributed to Saint Ignatius Loyola. It asks that God accept our surrender to him and that he use us to advance his loving will and to create a more just and peaceful world. It is a very appropriate prayer for private thanksgiving after receiving Holy Communion.

Receive, Lord, my entire freedom.
Accept the whole of my memory,
my intellect and my will.
Whatever I have or possess,
it was you who gave it to me;
I restore it to you in full,
and I surrender it completely
to the guidance of your will.

Give me only love of you
together with your grace,
and I am rich enough
and ask for nothing more.
Amen.

"Go and announce the Gospel of the Lord."
(Roman Missal)

In Jesus' parable of the judgment of the nations, the king said, "Whatever you did for one of these least brothers of mine, you did for me" (Matthew 25:40). This is what Jesus, the King, expected of his disciples, and this is what he expects of us. He expects us to be Good News and to bring Good News to others, especially to those who need us the most. The Good News is the Good News of God's love, and as the beloved disciple Saint John the Apostle wrote to his assembly, his local church, so long ago: "The way we came to know love was that [Christ] laid down his life for us; so we ought to lay down our lives for our brothers. . . . Children, let us love not in word or speech but in deed and truth" (1 John 3:16,18).

"Go in peace." *(Roman Missal)*

We have responded to Christ's invitation to come to him in the Sacrament of the Eucharist. He has given us his gift of peace. We go now to share that peace with a world that badly needs it.

Every dismissal formula encourages us to walk with the Lord as we leave the assembly, and reminds us to follow God's will in every event of our daily lives.

Live It!

The Challenge of Following Christ

In his encyclical "On the Progress of Peoples" (*"Populorum progressio"*), Pope Paul VI offers this challenge especially to young people: "Would that all those who profess to be followers of Christ might heed His plea: 'I was hungry and you gave me to eat; I was thirsty and you gave me to drink; I was a stranger and you took me in; naked and you covered me; sick and you visited me; I was in prison and you came to me" (Note 61; Matthew 25:35–36).

Consider this challenge in your own life: How can you help those who are hungry and thirsty? How can you help "the stranger" or visitors to your school, parish, or community? How can you help clothe those in need? How can you help give comfort to the sick or, as appropriate, encourage the growth in human and spiritual values among those in prison?

When you receive the Eucharist, talk to Jesus about these things that are so important to him.

The people's response to the dismissal is "Thanks be to God." Our thanksgiving for the entire Eucharistic celebration is wrapped up in this one phrase. We have so much to be thankful for: the Mass itself and all the gifts of God—especially the gift of his Son, Jesus Christ, given to us in his own Body and Blood in the Eucharist. Our thanksgiving is also a thanksgiving for what is to come after we leave this Eucharist, for God's gifts are never finished.

Before he leaves the altar, the priest, bowing, reverences it with a kiss. Then he bows with the other ministers and leaves. On Sundays there is usually a recessional—a procession from the altar to the back of the church—and a closing hymn.

Pay attention to the Dismissal at Mass this week. As you hear and respond to the priest's words, consider how you can bring peace, love, and the Good News to those you meet each and every day. ✝

Article 32 The Power of the Eucharist

The eating and drinking of the Body and Blood of Christ has certain effects within us, in our own hearts and lives, and within the Body of Christ, of which we are a part. The Eucharist changes us. In this article we discuss five powerful effects the Eucharist has on those who receive it and on the entire Church.

In the Gospel of John, the vine and the branches are symbols of our life in Christ. In fact, the union of vine and branch is so close that we usually cannot tell them apart. How can this be true of you and Christ?

© a454 / Shutterstock.com

The Eucharist Strengthens Our Union with Christ

This is the principal effect of receiving Holy Communion: the strengthening of our personal and intimate union with Jesus Christ. This primary effect reflects the words of the Lord himself: "I have called you friends" (John 15:15), and "Whoever eats my flesh and drinks my blood remains in me and I in him" (John 6:56).

The Eucharist gives us life. In the Last Supper discourse in the Gospel of John, Christ describes our connection with him as the life-giving connection between the vine and its branches. If a branch separates from the vine, it withers. In the Eucharist we are connected to Christ as branches to the vine. The Eucharist is the foundation of our new life in Christ. In every Eucharist we die to sin and rise to new life in him.

The Eucharist helps us to grow in the Christian life. Just as we need material food for growth and strength, so we need the spiritual food of the Eucharist to grow into the fullness of Christ during our entire lifetime. And, at the end of life, we may have the opportunity to receive the Sacrament of the Eucharist as viaticum, food for the journey from this life into eternal life. We discuss this further when considering the Sacrament of Anointing of the Sick.

The Eucharist Strengthens Our Union with the Church

"The Eucharist makes the Church" (*CCC*, 1396). Through our participation in the Eucharist, we are united more closely to Christ, and therefore our incorporation into the Church, which began at Baptism, is renewed and deepened. In Baptism we are called to form one body with the Church. The Eucharist fulfills this baptismal call. Saint Augustine explained the union of Christ and his Body, the Church, in this way:

> If you are the body and members of Christ, then it is your sacrament that is placed on the table of the Lord; it is your sacrament that you receive. To that which you are you respond "Amen" ("yes, it is true") and by responding to it you assent to it. For you hear the words, "the Body of Christ," and respond "Amen." Be then a member of the Body of Christ that your *Amen* may be true.[11] (*CCC*, 1396)

The Eucharist Encourages Our Prayer for the Unity of All Christians

Unfortunately, all who are baptized in the name of the Father, and of the Son, and of the Holy Spirit do not share a common table of the Lord in the Eucharist. We are called to pray for the full unity of all those who believe in Christ and have been baptized in him. Because we are not fully united, Eucharistic intercommunion is not permitted. This means the reception of Holy Communion in the Catholic Church by non-Catholics is not allowed. Neither are Catholics permitted to receive Communion in non-Catholic congregations. Eucharistic intercommunion is not possible with those faith communities that have not preserved Apostolic Succession through the Sacrament of Holy Orders. These include the faith communities usually described as Protestant.

However, in the Eastern Orthodox Churches (the Eastern Churches not in full communion with the Catholic Church), the line of Apostolic Succession has never been broken. The Eastern Orthodox Churches possess true Sacraments, especially in the priesthood and in the Eucharist. Therefore in certain circumstances, and with the approval of Church authority, the receiving of Communion in the Catholic Church by members of the Orthodox Churches is permitted.

We pray for unity with all of these Churches and faith communities, especially during the Week of Prayer for Christian Unity.

The Week of Prayer for Christian Unity

The Week of Prayer for Christian Unity begins each year on the Feast of the Chair of Saint Peter (January 18) and ends on the Feast of the Conversion of Saint Paul (January 25). Fr. Paul Wattson founded the Franciscan Friars of the Atonement, of Graymoor, New York, as an Episcopalian brotherhood dedicated to the atonement (making up for) of Christ for our sins and the ministry of "at-one-ment" (union) with all Christians. After much prayerful consideration, the friars eventually united as a community with the Catholic Church. Ecumenical efforts remained a focus of their ministry, and as early as 1908, they began to observe a week of intense prayer for Christian unity.

Currently, this Week of Prayer for Christian Unity is cosponsored by the Vatican's Pontifical Council on Promoting Christian Unity and the Commission on Faith and Order of the World Council of Churches. During this week parishes are urged to pray each day for a particular ecumenical intention. In some places the Week of Prayer for Christian Unity is celebrated by an ecumenical prayer service, hosted each year by a different Catholic parish, Orthodox church, or Protestant community.

The Eucharist Separates Us from Sin

Because the Body of Christ was "given up for us" and the Blood of Christ was "shed for the forgiveness of sins," the Eucharist not only unites us to Christ but also cleanses us from past sin and preserves us from future sin, with our freedom and cooperation. Saint Ambrose called the Body and Blood of Christ the remedy for sin (see *CCC,* 1393). We do not come to the Eucharist because we are perfect; we come because we need the nourishment of Christ and the forgiveness of our sins. When we come to the Eucharist, we come to Christ, the Divine Physician, who said, "Those who are well do not need a physician, but the sick do. . . . I did not come to call the righteous but sinners" (Matthew 9:12–13). Thus, as the Eucharist renews our charity and love, this very charity wipes away our venial sins. The Eucharist roots us deeper into the love of Christ, and thus we are able to extend that love to others.

The Eucharist, because it is a powerful sign of Christ's sacrificial love for us, also preserves us from mortal sin. It does not forgive mortal sin; for this we need the Sacrament of Penance and Reconciliation. But, because it strengthens the bonds between Christ and us, committing a mortal sin becomes more and more unthinkable—because it would separate us from the One who loves us.

The Eucharist Commits Us to the Poor

Saint Paul found it necessary to correct the Corinthian Church for its excesses. At one time it was the custom to partake of the Body and Blood of Christ as part of an entire meal. This led to a situation in which people began bringing their own food to eat—with some having plenty while others had little. Saint Paul scolded them for it, writing: "In eating, each one goes ahead with his own supper, and one goes hungry while another gets drunk. Do you not have houses in which you can eat and drink? Or do you show contempt for the church of God and make those who have nothing feel ashamed?" (1 Corinthians 11:21–22). Note that Saint Paul wrote that the selfishness and lack of sharing on the part of the Corinthians shows "contempt for the church of God," which is the Body of Christ. Saint Paul solved the immediate problem by telling everyone to eat at home! However, the root problem, lack of charity and love—for God, for our neighbors, and for our brothers and sisters in Christ—can be solved only by sharing our time, talent, and treasure with one another and with those in need. ✝

© Bill Wittman / www.wpwittman.com

Often a small group effort yields big benefits for those in need. Brainstorm ways your efforts to raise money or volunteer time might help a favorite cause in your area. Then put yourselves to work!

Article 33 Living the Eucharist

In the previous article, we discussed some effects of the Sacrament of the Eucharist, among them a stronger and deeper union with Jesus and the Church, and a commitment to those who are poor and in need. In this article we begin by discussing the importance of gathering for the Sunday Eucharist, and then we explore two of the many ways to live out our union with Christ and the Church: worship of the Eucharist and a commitment to people who are poor.

The Sunday Eucharist

The entire Church year revolves around the day of Christ's Resurrection: Sunday. Sunday is our day of rest, fulfilling and replacing the seventh day, the Sabbath day, of the Old Covenant as our weekly day of worship and rest. Sunday is, or should be, a day of "Heaven on earth," preparing us for that life of eternal praise and eternal rest for which we hope. As the Sabbath day commemorates the completion of the first creation of the world, so Sunday, the Lord's day, repre-sents the new creation made possible by the Resurrection of

© Bill Wittman / www.wpwittman.com

As we recognize the Body of Christ in the Eucharist, we are also called to recognize Christ in one another and in those in need.

Christ. For this reason the day we celebrate the Resurrection of Christ is often called the eighth day.

Celebrating the Resurrection of Christ at the Sunday Eucharist is "the foundation and confirmation of all Christian practice" (*CCC,* 2181). Because attending the Mass on Sundays and on holy days of obligation is so important, every Catholic is obliged to do so unless excused for a serious reason or dispensed by the pastor. Deliberately failing to do so is a grave sin. This obligation is the first precept, or rule, of the Church.

Resting from unnecessary work on Sundays, so that time may be set aside for worship and relaxation, is also a matter of obligation. Sunday is a day to spend time with family, to participate in social and cultural activities, and to spend time in quiet prayer and reflection. We must also avoid asking others to do any unnecessary work that would hinder their observance of Sunday worship and rest. However, the Church recognizes that some people must work on Sundays. In that case the Church urges those people to take advantage of another day of rest during the week.

Why is participating in the Eucharist on Sunday so important? Because it is a sign of faithfulness to Christ, and a way of thanking Christ for his total faithfulness to us. Gathering with others for the Mass on Sunday (or Saturday evening) also gives witness to our union with Christ and with one another in the solidarity of faith and love that is shared by the members of the Church. At the Eucharist, in word and action, we show that we are united in faith and love. Together the community gratefully acknowledges the holiness of God and his saving love for his people. By our very presence, we show that we trust in him for our salvation. In coming together to worship and to share the Bread of Life, we, as followers of Jesus, strengthen one another, and, with the guidance of the Holy Spirit, deepen our union with Christ as sons and daughters of the Father.

This union with Christ does not end when the Mass ends. There are many ways to live out this union with Christ, ways that flow directly from our active and reverent participation in the Eucharist. Two significant ways are the worship of the Eucharist and commitment to those who are poor and in need.

Catholic Relief Services

Catholic Relief Services (CRS) is the official international humanitarian agency of the Catholic Church in the United States. It operates under the auspices of the United States Conference of Catholic Bishops, and its mission is to assist the poor and vulnerable in other lands. Contributing to CRS is one way Catholics in the United States can live out our Eucharistic commitment to those who are poor or in need around the world.

Catholic Relief Services first began its work during World War II. At that time its focus was to help resettle European refugees who were fleeing war-torn countries. As conditions improved in Europe after the war, CRS turned its attention to other areas of need around the globe, with particular attention to those who are poor or oppressed.

As chair of the board of directors of Catholic Relief Services, Archbishop Timothy Dolan, the Archbishop of New York, wrote in a CRS brochure:

> For Catholic Relief Services, who we are and who we serve are even more important than what we do. . . . We are committed Christians. We serve the poor, in whom we see the reflection and the face of Jesus Christ. That is more important, and that gives rise to what we do. CRS serves people because of need, not creed. We don't help people because they're Catholic; we do it because we are.

Worship of the Eucharist

Eucharistic worship flows from the Real Presence of Christ, in his Body and Blood, in the Eucharist. Eucharistic worship is expressed in three important ways: reverence at the Mass and toward the Sacrament of the Eucharist, respect shown toward the tabernacle, and adoration of the Eucharist.

Reverence

Within the Eucharistic celebration, we show our reverence for the Body and Blood of Christ by certain gestures, among them, genuflecting or bowing deeply when approaching the altar (where the Body and Blood of Christ is consecrated) or the tabernacle. Reverence for the Eucharist means we must prepare ourselves well and prayerfully to receive the Body and Blood of Christ, realizing that we are in the presence of this great and holy Mystery of our faith. Such reverence extends to the way we treat the consecrated Hosts within and outside of the Mass. Our reverence for the Eucharist extends to those times when the Host is exposed to solemn veneration (as at a service of Benediction) and when it is carried in procession (as on the Feast of the Body and Blood of Christ).

The Tabernacle

Every church has a tabernacle set aside for the reservation of the Eucharist. The tabernacle contains the consecrated Hosts that are taken to those who are sick or dying. A light is kept burning before the tabernacle at all times. This is a symbol of the presence of Christ, who is always with us in the Eucharist. Quiet prayer before the tabernacle, in the presence of Christ in the Eucharist, has become an important tradition in the Church. These times of quiet prayer are often called visits to the Blessed Sacrament. In his encyclical "Mystery of Faith" (*"Mysterium fidei"*), Pope Paul VI (1897–1978) described such a visit as "a proof of gratitude, an expression of love, and a duty of adoration toward Christ our Lord" (*CCC*, 1418). The Church recommends that a special place for the tabernacle be reserved in every church.

Adoration

It is entirely appropriate that Christ, present in the Eucharist, be honored with our worship and adoration. In this way we express our gratitude and love for him who loved us so much, and loved us "to the end" (John 13:1). Many parishes today have obtained the privilege of having special times and days of Eucharistic adoration. The Host, placed in a sacred vessel called a monstrance, is set on the altar so it can be seen, for as little as an hour a day or

The practice of Eucharistic adoration emerged in the Middle Ages, when reception of the Eucharist was more rare than it is today. During adoration, the people could see, honor, and adore the Body of Christ.

for several hours at a time. In some places parishioners are urged to commit a certain hour of the day to spend in prayer before the Blessed Sacrament. Many find that in this way they answer the request Jesus made of his disciples during his agony in the garden at Gethsemane: "Could you not keep watch for one hour?" (Mark 14:37). By spending an hour in prayer before the Blessed Sacrament every so often—in quiet adoration and in prayer for ourselves, for our families and friends, and for the world—we will, in our own deepening connection with Christ, be all the more ready to share the love of Christ with those who so desperately need it.

No Longer for Ourselves

The Eucharist commits us to live for Christ and for his people, and therefore to serve those who are poor. Poverty is not only an absence of money. It can be that, and such poverty is devastating to human life. But someone can be in need—of a friend, of companionship, of a helping hand or a kind word—without being economically poor. How can you carry the love of Christ, the love you find in the Eucharist, to those in need around you, perhaps among your own family and friends?

And what, then, does the Eucharist have to do with those who suffer from poverty and grave injustices that threaten their welfare and even their existence? Everything, because when we reach out with love and care for those in need, we are serving and showing love for the Christ who comes to us and gives us his life in the Eucharist, and who identifies with "the least" among us (see Matthew 25:40).

Pope Paul VI, in his encyclical "On the Progress of Peoples," made this connection between the Eucharist and those in need. He alluded to the miracle of the loaves and fishes (you may recall that this is an anticipation of the Eucharist) when he wrote: "No one is permitted to disregard the plight of his brothers living in dire poverty, enmeshed in ignorance and tormented by insecurity. The Christian, moved by this sad state of affairs, should echo the words of Christ: 'I have compassion on the crowd'" (*Note 62*, Matthew 14:14).

Because in the Eucharist, we receive Christ himself within us, we also share in his dying and rising, his love, and his compassion. When we share in the Body and Blood of Christ, we share in the Love that gave itself for all. If Christ gave his life for us, surely, for the sake of love, we too can give our lives for others. We too, like Christ, must have compassion for the crowd, for the multitude who have been deserted, who have nowhere to turn and no one to speak for them.

Union with Christ in prayer and sharing the compassion of Christ in action are intimately related. The more we discover the real meaning of the Eucharist in our prayer and reflection, the more we will discover opportunities to share with others the dying and rising of Christ, his self-giving love, and his own compassion. The "crowd," in our own day, still calls forth the compassion of Christ, and may never know his love, except through us. ♱

Catholic Wisdom

God Is Love

The Church's commitment to those who are poor and in need flows from the very essence of who God is. In his first encyclical, "Charity in Truth" ("*Caritas in Veritate*"), Pope Benedict XVI wrote:

> Charity is at the heart of the Church's social doctrine. Every responsibility and every commitment spelt out by that doctrine is derived from charity which, according to the teaching of Jesus, is the synthesis of the entire Law (cf. Mt 22:36–40). . . . For the Church, instructed by the Gospel, charity is everything, because, as Saint John teaches (cf. 1 Jn. 4:8,16) . . . "God is love" . . . : *everything has its origin in God's love, everything is shaped by it, everything is directed towards it. Love is God's greatest gift to humanity, it is his promise and our hope.* (2)

Part Review

1. Name and describe the three elements of the Concluding Rites.

2. What is the message of the priest or deacon's exhortation to the assembly at the end of the Mass to "go in peace, glorifying the Lord by your life"?

3. Name the principal effect of receiving Holy Communion and explain what this means.

4. How does the Eucharist strengthen our union with the Church?

5. Another effect of the Eucharist is that it commits us to the poor. Describe what this means in your own life.

6. What is the relationship between Apostolic Succession and the prohibition of intercommunion between the Catholic Church and Protestant faith communities?

7. What is the goal of the Week of Prayer for Christian Unity?

8. Name and describe three aspects of Eucharistic worship.

9. How are union with Christ in prayer and sharing the compassion of Christ in action intimately related?

10. Name two symbols for the Eucharist and describe the meaning of each.

The Sacraments of Healing

Part 1

The Sacrament of Penance and Reconciliation

In this section we discuss the two Sacraments of Healing: the Sacrament of Penance and Reconciliation and the Sacrament of Anointing of the Sick. Even at first glance, it seems easy to see why both are called Sacraments of Healing: one is the Sacrament for the strengthening of those who are seriously ill, and the other is the Sacrament for the forgiveness of sins. Because all of us struggle with sin, we discuss the Sacrament of Penance and Reconciliation first. It is a wonderful Sacrament but, admittedly, a difficult one for many people. Even in this era of psychological sophistication, with wide availability of counseling and therapies for almost every human need, we, individually and as a culture, still seem averse to the kind of soul-searching and admitting of fault that this Sacrament requires. However, by the end of this section, you may find that, with a deeper understanding of this Sacrament, you will be more eager to ask God for the forgiveness that only he can give. There is no substitute for the Sacrament of Penance and Reconciliation.

The topics covered in this part are:

- Article 34: The Sacrament of Pardon and Peace (page 184)

- Article 35: Scriptural and Historical Background (page 188)

- Article 36: The Rite of Penance and Reconciliation (page 193)

- Article 37: Penance and Reconciliation in Our Lives (page 198)

Article

34 The Sacrament of Pardon and Peace

Penance and Reconciliation, Sacrament of

One of the Seven Sacraments of the Church, the liturgical celebration of God's forgiveness of sin, through which the sinner is reconciled with both God and the Church.

sin

Any deliberate offense, in thought, word, or deed, against the will of God.

mortal sin

An action so contrary to the will of God that it results in a complete separation from God and his grace. As a consequence of that separation, the person is condemned to eternal death. For a sin to be a mortal sin, three conditions must be met: the act must involve grave matter, the person must have full knowledge of the evil of the act, and the person must give his or her full consent in committing the act.

The **Sacrament of Penance and Reconciliation** is the Sacrament through which sins committed after Baptism can be forgiven, and reconciliation with God and community can be effected. In this Sacrament we are pardoned and reconciled with the Church through God's mercy. Because we are members of the Body of Christ, everything we do—for good or ill—has an effect on the rest of the Body. In the Sacrament of Penance and Reconciliation, our sins, which have brought harm to ourselves and others, are forgiven.

This Sacrament is a Sacrament of many names, because it is a Sacrament rich in meaning. It can be called the Sacrament of Conversion. The Greek word for *conversion* is *metanoia*. This word literally means "a turning around." When we realize that we have been going in the wrong direction, we turn around and take another path that will get us to where God wants us to be. This is what this Sacrament of Conversion does for us.

This Sacrament is also called the Sacrament of Confession, as the confession of sins is an integral part of the Sacrament. In confessing our sins, we must name them. And, to paraphrase a familiar slogan, "You name it, you own it." Therefore confession is a way of taking responsibility, a necessary step for the penitent. Our confession is also an acknowledgment of God's holiness and mercy.

Another name for this Sacrament is the Sacrament of Forgiveness, for in this Sacrament, through the priest's absolution, we receive pardon for our sins and the gift of God's peace. It is called the Sacrament of Penance because the action of penance (in prayer or in deed) on the part of the penitent—the recipient of God's forgiveness—is necessary for the completion of the Sacrament. This Sacrament is also called the Sacrament of Reconciliation, because by it, in God's love, we are reconciled to him and to our brothers and sisters in Christ.

The philosopher Socrates once said, "The unexamined life is not worth living." Does this apply to your life today?

The Sacrament: A Dialogue in Wholeness

Even though the Sacrament of Penance and Reconciliation is structured as a dialogue between the priest, who is the minister of the Sacrament, and the penitent, it is in reality one unified entity. It consists of four actions: the three actions of the penitent and the absolution of the priest. The actions of the penitent are: repentance, confession (admission of sins to the priest), and the intention to make amends for sin and do what is possible to repair the harm caused by sin. This last action on the part of the penitent is often called a penance. These elements are discussed in more detail in article 36, "The Rite of Penance and Reconciliation."

Heaven

A state of eternal life and union with God in which one experiences full happiness and the satisfaction of the deepest human longings.

venial sin

A less serious offense against the will of God that diminishes one's personal character and weakens but does not rupture one's relationship with God.

Sin

To understand the Sacrament of Penance and Reconciliation and its power of forgiveness, we must understand what sin is. **Sin** is "an utterance, a deed, or a desire contrary to the eternal law"[1] (*Catechism of the Catholic Church [CCC]*, 1849). It is a conscious and free choice to violate God's

Mortal and Venial Sin

Sin is divided into two categories, mortal sin and venial sin. To commit a **mortal sin** is to deliberately, knowingly, and willingly choose to commit a serious violation of God's Law and is contrary to the final goal of a human being: happiness with God forever in **Heaven**. Mortal sin is called mortal, or deadly, because it destroys charity, or love, within us. When we commit mortal sin, Heaven is closed to us, because Heaven is all love. An unrepented mortal sin leads to eternal separation from God.

Mortal sin is a choice. There are three conditions that make a sin a mortal sin: (1) it concerns a serious and grave matter; (2) it is committed with full knowledge that the action is sinful and in opposition to God's Law; and (3) it is committed freely and deliberately.

Venial sin is a sin committed in a less serious matter. Venial sin "constitutes a moral disorder" (*CCC*, 1875), but it does not destroy our relationship with God or his love within us. It does weaken our relationship with him and with the Church community, and weakens our ability to resist mortal sin. The repetition of sins, even venial ones, leads us to develop vices, which are sinful habits. Vices are often linked with the seven capital sins: pride, avarice, lust, wrath, gluttony, envy, and sloth.

Law; a failure in genuine love for God and neighbor; and a fault against reason, truth, and right conscience. Sin wounds human nature and injures human solidarity.

In our culture the attitude of "no harm, no foul" is common. This attitude can sometimes be an excuse for thinking that because the harm is not immediate or obvious, it does not exist. A sin that is temporarily hidden is still a sin, and making a habit of even less serious sin can lead to serious consequences that are suddenly not so hidden after all. And sometimes we can be lulled into thinking that if others are doing it, it can't be so bad. In fact, it is worse—because the sin is multiplied. A "group" does not have a conscience; only individuals do. And each individual is responsible for his or her own actions.

An individual's sin harms the Church because her members are intimately linked. We are one Body in Christ. Through the Sacraments we are united, and we influence one another in a deep and spiritual way. When sins are committed, this communion is damaged.

© Bill Wittman / www.wpwittman.com

Keys are a symbol of authority. Jesus is the Key of David who has the authority to open and close: to forgive sin. See Isaiah 22:21–23 and Revelation 3:6–8. The stole is the vestment worn during the Sacrament of Penance.

Forgiveness

God has given us a way to ask for and receive forgiveness and to heal our spiritual weaknesses. Jesus, the Son of God, has the authority to forgive sins, and he passed this authority to the Apostles, the first leaders of the Church. Through Apostolic Succession that authority has been passed down to the bishops and through them to priests, and it is administered in the Sacrament of Penance and Reconciliation.

Jesus forgave sins and reconciled sinners not only with God but also with the People of God. One sign of this reconciliation is Jesus' sharing of meals with sinners. Reconciliation with God meant reconciliation with the community as well. Similarly, in the Sacrament of Penance and Reconciliation, sinners are reconciled not only with God but with the Church. In fact, *"Reconciliation with the Church is inseparable from reconciliation with God"* (CCC, 1445).

In handing over the authority to forgive sins and to reconcile the sinner, Jesus said to Peter: "I will give you the keys to the kingdom of heaven. Whatever you bind on earth shall be bound in heaven; and whatever you loose on earth shall be loosed in heaven" (Matthew 16:19–20). And, in the Gospel of John, Jesus said to all the Apostles: "Receive the holy Spirit. Whose sins you forgive are forgiven them, and whose sins you retain are retained" (John 20:22–23). This forgiveness and reconciliation is extended to us today. The Church today has the same authority, given by Jesus, to forgive sins and to welcome back the sinner.

Only God can forgive, and he has given that same power to bishops and priests, not so they can "lord it over" us, but so, as servants of God, they can assure us that if we are forgiven

The Minister of the Sacrament

The ministry of the forgiveness of sin is exercised today by the bishops and by their coworkers, the priests. This ministry is given to them through the Sacrament of Holy Orders. Bishops regulate this ministry in which the priests collaborate. A priest, in order to exercise the ministry of the Sacrament of Penance and Reconciliation, must receive a commission from his bishop, his religious superior, or the Pope. Only priests who have received this commission from the authority of the Church can exercise this ministry. However, if someone is in danger of death, any priest can absolve the person's sins, even without an official commission.

A priest must be available for this Sacrament each time a Christian asks for it, as long as the requests are reasonable. As a confessor, a priest must have respect and sensitivity toward those who confess to him. He must have a good knowledge of human behavior with experience and understanding of ordinary human life. He must be faithful to the Magisterium, or teaching office, of the Church. It is his responsibility to encourage the penitent toward mature and responsible living of the Gospel and to help the penitent discover the healing love of Christ. The priest is also expected to pray and do penance for those who come to him in this Sacrament and to entrust them to the mercy of God (see CCC, 1466).

A priest may never reveal to anyone what he hears in the Sacrament of Penance and Reconciliation. This is called "the sacramental seal" or "the seal of the confessional." A confessor is bound to secrecy even when a serious crime, even murder, has been confessed. In smaller matters, if the priest wishes to discuss a particular confession with someone else, for advice or guidance, he must first ask permission of the penitent. If a priest violates the seal of the confessional, he is automatically excommunicated. Those who inadvertently overhear a confession are also bound to secrecy by the seal of the confessional. An interpreter who may be needed to help someone make a confession is also bound by the sacramental seal.

on earth in the Sacrament of Penance and Reconciliation, we are forgiven by God as well. ✝

conversion

A change of heart, turning away from sin and toward God.

^{Article} **35 Scriptural and Historical Background**

In this article we discuss certain Scripture passages important for understanding the Sacrament of Penance and Reconciliation and Jesus' institution of it. Then we explore the evolution of the Sacrament throughout the Church's history.

It is important to understand Jesus' institution of the Sacrament of Penance and Reconciliation in the context of his mission on earth. In his earthly ministry, Jesus, the Son of God, continually urged **conversion** (turning toward God), and, through his power to forgive sins, invited all people to share in his relationship with the Father, in the Holy Spirit. In this dual call to conversion and to forgiveness, the Sacrament of Penance and Reconciliation finds its roots in the words and actions of Christ.

Pray It!

An Act of Contrition

This Act of Contrition is given in the Rite of Penance. In the Sacrament of Penance and Reconciliation, you may use this, another Act of Contrition, or your own words.

My God,
I am sorry for my sins with all my heart.
In choosing to do wrong
and failing to do good,
I have sinned against you
whom I should love above all things.
I firmly intend, with your help,
to do penance,
to sin no more,
and to avoid whatever leads me to sin.
Our Savior Jesus Christ
suffered and died for us.
In his name, my God, have mercy.
(Rite of Penance, 45)

We have already discussed the important Scripture passage in which Jesus gives the power to forgive sins to Peter. This power has been passed on through the Sacrament of Holy Orders, to our present-day bishops and priests (see Matthew 16:19). This gift of Jesus to his Apostles, the power to forgive sins, is also recorded in John's Gospel. On the evening of the first day of the week after Jesus' death, when his followers were locked in the Upper Room out of fear, Jesus came and stood among them, and said, "Peace be with you" (John 20:19). He showed them the wounds in his hands and his side. He said to them again: "Peace be with you. As the Father has sent me, so I send you" (John 20:22). And then he gave them the means to pass on his own gift of peace and reconciliation to the entire Church and so to the world: "And when he had said this, he breathed on them and said to them, 'Receive the Holy Spirit. Whose sins you forgive are forgiven them, and whose sins you retain are retained'" (John 20:22–23). Note that the gift of this power to forgive sins, to offer peace and reconciliation to the followers of Jesus from that time forward, comes with the reception of the gift of the Holy Spirit. Only God—the Father, the Son, and the Holy Spirit—can forgive sins, and this power of forgiveness, given to the Apostles and to their successors, is exercised in the name of the Holy Trinity.

Forgiveness of the Paralytic

All through his public ministry, Jesus forgave sins and taught about God's loving mercy toward sinners. Let us look at one example in the Gospel of Mark. Mark records that Jesus was "at home" in Capernaum (Mark 2:1). So many people gathered to hear him preach that there was no room in the house, or even around the doorway. This posed a problem for the friends of a paralytic. They wanted to ask Jesus to heal their friend, but they could not get near Jesus. Then someone had an idea: Get him to Jesus through the roof!

So the friends broke through the roof above Jesus and lowered their paralytic companion down. "When Jesus saw their faith, he said to the paralytic, 'Child, your

This depiction of the paralyzed man being lowered by his friends through the roof is from a twelfth-century Greek manuscript of the Gospels. How do you bring your friends to Jesus?

© Erich Lessing / Art Resource, NY

concupiscence

The tendency of all human beings toward sin, as a result of Original Sin.

sins are forgiven'" (Mark 2:5). The scribes criticized Jesus in their hearts: "He is blaspheming. Who but God alone can forgive sins?" (2:7). Jesus knew what they were thinking and went on to prove that he had the authority to forgive sins by telling the paralytic, "I say to you, rise, pick up your mat, and go home" (2:11). The paralytic rose, picked up his mat "at once," and went home (2:12). In this way, Jesus proved his words ("Your sins are forgiven") by this action of healing.

When we hear in the Sacrament of Penance and Reconciliation "I absolve you from your sins" *(Rite of Penance, 46)*, we should remember this incident, for when the priest forgives our sins in this Sacrament, it is truly Jesus saying to us, "Child, your sins are forgiven."

Conversion after Baptism

You may remember from other studies that the first followers of Jesus expected his return to be soon after the Ascension. They believed in Jesus, were baptized, and then did their best to live by his teachings until he would come again. The early Christians had "put on Christ," but they found that following Jesus' teachings and avoiding sin was not easy. As the Apostle John wrote, "If we say, 'We are without sin,' we deceive ourselves" (1 John 1:8). Christian initiation did not abolish human nature, nor what is called **concupiscence**, the human tendency toward sin resulting from Original Sin. The life of the early Christians was a life of ongoing conversion— that is, a continual turning toward God, even after Baptism.

Baptism is, of course, the time and place for a person's first and fundamental conversion. In Baptism, as you remember, we renounce sin. All our sins are forgiven, and we are given new life in Christ.

Yet, for us, because we continue to struggle with sin after Baptism, we are called to conversion over and over again. This post-baptismal conversion is sometimes called a second conversion or an ongoing conversion. If by grace we are drawn to respond to God's merciful love, we can turn around again and, with contrite hearts, repent and believe again in the newness of life.

For an example of a second conversion, we can look to Saint Peter. (His first conversion was his answering of Jesus' invitation to follow him. See Mark 1:17–18.) After Jesus' arrest Peter denied his relationship with Jesus three times.

After the third denial, Jesus turned and looked at Peter. Peter was filled with remorse and wept bitterly. Later, after the Resurrection, Peter declared three times to Jesus, "You know that I love you" (John 21:15). Jesus also commanded Peter, "Feed my sheep" (21:17), which meant to care for the Church. Saint Peter's conversion restored him to right relationship not only with Jesus but also with the followers of Jesus, the Church (see Luke 22:61, John 21:15–17).

Jesus' call to conversion is an essential element of the proclamation of the Kingdom of God. He made this announcement when he "came to Galilee proclaiming the

The Second Plank

The Sacrament of Penance and Reconciliation is necessary for those in grave sin. These sinners have lost baptismal grace, cut off their relationship with God, and wounded the Body of Christ. The Fathers of the Church made clear that if you were drowning in sin, Baptism was the first plank of salvation. After Baptism the Sacrament of Penance and Reconciliation is "the second plank [of salvation] after the shipwreck which is the loss of grace"[2] (CCC, 1446).

As captains of our own vessels, we are each responsible for steering clear of rocks, shoals, and sandbars (sin) that will result in shipwreck. However, should we be caught in a storm, stray off course entirely, and be tossed into the crushing waves of sin, it is comforting to know that we can grab "the second plank" before we are completely lost!

© Corbis

gospel of God: 'This is the time of fulfillment. The kingdom of God is at hand. Repent, and believe in the Gospel'" (Mark 1:15).

In the Sacrament of Penance and Reconciliation, we focus on repentance and ongoing conversion. This movement of conversion, of turning again to God, also includes profound sorrow for our sins, a real disgust for them, and a firm commitment to avoid sin in the future. Of course we can and should repent in our hearts, but in the Sacrament of Reconciliation, we find the sure forgiveness of God and the grace we need to restore our relationships with him, with our family and friends, and with the entire Church.

Historical Notes

The way of celebrating the Sacrament of Penance and Reconciliation has varied through the centuries. In the early centuries, those who had sinned gravely and wanted to return to the Church underwent a rigorous program of public penance, which often lasted for years. This was for grave sins only, and was called the Order of Penitents. Admittance into the Order of Penitents was rare and could happen only once in a person's lifetime.

In the seventh century, the Irish missionary monks had some contact with monks of the Eastern Churches. The monks in the Eastern Churches practiced a more private form of penance. They confessed their sins privately to a spiritual father and did a private penance. Through the Irish monks, this custom gradually spread throughout the entire Church. This practice also had the advantage of being repeatable. It was not a once-in-a-lifetime conversion but rather a sacramental support to ongoing conversion in Christ. In this way both mortal sins and venial sins could be forgiven in one celebration. The Church's practice of the Sacrament of Penance and Reconciliation has followed this basic form ever since. Despite the variations over time, the fundamental structure of the Sacrament has remained the same through the centuries. ✞

Article 36 The Rite of Penance and Reconciliation

As mentioned in a previous article, the Sacrament of Penance and Reconciliation is a single entity made up of four actions: three actions of the penitent and one action of the priest. In this article we discuss each of these actions.

The Acts of the Penitent

Repentance or Contrition

Repentance, or contrition, is sorrow for one's sin and a hatred for sin, combined with the intention to avoid sin in the future. This is the primary act of the penitent. All contrition is based on faith in God's love for us. Contrition that springs

repentance (contrition)
An attitude of sorrow for a sin committed and a resolution not to sin again. It is a response to God's gracious love and forgiveness.

Live It!

How to Make a Good Confession

The Sacrament of Penance and Reconciliation is a good way to take a closer look at your life and make a fresh start, at least once a year. Many parishes offer communal Penance and Reconciliation services during Advent and Lent, and private Penance and Reconciliation is usually available at some time every week. Before you go to confession, ask God for help in remembering your sins, specific actions, and general patterns of behavior.

Following is an outline of what you can expect in confession. The priest will also be glad to help you.

- **Go to the priest.** You can kneel behind a screen or sit and face the priest. He will welcome you, and you will both make the Sign of the Cross. The priest will pray for you and may read a Scripture passage.
- **Confess your sins.** The priest will then discuss your sins with you and give you spiritual advice.
- **Receive a penance.** The priest will talk to you about doing something as a sign of your desire to change. It may be saying some prayers or doing a good action.
- **Tell God you are sorry.** You can use your own words or an Act of Contrition that you have memorized.
- **Receive absolution.** The priest proclaims the words of absolution, and God forgives your sins.
- **Conclude.** The priest says, "Give thanks to the Lord, for he is good," and you respond, "His mercy endures forever" *(Rite of Penance, 47)*. The priest then dismisses you, and you can respond, "Thank you" or "Amen."

When we celebrate the Sacrament of Penance and Reconciliation, the Holy Spirit is with us, helping us to be sorry for our sins and to listen to the advice of the priest. It is helpful to get to know a priest to whom you can confess regularly.

© Bill Wittman/www.wpwittman.com

reparation

Making amends for something one did wrong that caused harm to another person or led to loss.

absolution

An essential part of the Sacrament of Penance and Reconciliation in which the priest pardons the sins of the person confessing, in the name of God and the Church.

purely from our love for God is called "perfect contrition." Contrition for other good reasons (the ugliness of sin, the fear of Hell or earthly consequences) is called "imperfect." Both are gifts of God.

Confession of Sins

Even on a purely human level, as the saying goes, "Confession is good for the soul." Honest conversations—though difficult—in which we take responsibility for our actions and seek to make things right again are an important part of human life. If you have admitted wrongdoing and asked for someone's forgiveness, if you have ever had a misunderstanding with a friend and then helped restore that friendship, you have some idea of what this kind of honesty can mean.

In the Sacrament of Penance and Reconciliation, we go a step further along this path, and, by confessing our sins to the priest, we confess them to God. Thus confession is an essential part of the Sacrament. It is absolutely necessary, after an examination of conscience, to confess all mortal sins that are remembered so that they can be forgiven and the penitent can be reconciled with God and with the Church. The Church also highly recommends the confession of venial sins. By confessing venial sins, we help form and strengthen our conscience, nip evil tendencies in the bud, open our hearts to the healing of Christ, and make progress in the life of the Spirit. In receiving the Father's mercy, we are encouraged to be merciful to others as well.

Intention to Make Reparation

Within the Sacrament the opportunity is given to accept a penance, which is a prayer or action that repairs the harm caused by sin, from the priest. Sometimes this is a matter of justice: To repair the wrong we have done, we must return something stolen or pay for something we deliberately broke in anger. However, this is not the full reason for the act of **reparation**. "Absolution takes away sin, but it does not remedy all the disorders sin has caused"[3] (*CCC*, 1459). For example, if we had been stealing and smashing things, **absolution** takes away our sin, but there is still chaos within us that must be dealt with. The penance we are given, which will often include prayer or an action, such as an act of mercy, is aimed toward our own spiritual health and well-being, to help us deal with the chaos or disorder within ourselves that led us to sin. The penance, or "satisfaction," helps us to "reset" our hearts in the right direction and live, with reestablished good habits, as disciples of Christ.

examination of conscience
Prayerful reflection on, and assessment of, one's words, attitudes, and actions in light of the Gospel of Jesus; more specifically, the conscious moral evaluation of one's life in preparation for reception of the Sacrament of Penance and Reconciliation.

The Act of the Priest

Absolution is an essential part of the Sacrament of Penance and Reconciliation, in which the priest pardons the sins of the person confessing, in the name of God and of the Church. This is possible through the power Christ has given to the Church. In this absolution, Christ, the Good Shepherd, finds his lost sheep, and Christ, the Good Samaritan, binds up the wounds of the injured. In the forgiveness of sins, God our Father welcomes back his prodigal sons and daughters. In this absolution we are given the gift of pardon and peace.

© Bill Wittman / www.wpwittman.com

It is important to remember that in the Sacrament of Penance and Reconciliation, the priest absolves you from your sins, not in his own name, but in God's name. It is God who forgives you. What does this mean to you?

Celebration of the Sacrament

The Sacrament of Penance and Reconciliation is a liturgical action composed of these elements when celebrated by individual penitents:

1. **Preparation of priest and penitent** The priest prays for enlightenment from the Holy Spirit; the penitent makes an **examination of conscience** (see "The Word of God and

the Examination of Conscience" sidebar) and asks God for forgiveness.

2. **Welcoming the penitent** The priest greets the penitent graciously.

3. **Reading of the Word of God (optional)** This reading may be a verse the priest recites from memory, or it may be a reading the priest and penitent choose together.

4. **Penitent's confession and acceptance of the penance** The penitent may first say a general prayer ("I confess to Almighty God"), and then make a confession of sins. The priest may offer help and counsel as needed. He then proposes a penance, and the penitent agrees to do the penance.

5. **Penitent's prayer and priest's absolution** After the penitent prays an Act of Contrition, the priest extends his hands, or his right hand, over the head of the penitent and pronounces the words of absolution:

> "God, the Father of mercies,
> through the death and resurrection of his Son
> has reconciled the world to himself
> and sent the Holy Spirit among us
> for the forgiveness of sins;
> through the ministry of the Church
> may God give you pardon and peace,
> and I absolve you from your sins
> in the name of the Father, and of the Son, ✚
> and of the Holy Spirit."
> The penitent responds: Amen.
> (*Rite of Penance,* 46)

When the priest says the phrase beginning with "I absolve you," the essential words of absolution, he makes the Sign of the Cross over the penitent. The entire formula expresses the work of the Trinity in the Sacrament of Penance and Reconciliation: God the Father is the source of all mercy and forgiveness. Through the Paschal Mystery of his Son, Jesus Christ, the Father reconciled the entire world, including sinners, to himself. Through his gift of the Holy Spirit, the Father made forgiveness of sins possible. Through the work of the Church, forgiveness and reconciliation is offered today, in the name of the Trinity.

6. **Proclamation of praise and dismissal of the penitent** The priest says, "Give thanks to the Lord, for he is good." The penitent completes this psalm verse with, "His mercy

endures forever" (*Rite of Penance,* 47). The priest then dismisses the penitent with the words, "The Lord has freed you from your sins. Go in peace," or another similar option (47).

The Word of God and the Examination of Conscience

The immediate preparation for the Sacrament of Penance and Reconciliation ordinarily includes an examination of conscience, or an *examen.* This is a prayerful reflection on, and assessment of, our words, attitudes, and actions in light of the Word of God and particularly the Gospel of Jesus. Included in God's Word are important mandates given to us in the Ten Commandments. Other mandates for the moral Christian life include the teachings of Jesus, especially the Beatitudes (see Matthew 5:3–12); the moral teachings of the Gospels (especially the Great Commandment, see Matthew 22:34–40); the Sermon on the Mount (see Matthew, chapters 5–7); and the letters of the Apostles (see CCC, 1454).

The Communal Celebration

Most often the Sacrament of Penance and Reconciliation is administered to individuals in private. However, this Sacrament can also take place within a communal celebration. In this form the assembly celebrates the Liturgy of the Word and then participates in an examination of conscience together. This is followed by a communal prayer asking God for forgiveness, and then the Lord's Prayer. After a short prayer, the assembly is invited to approach the priests who are designated for individual confession and absolution.

When all have finished individual confession, a psalm or hymn of thanksgiving may be sung. The presiding priest offers a concluding prayer of thanksgiving. The Concluding Rites follow, and then there is a blessing and dismissal.

This communal rite reminds us that we are members of the Church, the Body of Christ, and that what we do has an effect on the entire Body. Of course every liturgical action, including the Sacrament of Penance and Reconciliation, is an action of the entire Body of Christ, whether it is celebrated for one individual or communally.

Another form of this Sacrament, called Communal Celebration of Reconciliation with General Confession and

General Absolution, is used only in cases of dire emergency. Such an emergency might arise if there is danger of death in the immediate future and there is no time for one priest to hear each individual confession, or if there are not enough priests to hear confessions in a reasonable length of time. The diocesan bishop decides whether this is the case in a particular situation. ✞

Article 37 Penance and Reconciliation in Our Lives

What difference does the Sacrament of Penance and Reconciliation make in our lives? Although it is a Sacrament that is celebrated very quietly, it can have dramatic effects. For many people this Sacrament has been a major turning point in their lives, because, by the grace of God given in this Sacrament, they were able to face themselves, be truly sorry, take responsibility for their sins, and be forgiven. They were able to carry their guilt, place it in God's hands, and move forward in hope. By the grace of this Sacrament, they turned from being burdened by the sins of the past to being open to God's promise of a different future.

© digitalskillet / iStockphoto.com

Friends are gifts from God. How can the Sacrament of Reconciliation help you to value your friendships and extend God's love to others?

Let us take a look at some of the effects of God's powerful action in this Sacrament, and how we can take them to heart in our everyday lives:

1. **The forgiveness of all sin** The Son of God shed his blood so that sin might be forgiven. Because bishops and priests have been given the authority to forgive sins in Christ's name, our sins can be forgiven in this Sacrament.

2. **Reconciliation with God** This is the purpose of the Sacrament. To those who are dead in sin, the Sacrament of Reconciliation brings a "spiritual resurrection" (*CCC*, 1468) and new life as a son or daughter of God.

3. **Reconciliation with the Church** If we are reconciled with God, we are also reconciled with the Church, the Body of Christ. The Sacrament of Reconciliation restores our relationship with all the members of Christ's Body, whether we know them personally or not. Sin harms or fractures our union, but the Sacrament of Penance and Reconciliation restores and repairs the broken places and, like bones in a human body, they grow stronger.

4. **Remission of punishment for sin** Someone who dies with unrepented mortal sin has chosen to live without God for all eternity. This state of eternal separation from God, in whom alone we can have the happiness for which we were created, is called **Hell**. However, God's forgiveness and grace received in the Sacrament of Penance and Reconciliation remits eternal punishment for mortal sins.

For both mortal and venial sins, the Sacrament remits, in part, the temporal, or temporary, punishment due to sin. Those who die in God's grace and friendship, but in a state of venial sin, must be purified in **Purgatory** to achieve the holiness necessary to enter the joy of Heaven. At the moment of death, each person is judged and receives a reward or punishment in keeping with how he or she has lived. This is called the particular judgment. Through God's forgiveness and the grace received in the Sacrament of Penance and Reconciliation, the period of purification is lessened.

We can also attain remission of the consequences of sin while we are still alive, through prayer, penance, and loving actions, especially the works of mercy. These works include actions that address physical or spiritual needs of others. Physical, or corporal, works include

Hell
The state of permanent separation from God, reserved for those who freely and consciously choose to reject God to the very end of their lives.

Purgatory
A state of final purification or cleansing, which one may need to enter following death and before entering Heaven.

Catholic Wisdom

Reconciled with All Creation

Pope John Paul II wrote the following in his apostolic exhortation "Reconciliation and Penance":

> This reconciliation with God leads, as it were, to other reconciliations, which repair the other breaches caused by sin. The forgiven penitent is reconciled with himself in his inmost being, where he regains his innermost truth. He is reconciled with his brethren whom he has in some way offended and wounded. He is reconciled with the Church. He is reconciled with all creation.[4] (*CCC*, 1469)

feeding the hungry, clothing the naked, visting the sick and those in prison, providing shelter for the homeless, and burying the dead. Spiritual works include forgiving those who hurt you, comforting those who suffer, being patient with others, sharing knowledge and advice with those who need it, and praying for others.

Another way remission of sins can be obtained is through indulgences, either for ourselves or for those in Purgatory. One common way to gain indulgences is to participate in certain devotional practices, such as making a Holy Hour or praying the Rosary. An indulgence may be partial, meaning it removes some temporal punishment for sin, or plenary, meaning it takes away all temporal punishment for sin.

5. **Peace and serenity of conscience, and spiritual consolation** Peace is a gift from God. It is not something we can manufacture for ourselves. If we are not at peace, it may be that something in ourselves is interfering with God's gift. One of the greatest effects of the Sacrament of Penance and Reconciliation is the restoration of peace and serenity to the heart and soul.

6. **An increase of spiritual strength for the Christian battle** We like to think of life as satisfying, fun, filled with love, and peaceful. And much of the time it is. But sometimes it is also a battle. Anyone who has dealt with temptation, peer pressure, bullying, or betrayal or rejection by a friend knows that this is true. But even when you experience such challenges, you are not alone. The angels and saints and the entire Church are there for you, and the grace of the Sacrament of Penance and Reconciliation will help you to choose and to stay on the right path in any difficulty.

Football players wear protective gear to guard against injuries. What spiritual "protective gear" does the Sacrament of Reconciliation give to you? Why do we call this Sacrament a Sacrament of Healing?

© Bill Grove / iStockphoto.com

A Life of Ongoing Conversion

The Sacrament of Penance and Reconciliation, with the individual and complete confession of grave sins, followed by absolution, is the only ordinary means of reconciliation with God and with the Church. However, the Sacrament was never meant to be a revolving door of sin, confess, be forgiven, sin, confess, be forgiven. We have seen that true sorrow requires a firm resolve not to sin again. Yes, we fail. But there is a difference between failing and not even trying. There is a difference between floating through life aimlessly, letting random thoughts and feelings carry you to one dead end after another, and choosing to live the Gospel life. The Sacrament of Penance and Reconciliation helps us to carry out our baptismal commitment to follow Jesus in love and service.

On the other hand, if you do find yourself confessing the same sins over and over again, do not let this discourage you. Continue to ask God for the grace to change, and continue participating in the Sacrament of Penance and Recon-

Advice from Pope Benedict XVI

In speaking with children who had just made their First Holy Communion, preceded by their First Penance, Pope Benedict XVI took questions. Livia asked: "Do I have to go to confession every time I receive Communion, even when I have committed the same sins? Because I realize that they are always the same."

In his reply, Pope Benedict made some remarks that apply to all ages:

Even if, as I said, it is not necessary to go to confession before each Communion, it is very helpful to confess with a certain regularity. It is true: our sins are always the same, but we clean our homes, our rooms, at least once a week, even if the dirt is always the same; in order to live in cleanliness, in order to start again. Otherwise, the dirt might not be seen but it builds up. Something similar can be said about the soul. For me myself: if I never go to confession, my soul is neglected and in the end I am always pleased with myself and no longer understand that I must always work hard to improve, that I must make progress. And this cleansing of the soul which Jesus gives us in the Sacrament of Confession helps us to make our consciences more alert, more open, and hence, it also helps us to mature spiritually and as human persons. ("Catechetical Meeting of the Holy Father with Children Who Had Received Their First Communion During the Year," October 15, 2005)

ciliation. You may find other spiritual practices helpful too, such as retreats, prayer services, attentive listening to Scripture and the homily at Sunday Mass, and reading Scripture or a spiritual book on your own. If you keep your heart (and your eyes and ears) open, the Holy Spirit will help you. ✝

Part Review

1. Explain how the authority to forgive sins and reconcile sinners was given by Jesus to Peter and the Apostles and extends to the Church today.

2. Give three other names for the Sacrament of Penance and Reconciliation and explain how each describes an essential element of the Sacrament.

3. Name and explain the three actions of the penitent in the Sacrament of Penance and Reconciliation.

4. Name and explain the action of the priest in the Sacrament of Penance and Reconciliation.

5. Explain the three conditions that must exist for a sin to be mortal, and the consequences of mortal sin.

6. Describe two Scripture accounts in which Jesus forgives sinners, and explain how these foretell the mercy God extends to us in the Sacrament of Penance and Reconciliation.

7. Why is the Sacrament of Penance and Reconciliation called "the second conversion" or "the second plank"?

8. Name the six effects of the Sacrament of Penance and Reconciliation. Choose two and explain their meaning.

Part 2

The Sacrament of Anointing of the Sick

As you probably learned in kindergarten, or even before, taking turns is a big part of life. It is one way to describe the human life cycle. First, it is your turn to be born. Then it is your turn to be a child, to go to school, and to learn to do things like swim or ride a bike. Then it is your turn to go to high school, to learn new skills, to find new interests. As the Book of Ecclesiastes says, "For everything there is a season, and a time for every matter under heaven" (3:1, NRSV).

We are each given a turn to live our lives on this beautiful earth. We are each given a turn to try to make human life better for others through love and service. But, within our own season of human life, most of us take a turn at minor illness. Some of us take a turn dealing with a major illness. All of us take our turn at dying, when it is our turn to relinquish our place, and to allow others who follow us to have their turn.

The Sacrament of Anointing of the Sick is God's gift for those who are taking their turn at serious illness, old age, or dying. It is a Sacrament of healing, strengthening, and, when death is near, preparation, so that, when their turn on earth is over, they will look forward to meeting God, and to hearing from him, "Well done, my good and faithful servant. . . . Come, share your master's joy" (Matthew 25:23).

The topics covered in this part are:

Article

38 The Sacrament of Healing and Strength

Anointing of the Sick, Sacrament of
One of the Seven Sacraments, sometimes formerly known as "the Sacrament of the dying," in which a gravely ill, aging, or dying person is anointed by the priest and prayed over by him and attending believers. One need not be dying to receive the Sacrament.

Illness is a reminder of our frailty and mortality as human beings, and can help us to realize, when our bodies fail us, how much we depend upon God.

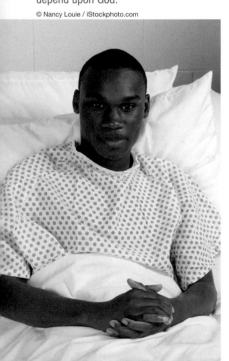

© Nancy Louie / iStockphoto.com

The **Sacrament of Anointing of the Sick** gives spiritual healing and strength to a person who is seriously ill. Sometimes physical recovery is granted as well.

The Sacrament's purpose is the bestowing of special grace on the Christian experiencing the difficulties of serious illness or old age. In this Sacrament, in the midst of our weakest moments, we encounter Christ, the Good Shepherd. In the words of the Prophet Ezekiel, whose prophecy of a true shepherd for God's People was fulfilled in Jesus Christ, we hear the voice of God saying: "I myself will pasture my sheep. . . . The lost I will search out, the strays I will bring back, the injured I will bind up, the sick I will heal. . . . I will shepherd them in judgment" (Ezekiel 34:15–16).

In this article we look at several aspects of the meaning of the Sacrament of Anointing of the Sick: the meaning of illness, Christ as Physician, faith and healing, the sufferings of Christ and our union with them, sharing the cross of Christ through illness, the Holy Spirit's gift of healing, and Christ's institution of the Sacrament of Anointing of the Sick. We will begin with the meaning of illness itself in human life.

The Meaning of Illness

At times of serious illness, our lives are disrupted and we are thrown into turmoil. We are extremely weak, both physically and mentally, and are vulnerable to fear, anguish, self-preoccupation, and sometimes even despair and revolt against God.

On the other hand, sometimes a serious illness can be a wake-up call, alerting us to the essentials of life. Serious illness stops us in our tracks and forces us to evaluate our lives, perhaps to search out the cause of our physical difficulties and then to plan for change in the future. Often an illness can bring about a *metanoia* in the heart, a conversion toward God and a greater appreciation of his gifts in our lives.

Thus illness can be a turning point. But God sends healing, either physical or spiritual, because illness and death have been conquered through his Son, Jesus Christ. The Prophet Isaiah spoke of a new Zion, a new Jerusalem (a figure of the Church of the New Covenant and of eternal life) in which God's People rejoice: "No one who dwells there will say, 'I am sick'; / the people who live there will be forgiven their guilt" (Isaiah 33:24). The Sacrament of Anointing of the Sick is the doorway to this healing.

Christ the Physician

Jesus Christ, the Son of God, came among us as a healer of body and soul. For some people who asked for physical healing, he both forgave their sins and sent them away whole. In these instances his healing of bodily afflictions was a sign of the deeper healing of sin. He never turned away from

Leprosy as Symbol

Leprosy, also called Hansen's disease, is a contagious disease. Until the 1970s, when a combination of drugs that kill the bacteria that causes the disease was developed, leprosy was incurable.

At the time of Jesus, those who suffered from this disease were forced to live in isolation. Those suffering from leprosy (or any skin disease that was thought to be leprosy) were told to leave their homes and live in perpetual quarantine on the outskirts of town. If somehow a person were cured, he or she was instructed to show the priests that the skin condition had healed and would then be given permission to go back home.

Even into the early twentieth century, leprosy was very much feared. It became a symbol for the worst of diseases and the worst of consequences: physical isolation, ostracism, and banishment. For that reason it became a symbol for separation from God and from the community—a symbol for sin.

This is why Jesus' healing of lepers is so significant. Jesus' healings are signs that even the worst separation from God and isolation from the community can be overcome and healed, that even the worst sin can be forgiven, and that the sinner can be restored to fullness of life.

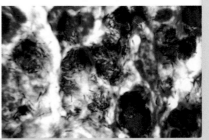

those who asked him for healing, not even from the most "untouchable" of his day, those who suffered from leprosy. In the Sacrament of Anointing of the Sick, we meet Christ the Physician, who heals our sin, our isolation, and, if it is in God's providence, our physical ailments as well.

Faith and Healing

What did Jesus ask of the sick whom he met along his way, the sick who asked him for healing? Only faith. Sometimes Jesus healed by his word alone, even from a distance (see Luke 7:7). Sometimes he offered his healing touch, and other signs: spittle and the laying on of hands (see Mark 7:32–36, 8:22–25), mud and washing (see John 9:6–7). (See also *Catechism of the Catholic Church [CCC]*, 1504.) Those who were sick tried to touch him, even the tassel of his cloak, in order to be healed (see Luke 8:44).

Christ's Suffering

The prophets foretold that the Messiah would heal, not only by his word and his touch but also by actually taking on the sufferings of God's People (see Isaiah 53:4).

While he was among us, Jesus did not heal every sick person. But through his individual healings, Jesus announced a message for all: that the Kingdom of God was coming and indeed was here. By his death and Resurrection, his message was made even more clear: "He himself bore our sins in his body upon the cross, so that, free from sin, we might live for righteousness. By his wounds you have been healed" (1 Peter 2:24). Through his Paschal Mystery, Christ conquered the consequences of Original Sin: sin and death, sickness and suffering. Because of Christ, these are only temporary. Through them we can become closer to Christ, we can align ourselves and our suffering to his on the cross, and thus we can be more closely united to him and to his Passion. In some small way, our suffering becomes a participation in Jesus' redemptive (saving) suffering. Because of Christ, sickness and suffering pave the way to an eternity of joy.

The Cross and Discipleship

Jesus invites each one of us to take up our own particular cross, whatever it might be, to follow him as his disciples (see Matthew 10:38). Certainly, illness is a heavy cross, but those of us who are healthy can share the ministry of Jesus toward the sick by offering our prayers and sacrifices for those who suffer illness, whether physical or mental. This can be our way of sharing the cross with those who suffer, and uniting ourselves with Christ's saving love for the sick.

Patient Endurance

The gift of healing is a gift of the Holy Spirit that some members of the Church are given to build up the Body of Christ. Yet even intense prayer does not always bring about healing of illness. Saint Paul the Apostle begged to be healed from what he called "a thorn in the flesh" (2 Corinthians 12:7), but his prayer was not granted. The answer he received was, "My grace is sufficient for you, for power is made perfect in weakness" (12:9). In enduring suffering with patience, we, like Saint Paul, are "filling up what is lacking in the afflictions of Christ on behalf of his body, which is the church" (Colossians 1:24). We can share one another's sufferings, we can bear one another's burdens, for we all belong to the one Body of Christ, the Church.

Pray It!

A Prayer for Protection

This prayer to Mary is an ancient one, and the oldest known version was found on an Egyptian papyrus from the third century. In Latin it is called the "*Sub tuum praesidium*," which means "Under Your Protection." (A Roman military fort was called a *praesidium*, and this word survives in the Spanish *presidio*.) This is a beautiful prayer to pray in times of illness, for yourself or others, because Mary is always happy to lead us closer to Jesus.

"Under Your Protection"

We fly to thy protection, O holy Mother of God.
Despise not our petitions in our necessities,
but deliver us always from all dangers,
O glorious and blessed Virgin.

(*Compendium*, page 184)

Christ Institutes the Sacrament of Anointing of the Sick

Oil of the Sick

Blessed olive oil used in the Sacrament of Anointing of the Sick to anoint the forehead and hands of people who are seriously ill or near death.

The Sacrament of Anointing of the Sick was instituted by Christ. We find the scriptural basis for this Sacrament in the Gospel of Mark (see 6:13) and the Letter of James (see 5:14–15). We examine these Scriptures more closely in the next article. ✝

Article 39 Scriptural and Historical Roots

The Sacrament of Anointing of the Sick has roots in the earliest period of the Church. In this article we look at both the scriptural and the historical roots of this Sacrament, including the meaning and use of oil, anointing in the early Church, and a short history of the Sacrament.

© PoodlesRock / Corbis

How does Jesus answer the question, "Who is my neighbor?" What can you do to make enemies into neighbors in your own life? (See Luke 10:36–37.)

The Meaning and Use of Oil

The Sacrament of Anointing of the Sick includes an anointing with a holy oil called the **Oil of the Sick**. It is pressed from olives and is blessed by the bishop. The oil is a sign of healing, strengthening, and the presence of the Holy Spirit.

The use of oil as a healing agent was familiar to the people of ancient times. It was a common remedy for wounds. In Jesus' Parable of the Good Samaritan, the Samaritan used it to help a man who had fallen into the hands of robbers: "He approached the victim, poured oil and wine over his wounds and bandaged them" (Luke 10:34). The wine, with its alcohol content, was a disinfectant; the oil eased the pain and soothed the skin.

Anointing in the Early Church

Scriptural accounts of the healing ministry of Jesus are numerous. In one scriptural account, in the Gospel of Mark, Jesus invites his Apostles to share in his healing ministry, using anointing with oil. Jesus sends them, two by two, to preach and to drive out demons. (In that time, some illnesses were believed to be caused by demons.) The account ends:

"So they went off and preached repentance. They drove out many demons, and they anointed with oil many who were sick and cured them" (Mark 6:12–13).

In the early Church, the anointing of those who were sick is attested to by the Letter of Saint James the Apostle. In his letter he wrote:

> Are there any who are sick among you? Let them send for the priests of the Church, and let the priests pray over them, anointing them with oil in the name of the Lord; and the prayer of faith will save the sick persons, and the Lord will raise them up; and if they have committed any sins, their sins will be forgiven them. (*Anointing of the Sick,* 117)

Tradition has recognized in this account the Sacrament of Anointing of the Sick. This is essentially the same rite used today: the anointing with oil by the priest and prayer for the sick person, with the laying on of hands.

A Short History of the Sacrament

Since her beginning, the Church has celebrated sacramental anointing of those suffering from illness. Gradually, over the centuries, these anointings were used only to prepare people for death. Because of this, the Sacrament became known as Extreme (or Last) Unction (or Anointing). However, the Sacrament itself, in its liturgy, always asked for healing if it would be helpful to the person's salvation.

The Second Vatican Council restored the original purpose of this Sacrament: to be a strengthening and healing grace for those who are seriously ill or in the frailty of old age. It is no longer necessary or advisable to wait until one is at the point of death before asking for this Sacrament.

Although every Sacrament is a liturgical and communal celebration of the entire Church, no matter how many people are participating, the Sacrament of Anointing of the Sick (in the form of Extreme Unction) had previously been celebrated with only the dying person

Parishes often offer a communal celebration of the Sacrament of Anointing of the Sick for those who are elderly or seriously ill. Why would you think a celebration with others in the parish church would be helpful to them?

© The Crosiers / Gene Plaisted, OSC

and perhaps the immediate family present. Today it is often celebrated within the Mass. We discuss the celebration of the Sacrament of Anointing of the Sick in the next article. ✝

The Minister of the Sacrament

The ministers of the Sacrament of Anointing of the Sick are bishops or priests. They use oil blessed by the bishop. If necessary, the oil can be blessed by the priest celebrating the Sacrament. Pastors and priests must teach their people about the importance of this Sacrament and its good effects, and should encourage them to call for a priest when they are in need of it. The local parish should also be encouraged to pray for those who are ill (see *CCC,* 1516). Many parishes publish prayer lists or use e-mail or telephone chains to do this. Parishioners also visit those who are ill or who find it difficult to come to Mass. They pray with the sick person, share the Word of God, and make sure the sick and the infirm are scheduled to receive the Eucharist regularly. If parishioners have been trained and commissioned to do so, they may bring the Eucharist to those who are ill.

Article

40 The Rite of Anointing of the Sick

"When the Church cares for the sick, it serves Christ himself in the suffering members of his Mystical Body" (*Sacred Congregation for Divine Worship, Prot. no. 1501/72 in Rites I,* 769). All through the centuries, the Church has cared for the sick, especially when others hesitated to do so for fear of contagion or even death. In the Early Middle Ages, monastic guest houses became the first hospitals. Out of concern for the needs of the sick, religious orders of brothers and sisters were founded. Saint Damien of Molokai (1840–1889) served the men and women suffering from leprosy on the island of Molokai, in what is now Hawaii, until he himself succumbed to the disease. In more recent times, Mother Teresa of Calcutta (1910–1997) began her society's work in India by taking in those who were literally dying in the streets and caring for them as for Christ himself.

However, the Church's greatest gift to the sick is the Sacrament of Anointing of the Sick. In this Sacrament the Church offers the grace of God for strength and healing.

This Sacrament may be celebrated in various places with various groups of people: in the home, in a hospital or assisted-care center, or in church. It can take place outside of the Mass or within the Mass. It may be offered to one person individually or to a group of people. It is often preceded by the Sacrament of Penance and Reconciliation and followed by reception of the Sacrament of the Eucharist.

Three Aspects of the Sacrament

There are three integral aspects of the Sacrament of Anointing of the Sick: the prayer of faith, the laying on of hands, and the anointing with the Oil of the Sick.

The Prayer of Faith

In the prayers of the Sacrament, the entire community asks God's help for the sick, in a spirit of trust and in response to God's Word. If possible, the sick person joins in these prayers.

The Laying On of Hands

This is a sign of blessing and, as you may recall, a gesture signifying the coming of the Holy Spirit. The laying on of hands by the minister of the Sacrament (a priest or bishop) is in direct imitation of Jesus, who often laid his hands on those who asked him for healing: "All who had people sick with

Live It!

Share Your Gifts

One of the worst consequences of serious illness or old age is isolation from family and friends. People in long-term care centers or other places for the care of the sick are vulnerable to this kind of isolation, not just for a few days, but for long stretches of time. Some have no families. Some have families who cannot visit as often as they would like. Most, if not all, have been separated from the everyday interactions of neighbors and friends.

Think about what you can do to bring the joy of Christ to those who are sick, either in your parish or in a nearby long-term care facility. Can you make cards? Can you form a singing group or a band for an evening's entertainment? Can you "adopt a grandparent" and visit on a regular basis? Find ways to share your gifts with those who are ill and isolated. You will be sharing Christ's love with those who will appreciate it most. And, in caring for the sick, you will be fulfilling one of the corporal works of mercy. (See Matthew 25:31–41.)

various diseases brought them to him. He laid his hands on each of them and cured them" (Luke 4:40).

The Anointing with Blessed Oil

The anointing with oil is a sign of the presence of the Holy Spirit. Through God's power and grace, the sick person is given strength to face serious illness, especially the physical and spiritual deterioration that can wear down every defense. The celebrating priest prays that the Lord will help the sick person with the grace of the Holy Spirit.

Though the laying on of hands is important to the rite, the essential elements of the Sacrament are "the anointing of the forehead and hands of the sick person (in the Roman Rite) or of other parts of the body (in the Eastern rite), the anointing being accompanied by the liturgical prayer of the celebrant asking for the special grace of this sacrament" (*CCC*, 1531).

The Celebration of the Sacrament

The Sacrament of Anointing of the Sick can be conferred within the Mass or outside of the Mass. Celebrating this Sacrament within the Mass emphasizes the union of those who are sick with the self-giving of Christ in the Eucharist. Because the Sacrament is celebrated in the midst of the community, it also emphasizes the prayerful concern of the local Church community for the sick persons within its midst.

Catholic Wisdom

Not Ended, But Changed

Many people see death as the end of everything. But when Jesus Christ came to redeem us, he redefined death. At a funeral Mass, we might hear these words from the Preface I for the Dead:

> Indeed, for your faithful, Lord,
> life is changed not ended,
> and, when this earthly dwelling turns to dust,
> an eternal dwelling is made ready for them in heaven.
>
> *(Roman Missal)*

Ask the Risen Christ to strengthen your faith in him and in the new and eternal life he has won for us.

If the Sacrament of Anointing of the Sick is celebrated during Mass, it begins after the Liturgy of the Word, and the litany for the Sacrament of Anointing of the Sick is prayed instead of the Prayer of the Faithful. The homily follows, and the Liturgy of Anointing begins, followed by the Liturgy of the Eucharist. The preface, the Eucharistic Prayer, and the other prayers of the Mass are adapted to include prayers and petitions for those who are in need of healing.

Celebration Outside of Mass

Whether celebrated within the Mass or outside of it, the rite of the Sacrament is essentially the same.

Greeting

If the Sacrament of Anointing of the Sick is celebrated outside of the Mass, the priest begins by greeting the sick person and those present with, "The peace of the Lord be always with you," or a similar blessing.

Sprinkling with Holy Water and Instruction

The priest may sprinkle holy water on the sick person and those present, as a reminder of Baptism and the death and Resurrection of Christ. He then gives a short instruction on the meaning of this Sacrament, ending with, "Let us therefore commend our sick brother/sister N. to the grace and power of Christ, that he may save him/her and raise him/her up" *(Rite of Anointing of the Sick Outside Mass)*.

If the Sacrament of Penance and Reconciliation is to be received, it is celebrated at this time.

Penitential Act and Liturgy of the Word

The Penitential Act follows, similar to the Penitential Act in the Eucharist, but directed toward the needs of those who are ill. (It is omitted if the Sacrament of Penance and Reconciliation has been celebrated.) This is followed by the Liturgy of the Word. A Gospel Reading is usually proclaimed, followed by a period of silence. The priest then gives a short homily addressed to the sick person, the family, and caregivers.

Who May Receive This Sacrament?

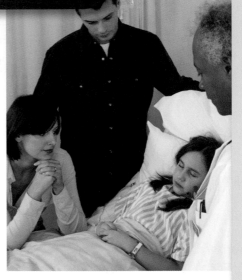

© Radius Images / Corbis

Any baptized Catholic above the age of reason (age seven) who is suffering from serious illness may receive the Sacrament, as well as those about to undergo serious surgery. Those suffering from alcoholism or other addictions may receive the Sacrament, as well as those suffering from mental illness.

The Sacrament of Anointing of the Sick may be received more than once. In fact, if a person should recover from a grave illness and then be confronted with the return of that illness or another grave illness, the Sacrament may and should be received again. If the person's condition becomes more serious in that same illness, the Sacrament may be repeated.

The Church especially encourages those who, because of illness or old age, are facing the near possibility of death to receive the strengthening grace of this Sacrament.

If you wonder whether you or someone dear to you may receive the Sacrament, discuss your concerns with a priest. The healing and strengthening power of Christ, with the Father and in the Holy Spirit, is available to you and to the ones you love.

The Liturgy of Anointing

The Liturgy of Anointing begins with a litany of prayers for the sick person, for relief of his or her sufferings, and for all who care for the sick. Then the laying on of hands takes place in silence. The priest lays both hands on the head of the sick person.

If the Oil of the Sick has already been blessed, the priest prays a prayer of thanksgiving to God. If it has not been blessed, the priest blesses it with this prayer:

God of all consolation . . .
Bless this oil ✚ and sanctify it for our use.
Make this oil a remedy for all who are anointed with it;
Heal them in body, in soul, and in spirit,
And deliver them from every affliction.

(*Anointing of the Sick,* 123)

The priest then anoints the sick person on the forehead with the blessed oil, saying:

"Through this holy anointing
may the Lord in his love and mercy help you
with the grace of the Holy Spirit."
All respond: Amen.

The priest then anoints the hands and says:

"May the Lord who frees you from sin
save you and raise you up."
All respond: Amen.

(*Anointing of the Sick,* 124)

© Bill Wittman / www.wpwittman.com

The vessel holding the Oil of the Sick is usually a clear bottle labeled OI (for "Oleum Infirmorum"). Review the sidebar on page 75 of this book to refresh your memory about all of the holy oils.

The priest may also, if he chooses, anoint the particular area of pain or injury in the body, but he does not repeat the prayer.

This is followed by a Prayer after Anointing. The rite provides prayer options especially suited for people in particular circumstances, including those who may be close to death, in advanced age, preparing for serious surgery, or for a child or young person with a serious illness. Then the priest leads all present in praying the Lord's Prayer.

Reception of Communion and Concluding Rite

The reception of Communion may follow. If not, the blessing of the sick person concludes the rite.

Viaticum

If someone is in danger of death, that person can, in addition to receiving the Sacrament of Anointing of the Sick, receive the Sacrament of the Eucharist as *viaticum.* This Latin word literally means "with you on the journey." In the Eucharist, Christ is with the dying person who is ready to make the journey from this life to eternal life.

Christ himself is with the dying son or daughter of God, to lead him or her to the Father. The Sacrament of the Eucharist is the sacrament of the death and Resurrection of Christ, and so it is the sacrament of passing over from death to life, and the pledge of life with God forever.

You may remember that the Sacraments of Baptism, Confirmation, and the Eucharist together are called the Sacraments of Christian Initiation. At the end of life, the Sacraments of Penance and Reconciliation and Anointing of the Sick, along with the Eucharist as *viaticum,* are the Sacraments through which we complete our journey here on earth. They are the Sacraments that prepare us for our final transition, with Christ, into eternal life. ☩

Article 41 Christ's Healing Power

In this article we consider the healing power of Christ in the Sacrament of Anointing of the Sick and its effect on the sick person receiving it.

The Effects of the Sacrament of Anointing of the Sick

First of all, does this Sacrament really work? Yes, it does, just as all the Sacraments really work, through the power and in the name of God—the Father, the Son, and the Holy Spirit. The effects, or gifts, of the Sacrament of Anointing of the Sick are many, including the following:

- **Union of the sick person to Christ in his Passion** Those who suffer are not useless; their sufferings, united to Christ's, can participate in his saving work. Suffering no longer is simply a consequence of Original Sin. It becomes redemptive.

- **Strength, peace, and courage to endure the sufferings of illness or old age** The grace of this Sacrament renews trust and faith in God, and gives strength to accept death peacefully. This is in itself a grace of healing.

- **Forgiveness of sins** If the person is contrite and was not able to receive absolution in the Sacrament of Penance and Reconciliation, he or she can receive it now.

Christ's Healing Power in Our Lives

Jesus Christ is alive and risen and with us today, especially in his Sacraments. The Sacrament of Anointing of the Sick teaches us that Christ's healing power is at work in the world, and that he is with us in all things, especially when we are weak and in need. This Sacrament helps us to understand more fully the last words of Jesus, just before his Ascension, in the Gospel of Matthew: "And behold, I am with you always, until the end of the age" (Matthew 28:20).

This Sacrament reminds us to reflect often on the healing power of Christ. Every time we receive the Eucharist, we pray to him, "But only say the word and my soul shall be healed" (*Roman Missal*). The healing power of Christ is at work in us, in body and in spirit, as he shares his risen life with us.

This Sacrament encourages us to offer up our sufferings for the good of the entire Body of Christ, the Church, and for the good of the entire world. It encourages us to bring the healing and compassion of Christ to those who suffer. It encourages us to accept pain, suffering, and death as the consequences of Original Sin—but it also encourages us to trust that we will be raised up with Jesus. Suffering and death are temporary. This Sacrament helps us to live with the hope that one day we will live in perfect and eternal union with God—Father, Son, and Holy Spirit.

- **Restoration of health if God wills it** The person's health will be restored if it would be a help toward the saving of the person's soul.

- **Ecclesial grace of union with the Body of Christ** Through this Sacrament, the sick person benefits from the intercession of the saints. He or she contributes to the holiness of the entire Church and, through union with Christ, to the good of the entire world.

- **Preparation for passing over to eternal life** The Sacrament is rightly given to those who are close to death and even at the point of departing from this life. In that case, the Sacrament is "also called *sacramentum exeuntium* (the sacrament of those departing)"[5] (*CCC*, 1523). Baptism begins our journey in Christ, in his death and in his Resurrection, and the Sacrament of Anointing of the Sick completes that journey on earth. It completes the anointings, which have marked us as Christ's own during our lifetime. "This last anointing fortifies the end of our earthly life like a solid rampart for the final struggles before entering the Father's house"[6] (*CCC*, 1523). ✝

Part Review

1. What is the purpose of the Sacrament of Anointing of the Sick, and who may receive it?

2. How can illness be a turning point in human life?

3. Why is the Sacrament of Anointing of the Sick "a true and proper Sacrament"?

4. Of what is the Oil of the Sick a sign and what are its scriptural roots?

5. Where and with whom may the Sacrament of Anointing of the Sick be celebrated?

6. What are the essential elements of the Sacrament of Anointing of the Sick?

7. How can physical suffering be a way for us to take up our cross with Jesus and, in our own small way, participate in his redemptive suffering?

8. Among all of Jesus' miracles of healing, why are his healings of lepers so significant in our understanding of the Sacraments of Healing?

9. What three Sacraments prepare us for our journey into eternal life, and what is the work of each in our transition to eternal life?

10. In what ways has the Church, from the earliest days of Christianity, provided for the care of those who are ill?

The Sacraments at the Service of Communion

Part 1

The Sacrament of Holy Orders

We begin our life in the Church as followers of Christ through the Sacraments of Christian Initiation—Baptism, Confirmation, and the Eucharist. These Sacraments are in themselves a call, a vocation, to personal holiness and to participation in the spread of the Good News of Jesus Christ to all the world.

Two other Sacraments—the Sacraments at the Service of Communion—give the grace and strength to serve others. These two Sacraments are the Sacraments of Holy Orders and of Matrimony. In this part we discuss the Sacrament of Holy Orders, and, in the next, the Sacrament of Matrimony.

The topics covered in this part are:

- Article 42: Consecrated to God's People (page 222)

- Article 43: The Priesthood of the New Covenant (page 226)

- Article 44: The Degrees of Ordination (page 231)

- Article 45: The Graces of the Sacrament (page 236)

42 Consecrated to God's People

Article

The People of God is a priestly people who participate in the one priesthood of Christ. We all share, through Baptism, in "the common priesthood of the faithful" (*Catechism of the Catholic Church [CCC]*, 1591). Yet springing from this baptismal call is another participation in Christ's priesthood, the ministerial priesthood of priests and bishops. The ministerial priesthood gives a sacred power through the Sacrament of Holy Orders for the purpose of serving the Church, helping all of us to fulfill our baptismal call. This ministry serves the People of God in the name of Christ and represents Christ within the community of the Body of Christ.

Those ordained to the ministerial priesthood (priests and bishops, who are also priests) are called to be "servant leaders": to serve and to lead the Church by teaching the Word of God, by offering divine worship in the liturgy, and by governing the Church as representatives of Christ, who is the Head of the Church. In this way they carry out the mission of Christ in the world today. Deacons are also ordained for service in the Church through the Sacrament of Holy Orders, but they do not participate in the ministerial priesthood. Because of their important work, they are mentioned throughout this part, as appropriate.

In this article we consider the origins of the term *ordination* and the priesthood of the Old Covenant. We also begin to explore the fulfillment of the Old Covenant priesthood by Christ and his institution of the priesthood of the New Covenant.

Many young men explore the idea of a priestly vocation during their high school and college years. Your diocesan vocation office may have materials and other helps to acquaint you with the work of priests in your area.

The Meaning of *Ordination*

The **Sacrament of Holy Orders** is the Sacrament by which baptized men are ordained for permanent ministry in the Church as bishops, priests, or deacons. In Rome, in ancient times, the word *order* referred to an established grouping that ordered Roman society. The Church uses this word to describe the state of life of various groups of people. Thus the liturgy names the order of bishops, the order of priests, the order of deacons. We have already learned about the order of catechumens. In the early Church, a person joined an *ordo,* or order, through a liturgical rite called *ordinatio.* At that time the rite was a sacrament, a blessing, or a consecration. Today we reserve the term *ordination* for the Sacrament of Holy Orders, through which men are integrated into one of three holy orders: bishop, priest, or deacon.

Holy Orders, Sacrament of

The Sacrament by which baptized men are ordained for permanent ministry in the Church as bishops, priests, and deacons.

The Priesthood of the Old Covenant

As you may remember, God chose the entire nation of Israel to be a holy and priestly people of his own. Aaron, the brother of Moses, was the first high priest. God then chose one of the Twelve Tribes of Israel, the tribe of Levi, to be priests and to carry out liturgical sacrifice and worship. The Levites alone had charge of the Dwelling Place of God, a special tent that held the stone tablets of the Ten Commandments and journeyed with the people wherever they went. Through Moses, God gave the Twelve Tribes of Israel a certain section of land as their inheritance: "But Moses gave no heritage to the tribe of Levi: the LORD, the God of Israel, is their heritage, as he had promised them" (Joshua 13:33).

This priesthood honored God with sacrifice and prayer and united the people in worship, but it could not bring salvation. Only the sacrifice of Christ would bring that about. The Church, however, sees in the priesthood of the Old Covenant a prefiguring of the ordained ministry that Jesus Christ himself established.

Thus the rites of ordination for bishops, priests, and deacons include references to the priesthood of the Old Covenant. At the ordination of bishops, reference is made to God's plan for salvation from the beginning:

"God the Father of our Lord Jesus Christ, . . .
by your gracious word
you have established the plan of your Church.

From the beginning,
you chose the descendants of Abraham to be your holy nation.
You established rulers and priests,
and did not leave your sanctuary without ministers to serve
you. . . ."[1]

(*CCC*, 1541)

When priests are ordained, the liturgy references the seventy wise men Moses chose to help him govern God's People and reminds us of the first high priest, Aaron. Addressing God the Father, we pray:

"You extended the spirit of Moses to seventy wise men. . . .
You shared among the sons of Aaron
the fullness of their father's power."[2]

(*CCC*, 1542)

I Come to Do Your Will, O God

The Letter to the Hebrews is addressed to Christians who understood the importance of the priesthood of the Old Covenant, with its yearly sacrifices in the Temple as offerings for sin. The writer instructs the people about the New Covenant of Jesus Christ in these same terms.

He explains the great difference between the Old Covenant and the New Covenant by focusing on the sacrifice of Jesus as the one and only sacrifice needed for the forgiveness of sins. The writer also understands that the entire life of Jesus was a "sacrifice" because the Divine Son of God gave up everything to do the Father's will and to become man. Mindful of Jesus' offering of his entire life for us, the writer of Hebrews wrote:

But in those sacrifices there is only a yearly remembrance of sins, for it is
impossible that the blood of bulls and goats take away sins. For this reason,
when [Jesus] came into the world, he said:
"Sacrifice and offering you did not desire,
but a body you prepared for me;
holocausts and sin offerings you took no delight in.
Then I said, 'As is written of me in the scroll,
Behold, I come to do your will, O God.'"

(Hebrews 10:3–7)

At the ordination of deacons, the sons of Levi are referenced:

> Almighty God . . . ,
>
> . . . .
>
> You established a threefold ministry of worship and service,
> for the glory of your name.
> As ministers of your tabernacle you chose the sons of Levi
> and gave them your blessing as their everlasting inheritance.[3]
>
> (CCC, 1543)

As Abraham is our "father in faith" ("Eucharistic Prayer I"), our bishops, priests, and deacons inherit the spiritual blessings given to the sons of Aaron and Levi.

Live It!

Discerning Your Vocation

Have you ever wondered if God is calling you to a special vocation? Well, of course he is! Through Baptism, God calls everyone—to ministry, to holiness, to Christian witness.

Here's a more difficult question: How can you figure out what vocation God is calling you to? Although a foolproof recipe for discerning your vocation hasn't been discovered yet, we do know many of the necessary ingredients:

- Trust that God wants you to discover your vocation. God has planted his call within your heart, and you simply need to be faithful in discovering it. Be honest about your deepest feelings, and do not be afraid of the vocation to which you are attracted.

- Look for clues. Do you enjoy being part of a community of people that is dedicated to God? Are you drawn to the idea of a life of prayer and of service to others in community? You should take a good look at religious life. Or perhaps you have given serious thought to the joys and sacrifices involved in a lifetime commitment between one man and one woman. Perhaps you love to be with children and cannot imagine not having children of your own. If so, it is probable that marriage is your vocation.

- Serve God in any way you can. Try out different ministries in the Church: liturgical ministries, catechetical (teaching) ministries, ministries of charity and social action. These will help you to discover your gifts and interests.

- Spend time with people you admire. Learn from them what a religious sister is and does, what the ministry of a deacon entails, how a married couple lives out their faith together.

- Seek out a spiritual director (a priest, sister, or qualified layperson) who can guide you through a prayerful process of discovering God's will for you. A spiritual director can help you follow God's path in truth and freedom.

Jesus Fulfills the Old Covenant

Jesus Christ fulfilled the priesthood of the Old Covenant through his institution of the Sacrament of Holy Orders. For Jesus Christ, our new High Priest, has entered not the earthly sanctuary of the Old Covenant but Heaven itself. His sacrifice was not the blood of lambs, but his own blood. This is the sacrifice of the New Covenant that conquered sin and brought salvation. This is the sacrifice we remember and celebrate, led by the ministry of the priesthood of the New Covenant, in the Sacraments and especially in the Eucharist.

The institution of the Sacrament of Holy Orders flows from Jesus' institution of the Church. The priesthood is the sacrament of Apostolic ministry. It is Christ's gift to the Church of his own authority and mission for the good of the whole Body of Christ. Through this Sacrament Christ's mission entrusted to his Apostles can be carried out in the Church until the end of time. ✝

These young men are being ordained priests by the Archbishop of Paris, France. Ask your parish priest where and by whom he was ordained. Then trace the line of his and his ordaining bishop's ordination.

© Pascal Deloche / Godong / Corbis

Article 43 The Priesthood of the New Covenant

Article 23, "What Is the Eucharist?" mentioned the priest Melchizedek whose Old Testament offering of bread and wine prefigured the offerings of bread and wine at the Eucharist. Melchizedek's priesthood is also a prefiguring of the unique priesthood of Christ. The Letter to the Hebrews notes the connection between Melchizedek as high priest and Jesus as the new High Priest:

In the days when he was in the flesh, he offered prayers and supplications with loud cries and tears to the one who was able to save him from death, and he was heard because of his reverence. Son though he was, he learned obedience from what he suffered; and when he was made perfect, he became the source of eternal salvation for all who obey him, declared by God high priest according to the order of Melchizedek. (Hebrews 5:7–10)

After the Resurrection of Christ, the Apostles understood that everything the priesthood of the Old Testament pointed toward found its fulfillment in Jesus Christ. He is the "one mediator between God and the human race" (1 Timothy 2:5), and, as High Priest of the New Covenant, gave himself as an offering "once for all" on the cross (Hebrews 7:27). Because we are baptized, we all participate in the one priesthood of Christ. Yet every bishop and priest participates in a unique way in this priesthood of Christ, our High

Christ's High Priestly Prayer

At the Last Supper, Jesus instructed his Apostles, "Do this in memory of me" (Luke 22:19). In this he commissioned them to offer this worship until the end of time. After the supper, as recorded in the Gospel of John, he offered what has been called his "high priestly prayer" of consecration for his Apostles and for all who would follow them. In this prayer Jesus prays to the Father for those he has loved and taught in his earthly life. In the following portion of the prayer, he prays that they will be true to his word and to his teachings:

> But now I am coming to you. I speak this in the world so that they may share my joy completely. I gave them your word, and the world hated them, because they do not belong to the world any more than I belong to the world. I do not ask that you take them out of the world but that you keep them from the evil one. . . . Consecrate them in the truth. Your word is truth. As you sent me into the world, so I sent them into the world. And I consecrate myself for them, so that they also may be consecrated in truth. (John 17:13–18)

You may want to finish reading this prayer, at John 17:20–26. In it Christ is praying for *you*—for all who believe in him through the word of the Apostles and their successors. At the very end, Jesus prays that the love of God the Father for his Son, Jesus, may be in us, and that Jesus himself may be in us.

Priest and our "source of eternal salvation" (Hebrews 5:9). The uniqueness of the ministerial priesthood lies in its call and commitment to serve the entire Church and to help all Christians live a life of grace in union with Jesus Christ. Through this ministry, Christ builds up and leads his Church (see *CCC*, 1547).

This unique participation in the priesthood of Christ and the leadership role that priests and bishops play in community life does not make them more important in the eyes of God than any other person; nor does it mean they are holier than laypeople—God calls us all to lives of perfect holiness according to our vocation. However, the ministerial priesthood is different in its essence from the common priesthood of all the baptized. It isn't that bishops and priests have *more* priesthood than the laity; they have a *different* priesthood, one that gives them unique responsibilities that no layperson can fulfill. These unique responsibilities fall into three areas: teaching the faithful, leading divine worship (the liturgy), especially the Eucharist, and governing the Church.

Representatives of Christ

Christ is the Head of the Church. He is the High Priest who has offered his life as a sacrifice, once and for all. He is the Good Shepherd who cares for his flock. He is the Teacher of Truth.

A parish priest is usually a "people person" who enjoys meeting with his parishioners, sharing their joys and sorrows. He finds that being Christ for his people, while burdensome at times, is also his greatest joy.

© Bill Wittman / www.wpwittman.com

Archbishop Oscar Romero

In the 1980s the tiny country of El Salvador, in Central America, was torn apart by a violent civil war. Archbishop Oscar Romero was the Archbishop of San Salvador. (An archbishop is a bishop of the highest rank, and he heads an archdiocese.)

Through weekly homilies broadcast by radio, he spoke out for peace and justice. Yet the violence continued. He told the people, "If some day they take away the radio station from us . . . if they don't let us speak, if they kill all the priests and the bishop too, and you are left a people without priests, each one of you must become God's microphone, each one of you must become a prophet."

They did not take the bishop's radio station. They took the bishop's life. On March 23, in his homily broadcast throughout the country, Archbishop Romero challenged the army: "Brothers, you are from the same people; you kill your fellow peasant. . . . No soldier is obliged to obey an order that is contrary to the will of God." After he was interrupted by applause, he went on, "In the name of God then, in the name of this suffering people I ask you, I beg you, I command you in the name of God: stop the repression."

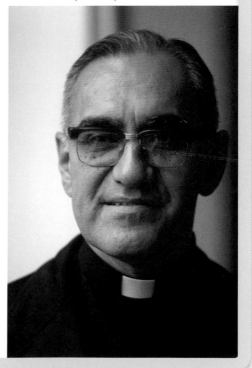

The archbishop received his answer the next day, when, as he was giving a homily during Mass, he was killed instantly by a sharpshooter. The day before he had said to a reporter, "You can tell the people that if they succeed in killing me, that I forgive and bless those who do it. Hopefully, they will realize they are wasting their time. A bishop will die, but the church of God, which is the people, will never perish."

(Adapted and quoted from Renny Golden, "Oscar Romero: Bishop of the Poor," *U.S. Catholic* Web site, February 25, 2009)

Archbishop Romero is now a candidate for sainthood.

The ordained minister, through his service to God's People, makes the presence of Christ—as high priest, shepherd, and teacher—visible. Through the Sacrament of Holy Orders, a priest is given the power to act "in the power and place of the person of Christ himself"[4] (*CCC,* 1548). An ordained minister, especially a bishop or priest, is head, high priest, teacher, and good shepherd for his people. This does not mean that the bishop, priest, or deacon is perfect as Christ is perfect. Because the ordained minister is human, he is not always a perfect model of Christ. Because of their leadership roles, bishops, priests, and deacons can either greatly help the Church and the spread of the Gospel, or they can hinder it. In the Sacraments, however, as mentioned in article 7, "Sacraments: Sign and Mystery," the sins and imperfections of the minister do not impede the sacramental grace. For example, absolution granted in the Sacrament of Penance and Reconciliation is still valid and imparts God's forgiveness even if the priest granting the absolution is himself not in a state of grace.

Bishops, priests, and deacons must always keep in mind that they were ordained not for privilege but for service. Acting "in the power and place" of Christ is a great responsibility. Christ himself warned his Apostles not to imitate the power of the authorities of this world but to be servants as he himself came to serve (see Mark 10:42–45). ✝

Pray It!

A Meditation

Blessed John Henry Cardinal Newman (1801–1890) was an Anglican priest in England when, after much prayer and study, he entered the Catholic Church in 1845. A scholar and writer, he contributed much to the life of the Church. This meditation hints at his own struggles to follow Christ no matter the cost:

> God has created me to do him some definite service; he has committed some work to me which he has not committed to another. I have my mission. . . . I am a link in a chain, a bond of connection between persons. He has not created me for naught. . . . Therefore, I will trust him. Whatever, wherever I am, I can never be thrown away. . . . He does nothing in vain. . . . He knows what he is about. He may take away my friends, he may throw me among strangers, he may make me feel desolate, make my spirits sink, hide my future from me—still he knows what he is about. (Newman Reader Web site)

44 The Degrees of Ordination

The ordained ministry consists of three degrees, or orders: the order of bishop (the episcopate), the order of priest (the presbyterate), and the order of deacon (diaconate). These three degrees are indispensable to the Church and its structure. Without each one of them, we would not be able to even speak of "the Church." In this article we discuss the differing, but complementary, ministries of each degree.

> **bishop**
> One who has received the fullness of the Sacrament of Holy Orders and is a successor to the Apostles.

The Role of the Bishop

When a priest is ordained a **bishop**, he receives the fullness of Holy Orders. This makes him a member of the college of bishops (the word *college* here means "gathering" or "group") and also makes him the visible head of the particular Church to which he has been assigned. (In this case *particular Church* means a diocese, as in "The Church of Cleveland.") Because the bishops are the successors to the Apostles and members of the college of bishops, their concern is not for their own dioceses alone. They have the responsibility of

Elements of the Rites of Ordination

Each degree of ordination has its own particular rite. However, these rites have certain elements in common:

- Bishops confer the Sacrament of Holy Orders in all three degrees.
- The essential elements of the Sacrament of Holy Orders are the laying on of hands and the speaking of the prayer of consecration. In this prayer the presiding bishop asks God to grant the *ordinand* (the one to be ordained) the graces of the Holy Spirit required in his ministry as bishop, priest, or deacon.
- The Sacrament of Holy Orders imprints an indelible spiritual character.

© DARIO PIGNATELLI / Reuters / Corbis

priest
One who has received the ministerial priesthood through the Sacrament of Holy Orders. The priest serves the community of faith by representing and assisting the bishop in teaching, governing, and presiding over the community's worship.

caring for the entire Church under the authority of the Pope, the Bishop of Rome and the successor to Saint Peter.

Each bishop ordained is in the line of Apostolic Succession that extends back to Saint Peter and thus to Christ himself. This gives the bishop a place of chief dignity in the Church. The gift of the Holy Spirit, first given to the Apostles, is transmitted to bishops through the Sacrament of Holy Orders. Thus, through episcopal ordination, the bishop represents Christ himself as teacher, shepherd, and priest, and acts as Christ's representative (see *CCC*, 1558).

The ordination of a new bishop must be approved by the Bishop of Rome, the Pope, as he is the visible sign of the union of all the particular Churches. As a sign of the unity of the Church and of the unity of the college of bishops, since ancient times it has been a practice of the Church for several bishops to participate in the ordination and consecration of a new bishop.

The Eucharist celebrated by the bishop has special significance: With the bishop present, the complete local Church is assembled in worship, and the representative of Christ—Good Shepherd and Head of the Church—presides.

The Role of the Priest

When a man is ordained a **priest**, he is ordained as a coworker of the bishop. He is united with the bishop in priestly dignity, and will look to the bishop for guidance in his pastoral assignment and duties. The priests of a diocese form a *presbyterium*, or body of priests, around the bishop, to help and advise him. With the bishop each priest is responsible for a particular Church. It is the responsibility of the bishop to determine the pastoral assignment or other official responsibility for each priest in his diocese.

During the Rite of Ordination, the unity of the priests of the diocese is expressed by their laying on of hands, after the bishop, upon the head of the new priest. Every priest shares with the bishop in the authority of Christ himself in building up, making holy, and ruling his Body, the Church. This authority is given through the Sacrament of Holy Orders. At ordination the new priest's bond with the bishop is expressed by the priest's promise of obedience to the bishop and by the sign of peace the bishop gives to the new priest. Together these two actions mean that the bishop considers the new priest his coworker, his son, his brother, and his friend, and that the new priest owes the bishop his love and obedience in return.

By the anointing of the Holy Spirit and the character of Holy Orders, the priest is authorized to act in the person of Christ. He is consecrated to preach the Gospel, to guide the People of God, and to celebrate the liturgy of the Church as a priest of the New Covenant. Even though he is assigned to a particular ministry in a diocese, mission, or parish, he in fact shares in the universal mission of Christ, to preach the Gospel to the ends of the earth.

It is especially at the Eucharist, in the assembly of the faithful, that priests fulfill their priestly office, for at the Eucharist, acting in the person of Christ, they make present again the one sacrifice of Christ's offering himself for

Requirements for Ordination

The Church ordains only baptized men who have been recognized as suitable for the ministry. Becoming an ordained minister (a bishop, priest, or deacon) is not a right or a purely personal decision but is based in the call of the Church. The Church alone has the right and responsibility to call someone to receive the Sacrament of Holy Orders. The Sacrament of Holy Orders is received as pure gift.

Other requirements are a commitment to celibacy (in the Latin Church, with the exception of permanent deacons), adequate education and formation, good mental health, a lifelong commitment to personal prayer and devotion, and willingness to be a servant leader in the name of Christ.

Priests undergo an extensive education and formation before being ordained. Candidates for the priesthood are usually admitted to a seminary. This is a house of formation in which candidates take college-level courses relevant to their future work. The program of study usually requires about five years of higher-level education beyond the college level. However, education for the priesthood is not only intellectual. Formation in three other areas—human growth, spiritual life, and pastoral practice—is equally important. Seminarians are given opportunities to help in parishes and other pastoral settings, especially in the summer. In this way they are guided to a greater self-knowledge and a greater understanding of the vocation of the priest.

all: "From this unique sacrifice their whole priestly ministry draws its strength"[5] (*CCC,* 1566).

The Role of the Deacon

deacon

One who is ordained for service and ministry, but not for ministerial priesthood, through the Sacrament of Holy Orders. Deacons are ordained to assist priests and bishops in a variety of liturgical and charitable ministries.

The word **deacon** comes from the Greek word *diakonia,* which means "service." The ministry of deacons is expressed in their title: They are ordained for service in the Church. Ordination bestows on them important functions in the ministry of the Word, divine worship, pastoral governance, and the service of charity and good works. These are all carried out under the authority of the bishop.

For deacons the character of the Sacrament of Holy Orders unites them to Christ, who came not "to be served but to serve" (Mark 10:45). Their service includes assisting at the liturgy, above all in the Eucharist; distributing Holy Communion; baptizing; assisting at and blessing marriages; proclaiming the Gospel; preaching; presiding over funerals; and serving those who are poor or in need.

There are two types of deacons: transitional deacons, who intend to be ordained to the priesthood in the future; and permanent deacons, who intend to remain lifelong deacons. They may be married or single. Deacons intending to be priests in the future, and deacons who are single, make a promise of celibacy at ordination. If a deacon is married, he promises not to remarry if his spouse should pass away. ✟

Catholic Wisdom

A Civilization of Love

What is the task of the priest today? This is what Pope John Paul II told a group of American bishops in answer to this question:

In collaborating closely with the laity, priests must encourage them to see the Gospel as the principal force for the renewal of society—the vast and complex world of politics and economics, but also the world of culture, of science and the arts, of international life, of the mass media (cf. *Evangelii nuntiandi,* 70). A priest need not be an expert in all these things, but he should be an expert in discerning the "higher gifts" which the Holy Spirit abundantly pours out for the building of the kingdom (cf. 1 Cor 12:31), and he should help his people apply those gifts in advancing a civilization of love.

Symbols of Grace and Mission

Sacred signs and symbols in the Rite of Ordination highlight aspects of the grace of the Sacrament. These are a few examples:

- Both bishop and priest are anointed with Sacred Chrism. The bishop is anointed on his head, and the priest on the palms of his hands. This anointing is a sign of the anointing by and presence of the Holy Spirit.

- In the ordination of a bishop, two assisting priests hold the Book of the Gospels above the new bishop's head while a special prayer of consecration is prayed for him. The Book of the Gospels is then given to the new bishop as a sign of his call and authority to teach the truth and to proclaim the Word of God. He is then given the ring as a sign of his fidelity to the Church, and the crosier (the shepherd's crook) as a sign of his call to model his leadership after Jesus, the Good Shepherd. He is also given the mitre (the unique pointed hat), which is a symbol of his authority.

- The new priest is given a paten and chalice as a sign of his role in the Eucharist.

- The new deacon is given the Book of the Gospels as a sign of his call to read and to proclaim the Gospel of Christ.

Article 45 The Graces of the Sacrament

The Holy Spirit gives those who receive the Sacrament of Holy Orders certain effects and graces. Like the Sacraments of Baptism and Confirmation, the Sacrament of Holy Orders marks the recipient with an indelible spiritual character. It is never conferred temporarily nor is it repeated.

There can be good and serious reasons for an ordained minister's being released from the obligations that he accepted at his ordination. Or, again for serious reasons, an ordained minister can be forbidden to exercise his ministry. However, even in such circumstances, an ordained minister never returns to the lay state. The character of ordination is forever. For example, in an emergency, when no other priest is available, a priest who has been relieved of his priestly responsibilities and is living as a layperson may still celebrate the Sacrament of Anointing of the Sick with someone who is dying.

© Robyn Mackenzie/shutterstock

Help Wanted

Is Christ calling you to be a priest, deacon, brother, or sister? All personality types welcomed. Sense of humor a definite plus. Pay negotiable. Excellent opportunity for a life well lived in prayer, good works, deep satisfaction, happiness, and genuine love. Inquire in person to your nearest parish priest, deacon, religious brother or sister, or school counselor.

The Grace of the Holy Spirit

The grace of the Sacrament of Holy Orders is union with Christ and being given a share in his mission as Priest, Teacher, and Pastor. The special grace of this Sacrament for the bishop is the grace of strength—strength to govern and guide; strength to love all, especially those in need; and strength to proclaim the Gospel to all. The bishop is given strength to be a role model for his people, to walk the way of holiness ahead of them as a shepherd leads his flock, and to lead them to the life-giving Eucharist, in which he identifies with Christ. In this Sacrament he is given strength to give his life, day by day, for his sheep.

A prayer from the Byzantine liturgy expresses the grace of this Sacrament for priests. In this rite, the bishop, while laying his hand on the priest, prays to the Father that the new priest may be filled with the Holy Spirit, saying the following:

> That he may be worthy to stand without reproach before your
>   altar,
> to proclaim the Gospel of your kingdom,
> to fulfill the ministry of your word of truth,
> to offer you spiritual gifts and sacrifices,
> to renew your people by the bath of rebirth.[6]

(*CCC*, 1587)

The prayer continues with the petition that the priest may, at the second coming of Christ, meet our Savior Jesus Christ and receive a just reward for "a faithful administration of his order"[7] (1587).

The sacramental grace for deacons is a whole-hearted commitment to the People of God. In this commitment deacons cooperate with the bishop and priests, offer service (*diakonia*) in the liturgy, proclaim the Word of God, and reach out in works of love toward those who are in need.

The grace of ordination, as all graces, requires the cooperation and continual conversion of the one who receives it. Grace is a gift. It is not a thing but a relationship. The closer the bishop, the priest, and the deacon come to God, the more faithfully they will live out their commitment to serve God's People. The ordained clergy are ordained not as leaders alone, but as servant leaders, following in the footsteps of Christ. They are ordained to help the People of God follow their own baptismal call—to follow Christ in the path of their own vocations. In this the ordained ministers can have no greater model of service than Jesus, the Good Shepherd, who gave up his life for his sheep. ✝

Care for the vulnerable (those who are poor or in need) has been a special grace and responsibility of deacons since the early days of the Church. See Acts of the Apostles 6:1–6. A moment of caring can make someone's day!

© Bill Wittman / www.wpwittman.com

A Prayer for Vocations

The United States Conference of Catholic Bishops (USCCB) has suggested this prayer as a prayer for vocations in service to God's People. The Church will always be in need of generous men and women to give of themselves in service. This is one way we can help to support our bishops, priests, deacons, religious, and lay ministers in their efforts to serve us—by praying that God will send more workers into the vineyard of the Church!

Loving and Generous God,
it is You who call us by name
and ask us to follow You.

Help us to grow in the Love
and Service of our Church
as we experience it today.

Give us the energy and courage
of Your Spirit
to shape its future.

Grant us faith-filled leaders
who will embrace Christ's
        Mission
of love and justice.

Bless the Church of _____ (name your diocese)
by raising up dedicated and generous leaders
from our families and friends
who will serve Your people as Sisters,
Priests, Brothers, Deacons, and Lay Ministers.

Inspire us to know You better
and open our hearts
to hear Your call.

We ask this through our Lord.
Amen.

                        (USCCB Web site)

Part Review

1. What are the three orders of ministry to which men can be ordained?

2. Why do the rites of ordination for bishops, priests, and deacons include references to the priesthood of the Old Covenant? Select one Old Testament reference and explain its significance in the Rite of Ordination.

3. How does the priesthood of the men called to ordained ministry differ from the common priesthood of all the baptized?

4. What are the three areas of responsibility for those in ordained ministry? Give one example of each.

5. To what vocation does God call each of us?

6. How did the priesthood of the Old Testament find its fulfillment in Jesus Christ?

7. How does a bishop or priest act in the person of Christ?

8. What are the essential elements of the Sacrament of Holy Orders?

9. What is the role of the bishop? the priest? the deacon?

10. Describe the special grace the Sacrament of Holy Orders gives to bishops, priests, and deacons.

Part 2

The Sacrament of Matrimony

Marriage is a calling to a particular person and to a particular way of life. Married life brings many joys to a husband and wife: the joy of devoted and caring companionship, a sharing of mutual goals, the nurturing and support of a loving spouse in times of challenge as well as times of celebration, and, for most married couples, the joy of raising children together. Of course, this does not mean that each and every day of married life is filled with boundless joy and no challenges. As many newly married husbands and wives might tell us, it is not long after the wedding, when the guests have gone, the honeymoon is over, and everyday life takes center stage once again that, surely by the grace of God, the idea hits home: A happy marriage takes *work*.

Marriage takes a lifetime of hard work, and it is not possible without mutual respect and mutual love. This is what the Sacrament of Matrimony is all about. It is not just about having a church wedding. It is about the lifetime commitment to be one in love.

The Church, through the Sacrament of Matrimony, asks this commitment of every married man and woman because God does, because it is part of his plan for the happiness of the human family. Naturally, a lifetime commitment takes preparation.

The topics covered in this part are:

Article 46 Lifelong Covenant

Through your previous study of religion, you probably became familiar with the importance of God's covenant with his people. The Old Covenant was a gift of God to the people of Israel, and it has never been dissolved. The New Covenant is a gift of God to us, in Jesus Christ, his Son, and we live by it today. We renew it at every Eucharist. Through the words and actions of the priest and the power of the Holy Spirit, the sacrifice of Jesus Christ is made present, and we participate in it by receiving, as did the Apostles at the Last Supper, his Body and Blood.

The union of a baptized man and a baptized woman in Marriage is a sign and symbol of God's covenant with his people, a covenant of love and grace in Jesus Christ. In the wedding Mass, we may hear these words at the Preface:

> In the union of husband and wife
> you gave a sign of Christ's loving gift of grace,
> so that the Sacrament we celebrate
> might draw us back more deeply
> into the wondrous design of your love.
>
> (*Roman Missal,* "Preface, Marriage II")

In this article we explore the meaning of the Marriage covenant through the history of this Sacrament and its scriptural sources.

God's Plan for Marriage

God created marriage, and it is part of his wonderful plan for human life. Because we are made in the image and likeness of God, we are made for love. Thus marriage is not a purely human institution but is God's loving way of bringing happiness to his sons and daughters and assuring them that they need not be alone as they journey through life. Marriage has been planned by God to bring about two

The cross is a symbol of Christ, who, in Christian Marriage, is joined with two individuals (symbolized by the rings) into an unbreakable union. The color of the rays (red) is the color of love and sacrifice.

© The Crosiers / Gene Plaisted, OSC

great goods: the good of the man and woman pledged to each other, and the procreation and education of children. In their intimate union in both body and spirit, the marital love of man and woman is an image and likeness of God's love for all of us. And if God blesses the husband and wife with the gift of a child, there is all the more reason to rejoice!

When Jesus taught about the divine plan for marriage, he went all the way back to the Book of Genesis and drew upon the following passage: "That is why a man leaves his father and mother and clings to his wife, and the two of them become one body" (2:24, see Matthew 19:5). Jesus concluded that this was the reason why marriages cannot be dissolved: "So they are no longer two, but one flesh. Therefore, what God has joined together, no human being must separate" (Matthew 19:6). Thus Christ raised marriage in the New Covenant, marriage between Christians, to the dignity of a Sacrament.

Marriage and the Old Covenant

As in all other areas of life, the reality of evil and sin is present in the relationships between men and women. In society as a whole, relationships between men and women can result in misunderstandings and conflict. This is due not to the nature of men and women, or to the quality of their relationships, but to sin. Within marriage, misunderstandings and conflicts can escalate into domination, jealousy, and infidelity. The first sin—the sin of the first man and woman—resulted in a break in the original communion between man and woman. The consequences of this Original Sin, the necessity of toil and the pain of childbirth, became part of human life.

But God continues to offer mercy to his people. The consequences of the first sin also became a means of healing. In marriage the need to work to sustain themselves and their families and the rearing of children necessitate that a man and a woman support each other through life. The self-giving that this mutual support requires helps the married couple to grow in God's love and grace.

Under the Old Covenant, the unity and indissolubility of marriage was a moral concept that developed gradually. The polygamy of kings and patriarchs was not explicitly rejected; however, the Law of Moses protected the wife from

The Book of Tobit

The Book of Tobit is a rather short book found in the Old Testament. It tells the story of a family consisting of Tobit, a faithful Jew who is afflicted with blindness; his wife, Anna; his son, Tobiah; and a young woman, Sarah. Tobit sends Tobiah on a journey to recover some money he had left behind in his home country. (Tobiah is not completely alone though; his dog follows him and is with him every step of the way.) His father also suggests that when Tobiah reaches the home of their people, he might look for a woman to marry. The Angel Raphael joins Tobiah on his journey to help and guide him. When the young woman, Sarah, enters the story, Raphael's guidance becomes very important indeed!

The story told by the inspired author of the Book of Tobit is not a historical account. It is a religious novel that uses fictional elements to convey God's truth. The reader of Tobit is urged to be faithful to God's Law, to act respectfully toward parents, to honor marriage, and to value almsgiving, prayer, and fasting.

The Book of Tobit is beautifully written and has a happy ending for all its characters. You may want to read it for yourself.

being at the mercy of her husband, even though it still permitted a man to divorce his wife.

The prophets, however, aimed at a higher standard. They saw God's covenant as one of an exclusive married love, with God as the Bridegroom and Israel as the Bride:

> For as a young man marries a virgin,
>> your Builder shall marry you;
> And as a bridegroom rejoices in his bride
>> so shall your God rejoice in you.
>
>> (Isaiah 62:5)

Thus in their prophetic teaching, the prophets prepared the people for a deeper understanding of the unity and indissolubility of married love between a man and a woman. The Book of Ruth and the Book of Tobit both describe a tender and exclusive married love. The Song of Songs—on the surface, a human love story—has traditionally been seen as a metaphor for God's covenantal love for his people. It was this abiding love of God for his people that prepared the way for the New Covenant in which the incarnate Son of God gave himself as the Bridegroom to all humankind.

The Wedding at Cana

The Church has always seen marriage as part of the divine plan, and sees in Jesus' presence at the marriage at Cana a sign of his blessing upon the state of marriage itself. At Cana, at the urging of his mother, Jesus came to the rescue of a newly married couple who had run out of wine for their guests. Through the miracle of changing water into wine, Jesus "revealed his glory" and announced that a New Covenant in himself had arrived (see John 2:1–11.) Jesus' presence at the wedding affirmed the goodness of marriage and revealed that the Sacrament of Matrimony, from then on, would be a sign of his presence. (We might also recall that at the Last Supper, Jesus blessed the wine and made it the sign of the New Covenant in his blood.)

Jesus' affirmation of the goodness of Marriage forms the background of his teaching on other issues related to marriage and family. For example, Jesus prohibited divorce and remarriage (see Matthew 19:1–12, 5:31–32). He taught that Marriage is truly a covenantal relationship, like the covenantal relationship between God and his people, and as such, cannot be dissolved. God's plan for human relationship, for the majority of people, includes a lifetime of love to reflect, mediate, and witness his own deep and faithful covenantal love.

Jesus also demonstrated his love of children and stated that the Kingdom of Heaven belongs to them (see Matthew 19:13–15). "Children are the supreme gift of marriage"[8] (*Catechism of the Catholic Church [CCC]*, 1652) and, as gifts, bring great good to their parents. In marriage a man and a woman cooperate with God in bringing new life into the world.

Is Jesus' insistence on a lifetime commitment for married couples an impossible burden? Is it impossible to accomplish? Jesus said that with God's help, and the grace and strength of the Sacrament of Marriage, faithfulness to one person for life is possible. This is, of course, with the understanding that there is no Christian life for anyone, married or not, without the cross. Marriage in Christ, in the New Covenant, is not trouble free, but, for those who follow Christ, it is not only possible but also loving and joyful. ✞

Article 47 Witnesses to Love

Marriage is an exclusive, permanent, and lifelong contract between a man and a woman in which they commit themselves to care for each other and to procreate and raise children. When a marriage takes place between

© Monkey Business Images / Shutterstock.com

"Charity begins at home"—but it doesn't end there. A loving marriage contributes to the stability of the entire family, and the influence of family love can reach around the world. How does your family share love with others?

Ask Father Steven

Father Steven writes a question-and-answer column for a diocesan newspaper. Here are some questions he found in his e-mail recently.

Dear Father Steven,
I have noticed that sometimes people are married during Mass and sometimes not. What is the normal Catholic practice? Thank you much! Emily

Dear Emily,
When two Catholics marry, the Rite of Marriage is normally celebrated during the Eucharist. This is because all the Sacraments unite us with the Paschal Mystery of Christ. Just as we celebrate, particularly in the Eucharist, that Christ gave up his life for us, so at a Catholic wedding, we celebrate the gift of life that the bride and bridegroom are and will be for each other. If celebrating the rite during Mass is not possible, then a Liturgy of the Word, followed by the vows of the Sacrament of Marriage, may be celebrated.

Dear Father Steven,
What is a mixed marriage? Jason

Dear Jason,
One kind of mixed marriage is a marriage between a Catholic and a baptized non-Catholic. This kind of marriage is not forbidden but it does present obstacles to complete unity in marriage. It can have consequences in the education of children, and tensions can arise, even to the point of abandoning the Catholic faith.

Another kind of mixed marriage is called *disparity of cult*, which is a marriage between a Catholic and a person who is not baptized. In these cases care must be taken on the part of pastors and the engaged couple to ensure that all misunderstandings about the life of faith are discussed before the marriage. Both kinds of mixed marriages require special permission from Church authority.

Dear Father Steven,
My mother is Catholic but my father is not. We kids were raised Catholic, but now that we are older, we are discussing religion a lot more, and even arguing about it. It is causing problems. Do you have any ideas on ways to help us? Amy

Dear Amy,
I would suggest you talk with your parish priest. You did not say whether your father practices any religion, but in many regions, a pastoral plan for families in mixed marriages has been worked out. It encourages families to nourish those things they agree on and respect those things on which they differ. If your father has no faith at all, continue to love him and pray for him. We can never go wrong with love and prayer, and my prayers are with you!

baptized persons who enter into a covenant modeled on that between Christ and the Church, it is recognized as the **Sacrament of Matrimony**. The terms *Marriage* and *Matrimony* are often interchanged.

We have already discussed the "lifelong contract between a man and a woman" mentioned in this definition. Let us move on to the next phrase, "a covenant modeled on that between Christ and the Church."

In the previous article, we briefly touched on Christ's love for the Church. In this article we explore this reality in more depth, particularly in the writings of Saint Paul the Apostle, and consider its relationship to Marriage.

In his Letter to the Ephesians, Saint Paul writes this about Christian marriage: "Wives should be subordinate to their husbands in everything" (Ephesians 5:24). In the cultural context of the Greco-Roman Empire, this is, in fact, how things worked. However, in the Rite of Marriage today, there is no mention of the wife's obeying her husband in everything; rather, in the nuptial blessing, the priest prays for the married couple and refers to the wife in the following words:

> May her husband entrust his heart to her,
> so that, acknowledging her as his equal
> and his joint heir to the life of grace,
> he may show her due honor. . . .
>
> (*Roman Missal,* "Nuptial Blessing A")

As equal partners, a husband and a wife talk things over and make mutual decisions as adults. In fact, to give due credit to Saint Paul, he begins his discussion by writing, "Be subordinate to one another out of reverence for Christ" (Ephesians 5:21). At the very least, this means sharing ideas honestly and coming to decisions that both can live with.

However, the most important point in Saint Paul's letter is that married couples are signs of Christ's love for the Church:

> Husbands, love your wives, even as Christ loved the church and handed himself over for her to sanctify her. . . . So [also] husbands should love their wives as their own bodies. He who loves his wife loves himself. For no one hates his own flesh but rather nourishes and cherishes it, even as Christ does

Matrimony, Sacrament of

A lifelong covenant, modeled on that between Christ and the Church, in which a baptized man and a baptized woman make an exclusive and permanent commitment to faithfully love each other and to cooperate in the procreation and education of children.

the church, because we are members of his body. (Ephesians 5:25–30)

Saint Paul then goes on to quote the same passage from Genesis that Jesus quoted, ending with, "and the two shall become one flesh" (Ephesians 5:31). He then concludes, "This is a great mystery, but I speak in reference to Christ and the church" (5:32).

Saint Paul states that he knows no greater union than that of Christ and the Church. The Sacrament of Matrimony is a sign of that union. In this Sacrament a man and a woman are given the grace to love each other with the same love with which Christ loves the Church. The Sacrament of Matrimony, through its graces, brings human love to fulfillment and to unbroken unity. The grace of the Sacrament of Matrimony joins a man and a woman and makes them holy as they journey together on the path to eternal happiness.

If married couples continually try to love each other as much as Christ loves the Church, they will have formed a true and lasting marriage in Christ, and will be witnesses to his love their entire lives. ☦

Pray It!

Anniversary Prayer

Praying for parents, relatives, and friends who are married is an important way to support married couples. This prayer is a prayer for an anniversary. You might like to write it in a card for the next wedding anniversary of a couple you know.

Dear God,
Bless _____ and _____ on their anniversary.
In their love for each other, they reveal your love to the world.
Give them grace to live out their Marriage covenant,
provide them with strength when times are hard,
and shower them with joy in the company of family and friends.
Open their eyes to the gifts you have given them
in order to serve you by serving others.
May they enjoy many more years together,
growing closer to each other and to you.
May they love and honor each other all the days of their lives.
Amen.

Article 48 The Rite of Marriage

Marriage is a public vocation. Thus the Sacrament of Matrimony is never private but always public and always in church. The Sacrament of Matrimony establishes the matrimonial covenant as a religious action, an act of worship, and emphasizes that in this action and as a result of it, God's love will be shared not only between the married couple but also with the community. Thus it is fitting that the ceremony be public, within a liturgical celebration, and before a priest (or deacon), two other witnesses, and the assembly. The presence of the minister and the witnesses is a tangible sign that sacramental marriage is a communal and ecclesial reality, not a private or secular matter.

Note that the priest or deacon is not the minister of the Sacrament, but a witness representing the Church. The actual ministers of the Sacrament are the bride and the groom, who give their free consent to the Marriage.

© The Crosiers / Gene Plaisted, OSC

The Marriage covenant is a covenant of mutual consent.

Marriage and Family Life

In one of the seven themes of Catholic social teaching, the United States Conference of Catholic Bishops declares, "Marriage and the family are the central social institutions that must be supported and strengthened, not undermined" (USCCB Web site). The organization of society (in economics, politics, law, and policy) directly affects marriage and family. Think of the many obstacles to family life in our society: lack of affordable, quality child care; issues of employment for parents (low-wage or part-time work); or the lack of any employment at all, resulting in poverty and hunger. Even economically stable families have difficulty scheduling family time due to parents' work demands, children's over-involvement in organized sports and other activities at younger and younger ages, and lack of extended family nearby to help in times of need. All of us, whether married or not, have a right and a duty to care about families—others' as well as our own—especially families struggling with poverty and need. All of us have a right and duty to participate in society's decisions that affect the well-being of families.

The Requirements of Marriage

These three elements are essential to a marriage:

- **Unity** Marriage unites the husband and wife in an unbreakable and exclusive union. Adultery and polygamy are sins against the unity of Marriage.
- **Indissolubility** The Marriage bond can never be dissolved. The husband and the wife make a commitment to lifelong fidelity. Divorcing one's lawful spouse and marrying another person is a sin against the permanence of Marriage.
- **Openness to children** Husbands and wives must be open to children and accept them as gifts from God. Artificial contraception is a sin against the openness to new life. It is intrinsically evil because it makes procreation impossible. The essence of conjugal love is total self-gift to the other, and using contraception, a refusal to be open to the possibility of new life, makes this gift a lie.

© Bill Wittman / www.wpwittman.com

(In the Eastern Churches, the priest witnesses the consent of the bride and groom, but, for the Sacrament to be valid, his blessing is also required. Thus in the Eastern Churches, the priest is the minister of the Sacrament.)

This consent, which must be freely given, is an essential element of the Sacrament of Matrimony. Consent is the will of the man and woman to give themselves to each other in order to live a lifelong covenant of faithful love, and to be open to sharing that love with children. This consent is expressed in the vows of Matrimony: "I, N., take you, N., to be my wife [or husband]" (*Rite of Marriage*, 45).

The priest or deacon, as the Church's witness, receives this consent, and gives the blessing of the Church with the following words: "You have declared your consent before the Church. May the Lord in his goodness strengthen your consent and fill you both with his blessings. What God has joined, men must not divide" (*Rite of Marriage*, 46).

If free consent is lacking on either side, there is no Marriage bond. To be free when expressing consent means: (1) not being under any constraint (coercion or pressure, even if subtle) and (2) not being barred from Marriage by any natural or Church law.

A *constraint* is an obstacle that prevents free and full consent to a marriage. Let us look at some examples of constraint. Pregnancy, mental illness, or a secret addiction could all be obstacles that prevent free and full consent. Where there is constraint, or obstacles to free and full consent, there is no valid Marriage bond. This is one reason why the Church requires a period of preparation before the Sacrament of

Catholic Wisdom

The Nuptial Blessing

The nuptial blessing is a special blessing prayed after the Lord's Prayer in the wedding Mass. The following is an excerpt. Extending his hands over the couple, the priest prays for the bride and groom:

> In happiness may they praise you, O Lord,
> in sorrow may they seek you out;
> may they have the joy of your presence
> to assist them in their toil,
> and know that you are near
> to comfort them in their need;
> let them pray to you in the holy assembly
> and bear witness to you in the world,
> and after a happy old age,
> together with the circle of friends that surrounds them,
> may they come to the Kingdom of Heaven.
> Through Christ our Lord.
>
> (*Roman Missal*, "Nuptial Blessing C")

Marriage, often with some kind of assessment to determine a couple's readiness. Free consent is very important to a faithful and fruitful marriage.

"Not being barred from Marriage by natural or Church law" means that one must be legally and ecclesiastically free to marry. For example, a person who has taken religious vows in the Church is not free to marry until he or she is released from those vows. Someone who is already married to someone else cannot contract a new bond of Marriage. There are also instances in which natural law prohibits marriage, such as marriage between family members.

When a marriage has been entered into under constraint, or for other reasons, the Marriage bond can be declared null and void by the Church. The Church's declaration of nullity is called an annulment. This declaration means that a true Marriage bond, as a Sacrament, never existed in the eyes of the Church. It does not mean that the children of that marriage are illegitimate or are now orphans. It simply means that, for some reason, free consent to the marriage by one of the partners was never given.

An annulment declared by the Church is not the same as a civil divorce. Those who have been civilly divorced from a spouse still living, and have remarried without a Church annulment, have gone against God's Law as taught by Christ. They are still members of the Church, but may not receive the Eucharist. The Church encourages them to educate their children in the faith, to attend Mass and listen to the Liturgy of the Word, to pray, to do works of love and justice, to do penance, and to strengthen their relationship with God through prayer, asking for his grace for themselves and their families. ✝

Article 49 Lifelong Journey

The grace of the Sacrament of Matrimony is the grace to bring the couple's love for each other to its fullness and to strengthen their bond with each other. This grace helps the husband and wife to live the responsibilities of married life, so that, in their love and companionship, they may help bring each other through this life and into the eternal and heavenly Kingdom prepared for them for all eternity.

The grace of the Sacrament of Matrimony prepares the newly married couple for a lifelong journey of fidelity. The gift of self cannot truly be made on a tentative basis: "Maybe I love you enough to stay with you, and maybe I don't." It cannot be a "Let's see how things turn out" proposition. That is not unconditional love, and that undermines the stable commitment upon which a lifetime of happiness for both the spouses and their children is built. Unconditional love is the only basis for a lasting marriage.

In addition, as we learned previously, Christian Marriage is a symbol of the fidelity of Christ to his Church. Husbands and wives, strengthened by the grace of the Sacrament of Matrimony, are called to this same fidelity. In this fidelity they proclaim the faithful love of God for all and can love each other because they share in God's love.

The entire community must support those in the married state with their prayers and encouragement. If, for serious reasons, a couple can no longer live together in harmony, they may separate. However, a separated husband and wife are still married and may not contract another union. The ultimate goal of a separation is reconciliation, and a renewed commitment to the matrimonial covenant. This may be accomplished through the guidance of a spiritual advisor and other counselors, as well as the support of trusted family members and friends. Most of all, it requires the firm and mutual resolve of the couple.

The grace of the Sacrament of Matrimony is a lifelong grace. Those who seek to cooperate with this grace find that, at times, enriching their marriage through reflection and education is helpful. Retreat houses offer weekend retreats or days of recollection for married couples. Dioceses and parishes often offer courses on human relationships and communication, taught from the perspective of faith. Many

© Jonathan Cook / iStockphoto.com

A married couple freely promises to love and honor each other all the days of their lives, in good times and in bad, in sickness and in health; to lovingly accept children; and to bring them up in the faith of the Church.

Preparing for a Catholic Marriage

Preparing for a Catholic marriage is more than preparing for a Catholic wedding, but sometimes the two overlap. Here are some key considerations from the article "Getting Married Catholic," found on the For Your Marriage Web site, a Web site sponsored by the United States Conference of Catholic Bishops:

1. Meet with your parish priest as soon as you become engaged.
2. Prepare for your marriage. Set aside at least six months to give time not only to arranging the practical wedding details but also to discussing and reflecting on your relationship and your plans for the future. Also give yourselves time for prayer—both individually and together.
3. Attend an approved marriage preparation program in your area. There are also national programs. Check for these by contacting your diocesan family life office.

What does a marriage preparation program involve? Usually the engaged couple meets with a team consisting of a married couple and a priest or deacon. Sometimes a parish may offer a Mentor Couple program, in which a married couple, especially trained for this work, meets with an engaged couple to discuss various issues related to marriage. Most preparation programs include a marriage preparation inventory taken by the engaged couple. In highlighting various areas of life, this inventory points to areas of agreement as well as areas that could benefit from further discussion between the potential spouses.

© Tom Grill / Corbis

dioceses sponsor an Office of Family Life or Family Minis-tries, and offer various resources on their diocesan Web sites.

The Domestic Church

The Sacrament of Matrimony is the foundation for the Christian family. The Christian family is the place where children first learn the love of God through the love of their parents. The family is the domestic church. It is "the church at home," where children first hear the faith proclaimed. The family is a domestic church because, as a community of grace and prayer, it fosters growth in human virtues and, especially, practice in Christian love.

Parents are the children's first teachers in the faith. When children are young, parents—exercising their author-ity as members of the "common priesthood of the faith-ful"—should set a routine of family prayer and reading from Scripture. As children grow, parents should set an example of regular participation in the Sacraments. Children should see their parents praying, helping those in need, serving others, and forgiving each other as often as the need arises. Children should learn the dignity and satisfaction of work, as they are gradually included in the daily chores of household living.

Families are the backbone and the lifeblood of the Church. Single people can make significant contributions to family life as aunts and uncles, godparents, or family friends. They certainly should not be left out of the love and support of the Christian community. Families should often include their single friends and fellow parishioners in their celebrations, particularly at important seasons of the Church year, like Christmas and Easter. Some single people, such as those living in senior residences or long-term care facilities, can easily be marginalized. Those who are homeless are in special need, as are those who are living alone in poverty. Pastors and families, as well as charitable organizations, should always seek to find ways to open the doors of the par-ish family to them.

The Gift of Children

As mentioned previously, a man and woman united in Christian Marriage must also be open to the gift of chil-dren and ready to take on responsibility for their growth and education, especially in morality and the spiritual life. For the parents this is a cooperative work with God and his love. Each child is unique and comes with unique gifts and talents. As far as possible, parents are called to notice and to nurture these gifts, not only for the child's own good but also for the good of the world.

Parents are called to encourage each child, according to each one's particular gifts, in a suitable vocation. Parents are also called to encourage and nurture a religious vocation, should they discern that one or more of their children might be suited to this calling.

Those couples unable to bring children into the world can still live a meaningful married life, in love for others, in hospitable welcome to friends and neighbors, as adoptive parents or mentors, and of sacrificial love for those in need. ✝

Live It!

Are You Ready for Marriage?

Marriage is a decision best made by mature and responsible people who have reached adulthood. However, how you handle friendships now is a good indicator of the way you might handle a married relationship in the future. The following questions might be helpful in assessing attitudes in regard to some aspects of friendship that will loom large in married life. Test yourself!

1. How well do I listen? Am I always looking to argue small points? Do I allow others to have their own choices and ideas in a friendship, or do I dominate the relationship?

2. How do I handle conflict? Do I fly off the handle, or do I find an appropriate time and place to discuss the issue with the other person?

3. How do I feel when my plans are upset for some reason? Am I angry? resentful? Or can I be flexible and look for ways to include the needs of others in a "plan B"?

4. Do I apologize when I am in the wrong? Even when I am in the right, do I seek to repair a misunderstanding? Do I constantly bring up past mistakes?

We can all grow in these friendship areas, but building good attitudes now is especially important for the future success of a Marriage. More information on readiness for Marriage can be found at the For Your Marriage Web site, which is sponsored by the USCCB.

Part Review

1. What is God's plan for marriage?

2. What is the definition of the Sacrament of Matrimony? Choose two key elements from this definition and explain why each is important in Christian Marriage.

3. How did the idea of the unity and indissolubility of marriage gradually develop in the Law of Moses, the teachings of the prophets, and finally, in the New Covenant established by Christ?

4. How do Saint Paul's words in Ephesians 5:25–30 relate to the union of husband and wife in the Sacrament of Matrimony?

5. Why is it important that consent in the Sacrament of Matrimony be free? What are some circumstances that may create constraint or pressure to marry, leading to a marriage contracted without free consent?

6. Who are the ministers of the Sacrament of Matrimony? What is the role of the priest or deacon in the Sacrament in the Latin Rite? in the Eastern Churches?

7. What three requirements are essential to Marriage?

8. What are some ways those who are single can contribute to family life? How can married couples provide those who are single, especially those who may be isolated because of old age or illness, an opportunity to share in family life?

9. When might the Church issue a declaration of nullity, called an annulment, and what does this declaration mean?

Glossary

A

absolution An essential part of the Sacrament of Penance and Reconciliation in which the priest pardons the sins of the person confessing, in the name of God and the Church. *(page 195)*

actual graces God's interventions and support for us in the everyday moments of our lives. Actual graces are important for conversion and for continuing growth in holiness. *(page 40)*

anamnesis The Greek word for memory. In the Eucharist, this refers to the making present of the Paschal Mystery, Christ's work of salvation. The *anamnesis* refers also to a particular section of the Eucharistic Prayer after the words of institution in which the Church remembers Christ's saving deeds: his Passion, Resurrection, and glorious return. *(page 119)*

Anointing of the Sick, Sacrament of One of the Seven Sacraments, sometimes formerly known as "the Sacrament of the dying," in which a gravely ill, aging, or dying person is anointed by the priest and prayed over by him and attending believers. One need not be dying to receive the Sacrament. *(page 204)*

Apostolic Succession The uninterrupted passing on of apostolic preaching and authority from the Apostles directly to all bishops. It is accomplished through the laying on of hands when a bishop is ordained in the Sacrament of Holy Orders as instituted by Christ. The office of bishop is permanent, because at ordination a bishop is marked with an indelible, sacred character. *(page 96)*

assembly Also known as a congregation, a community of believers gathered for worship as the Body of Christ. *(page 138)*

B

Baptism, Sacrament of The first of the Seven Sacraments and one of the three Sacraments of Christian Initiation (the others being Confirmation and the Eucharist) by which one becomes a member of the Church and a new creature in Christ. *(page 55)*

bishop One who has received the fullness of the Sacrament of Holy Orders and is a successor to the Apostles. *(page 231)*

C

catechesis, catechists Catechesis is the process by which Christians of all ages are taught the essentials of Christian doctrine and are formed as disciples of Christ. Catechists are the ministers of catechesis. *(page 61)*

catechumen An unbaptized person who is preparing for full initiation into the Catholic Church by engaging in formal study, reflection, and prayer. *(page 59)*

Christian Initiation, Sacraments of The three Sacraments—Baptism, Confirmation, and the Eucharist—through which we enter into full membership in the Church. *(page 60)*

Church The term *Church* has three inseparable meanings: (1) the entire People of God throughout the world; (2) the diocese, which is also known as the local Church; (3) the assembly of believers gathered for the celebration of the liturgy, especially the Eucharist. In the Nicene Creed, the Church is recognized as One, Holy, Catholic, and Apostolic—traits that together are referred to as "marks of the Church." *(page 136)*

common priesthood of the faithful The name for the priesthood shared by all who are baptized. The baptized share in the one priesthood of Jesus Christ by participating in his mission as priest, prophet, and king. *(page 87)*

concupiscence The tendency of all human beings toward sin, as a result of Original Sin. *(page 190)*

Confirmation, Sacrament of With Baptism and the Eucharist, one of the three Sacraments of Christian Initiation. Through an outpouring of the special Gifts of the Holy Spirit, Confirmation completes the grace of Baptism by confirming or "sealing" the baptized person's union with Christ and by equipping that person for active participation in the life of the Church. *(page 94)*

conversion A change of heart, turning away from sin and toward God. *(page 188)*

D

deacon One who is ordained for service and ministry, but not for ministerial priesthood, through the Sacrament of Holy Orders. Deacons are ordained to assist priests and bishops in a variety of liturgical and charitable ministries. *(page 234)*

E

Easter The day on which Christians celebrate Jesus' Resurrection from the dead; considered the most holy of all days and the climax of the Church's liturgical year. *(page 72)*

Eastern Catholic Churches The twenty-one Churches of the East, with their own theological, liturgical and administrative traditions, in union with the universal Catholic Church and her head, the Bishop of Rome. *(page 26)*

elect The title given to catechumens after the Rite of Election while they are in the final period of preparation for the Sacraments of Christian Initiation. *(page 66)*

Eucharist, the Also called the Mass or Lord's Supper, and based on a word for "thanksgiving," it is the central Christian liturgical celebration, established by Jesus at the Last Supper. In the Eucharist the sacrificial death and Resurrection of Jesus are both remembered and renewed. The term sometimes refers specifically to the consecrated bread and wine that have become the Body and Blood of Christ. *(page 116)*

evangelization The proclamation of the Good News of Jesus Christ through word and witness. *(page 64)*

examination of conscience Prayerful reflection on, and assessment of, one's words, attitudes, and actions in light of the Gospel of Jesus; more specifically, the conscious moral evaluation of one's life in preparation for reception of the Sacrament of Penance and Reconciliation. *(page 195)*

H

Heaven A state of eternal life and union with God in which one experiences full happiness and the satisfaction of the deepest human longings. *(page 185)*

Hell The state of permanent separation from God, reserved for those who freely and consciously choose to reject God to the very end of their lives. *(page 199)*

Holy Orders, Sacrament of The Sacrament by which baptized men are ordained for permanent ministry in the Church as bishops, priests, and deacons. *(page 223)*

L

liturgical year The annual cycle of religious feasts and seasons that forms the context for the Church's worship. During the liturgical year, we remember and celebrate God the Father's saving plan as it is revealed through the life of his Son, Jesus Christ. *(page 19)*

liturgy The Church's official, public, communal prayer. It is God's work, in which the People of God participate. The Church's most important liturgy is the Eucharist, or the Mass. *(page 10)*

Liturgy of the Hours Also known as the Divine Office, the official, public, daily prayer of the Catholic Church. The Divine Office provides standard prayers, Scripture readings, and reflections at regular hours throughout the day. *(page 46)*

Logos A Greek word meaning "word." *Logos* is a title of Jesus Christ found in the Gospel of John that illuminates the relationship between the Three Persons of the Holy Trinity. (See John 1:1,14.) *(page 116)*

M

Magisterium The Church's living teaching office, which consists of all the bishops, in communion with the Pope. *(page 13)*

Matrimony, Sacrament of A lifelong covenant, modeled on that between Christ and the Church, in which a baptized man and a baptized woman make an exclusive and permanent commitment to faithfully love each other and to cooperate in the procreation and education of children. *(page 247)*

mortal sin An action so contrary to the will of God that it results in a complete separation from God and his grace. As a consequence of that separation, the person is condemned to eternal death. For a sin to be a mortal sin, three conditions must be met: the act must involve grave matter, the person must have full knowledge of the evil of the act, and the person must give his or her full consent in committing the act. *(page 185)*

mystagogy A period of catechesis following the reception of the Sacraments of Christian Initiation that aims to more fully initiate people into the mystery of Christ. *(page 75)*

O

Oil of the Sick Blessed olive oil used in the Sacrament of Anointing of the Sick to anoint the forehead and hands of people who are seriously ill or near death. *(page 208)*

Original Sin From the Latin *origo*, meaning "beginning" or "birth." The term has two meanings: (1) the sin of the first human beings, who disobeyed God's command by choosing to follow their own will and thus lost their original holiness and became subject to death, (2) the fallen state of human nature that affects every person born into the world. *(page 77)*

P

Paschal candle Also called the Easter candle, this is the large, tall candle lit at the Easter Vigil by a flame from the new fire; the symbol of the Risen Christ. It is lit in the sanctuary for Masses during the Easter season, and during the year is kept near the baptismal font. It is lit at Baptisms and at funeral services throughout the year as a sign of the presence of the Risen Christ among us. *(page 71)*

Paschal Mystery The work of salvation accomplished by Jesus Christ mainly through his life, Passion, death, Resurrection, and Ascension. *(page 36)*

Passion The sufferings of Jesus during his final days in this life: his agony in the garden at Gethsemane, his trial, and his Crucifixion. *(page 115)*

Passover The night the Lord passed over the houses of the Israelites marked by the blood of the lamb, and spared the firstborn sons from death. It also is the feast that celebrates the deliverance of the Chosen People from bondage in Egypt and the Exodus from Egypt to the Promised Land. *(page 118)*

Penance and Reconciliation, Sacrament of One of the Seven Sacraments of the Church, the liturgical celebration of God's forgiveness of sin, through which the sinner is reconciled with both God and the Church. *(page 184)*

prayer Lifting up of one's mind and heart to God or the requesting of good things from him. The five basic forms of prayer are blessing, praise, petition, thanksgiving, and intercession. In prayer we communicate with God in a relationship of love. *(page 47)*

priest One who has received the ministerial priesthood through the Sacrament of Holy Orders. The priest serves the community of faith by representing and assisting the bishop in teaching, governing, and presiding over the community's worship. *(page 232)*

Purgatory A state of final purification or cleansing, which one may need to enter following death and before entering Heaven. *(page 199)*

R

redemption From the Latin *redemptio,* meaning "a buying back"; referring, in the Old Testament, to Yahweh's deliverance of Israel and, in the New Testament, to Christ's deliverance of all Christians from the forces of sin. *(page 44)*

reparation Making amends for something one did wrong that caused harm to another person or led to loss. *(page 195)*

repentance (contrition) An attitude of sorrow for a sin committed and a resolution not to sin again. It is a response to God's gracious love and forgiveness. *(page 193)*

Rite of Christian Initiation of Adults The process by which an unbaptized person, called a "catechumen," and those who were baptized in another Christian denomination, called "candidates for full communion," are prepared to become full members of the Church. *(page 61)*

Rite of Election The Rite, which takes place on the first Sunday of Lent, by which the Church elects or accepts the catechumens for the Sacraments of Christian Initiation at the Easter Vigil. The Rite of Election begins a period of purification and enlightenment. *(page 66)*

ritual The established form of the words and actions for a ceremony that is repeated often. The actions often have a symbolic meaning. *(page 33)*

S

Sacrament An efficacious and visible sign of God's grace, instituted by Christ and entrusted to the Church, by which divine life is dispensed to us. The Seven Sacraments are Baptism, the Eucharist, Confirmation, Penance and Reconciliation, Anointing of the Sick, Matrimony, and Holy Orders. *(page 37)*

sacramental economy The communication or dispensation of the fruits of Christ's Paschal Mystery in the celebration of the Church's sacramental liturgy. *(page 39)*

Sacred Chrism Perfumed olive oil consecrated by the bishop that is used for anointing in the Sacraments of Baptism, Confirmation, and Holy Orders. *(page 80)*

sanctifying grace The grace that heals our human nature wounded by sin and restores us to friendship with God by giving us a share in the divine life of the Trinity. It is a supernatural gift of God, infused into our souls by the Holy Spirit, that continues the work of making us holy. *(page 40)*

scrutinies Rites within the Rite of Christian Initiation of Adults that support and strengthen the elect through prayers of intercession and exorcism. *(page 69)*

sin Any deliberate offense, in thought, word, or deed, against the will of God. *(page 185)*

symbol An object or action that points us to another reality. It leads us to look beyond our senses to consider a deeper mystery. *(page 33)*

T

Tradition This word (from the Latin, meaning "to hand on") refers to the process of passing on the Gospel message. Tradition, which began with the oral communication of the Gospel by the Apostles, was written down in the Scriptures, is handed down and lived out in the life of the Church, and is interpreted by the Magisterium under the guidance of the Holy Spirit. *(page 14)*

Transubstantiation In the Sacrament of the Eucharist, this is the name given to the action of changing the bread and wine into the Body and Blood of Jesus Christ. *(page 148)*

Trinity From the Latin *trinus*, meaning "threefold," referring to the central mystery of the Christian faith that God exists as a communion of three distinct and interrelated Divine Persons: Father, Son, and Holy Spirit. The doctrine of the Trinity is a mystery that is inaccessible to human reason alone and is known through Divine Revelation only. *(page 14)*

V

venial sin: A less serious offense against the will of God that diminishes one's personal character and weakens but does not rupture one's relationship with God. *(page 185)*

Index
Page numbers in italics refer to illustrations.

Acknowledgments

The scriptural quotation on page 203 is from the New Revised Standard Version of the Bible, Catholic Edition. Copyright © 1993 and 1989 by the Division of Christian Education of the National Council of the Churches of Christ in the United States of America. All rights reserved.

All other Scripture texts used in this work are taken from the *New American Bible, revised edition* © 2010, 1991, 1986, 1970 Confraternity of Christian Doctrine, Inc., Washington, D.C. All Rights Reserved. No part of this work may be reproduced or transmitted in any form or by any means, electronic or mechanical, including photocopying, recording, or by any information storage and retrieval system, without permission in writing from the copyright owner.

The excerpts marked *Catechism of the Catholic Church* and *CCC* are from the English translation of the *Catechism of the Catholic Church* for use in the United States of America, second edition. Copyright © 1994 by the United States Catholic Conference, Inc.—Libreria Editrice Vaticana (LEV). English translation of the *Catechism of the Catholic Church: Modifications from the Editio Typica* copyright © 1997 by the United States Catholic Conference, Inc.—LEV. Used with permission of the United States Conference of Catholic Bishops (USCCB).

The excerpts marked *Roman Missal* are from *The Roman Missal* © 2010, International Commission on English in the Liturgy Corporation (ICEL). English translation prepared by the ICEL. Used with permission of the ICEL.

The excerpts marked *RCIA* are from the English translation of *Rite of Christian Initiation of Adults* © 1985, ICEL; the excerpts marked *Rite of Baptism for Children* are from the English translation of *Rite of Baptism for Children* © 1969, ICEL; the excerpts marked *Rite of Confirmation* are from the English translation of *Rite of Confirmation (Second Edition)* © 1975, ICEL; the excerpts marked *Rite of Penance* are from the English translation of *Rite of Penance* © 1975, ICEL; the excerpts marked *Anointing of the Sick*, and the excerpt on page 213 are from the English translation of *Pastoral Care of the Sick: Rites of Anointing and Viaticum* © 1982, ICEL; the excerpts marked *Rite of Marriage* are from the English translation of *Rite of Marriage* © 1969, ICEL; in *The Rites of the Catholic Church*, volume one, prepared by the ICEL, a Joint Commission of Catholic Bishops' Conferences (Collegeville, MN: Liturgical Press, 1990]. Copyright © 1990 by the Order of St. Benedict, Collegeville, MN. Used with permission of the ICEL.

The excerpt on page 19 is from "Egeria's Description of the Liturgical Year in Jerusalem: Translation," based on the translation reproduced in Louis Duchesme's *Christian Worship* (London, 1923), found at *users.ox.ac. uk/~mikef/durham/egetra.html*.

The words from the Eastern Church liturgy on pages 25 and 138 are from *The Divine Liturgy*, Orthodox Church in America (Sea Cliff, NY: Olga Poloukhine, 1989), pages 7 and 75. Copyright © 1989. English text taken from the *Service Book of the Orthodox Church in America*, second edition, 1977.

The excerpt on page 33 is from *Julian of Norwich: Showings*, translated from the critical text by Edmund Colledge and James Walsh (New York: Paulist Press), page 186. Copyright © 1978 by the Missionary Society of St. Paul the Apostle in the State of New York.

The quotation from Benedict XVI on page 93 is from "Address of His Holiness Benedict XVI to Participants in a Meeting Organized by the Catholic Fraternity of Charismatic Covenant Communities and Fellowships," at *www.vatican.va/holy_father/benedict_xvi/speeches/2008/october/ documents/hf_ben-xvi_spe_20081031_carismatici_en.html*. Copyright © 2008 LEV.

The prayer on page 106 is from "Translation of the Pentecost Sequence," by Sr. Irene Nowell, at *www.mountosb.org/music/sequence. html*. Used with permission of the author.

The excerpts on page 122 are from *Church of the Eucharist (Ecclesia De Eucharistia)*, numbers 5 and 8, at *www.vatican.va/holy_father/special_ features/encyclicals/documents/hf_jp-ii_enc_20030417_ecclesia_ eucharistia_en.html*. Copyright © LEV.

The quotation from Oscar Romero on page 131 is from *A Martyr's Message of Hope: Six Homilies by Archbishop Oscar Romero* (Kansas City, MO: Celebration Books, 1981), page 166, as quoted in *A Eucharist Sourcebook*, compiled by J. Robert Baker and Barbara Budde (Chicago: Liturgy Training Publications, 1999), page 53. Copyright © 1999 by the Archdiocese of Chicago.

The excerpts on pages 137 and 144 are from *Constitution on the Sacred Liturgy (Sacrosanctum Concilium*, 1963), numbers 116 and 52, at *www.va/archive/hist_councils/ii_vatican_council/documents/vat-ii_ const_19631204_sacrosanctum-concilium_en.html*. Copyright © LEV.

The second excerpt on page 144 is from *Lectionary for [Sunday] Mass: For Use in the Dioceses of the United States of America*, second typical edition, by the USCCB (New Jersey: Catholic Book Publishing Company, 1998), number 24, page 18. Illustrations and arrangement copyright © 1998 by the Catholic Book Publishing Company. Used with permission of the ICEL.

The prayer on page 238 is from the USCCB Web site, at *www.usccb. org/vocations/prayereng.shtml*.

The anniversary prayer on page 248 is from *The Catholic Faith Handbook for Youth*, Second Edition, by Brian Singer-Towns (Winona, MN: Saint Mary's Press, 2008), page 201. Copyright © 2008 by Saint Mary's Press. All rights reserved.

The quotation on page 249 is from "Themes of Catholic Social Teaching," by the USCCB, at *www.usccb.org/sdwp/projects/socialteaching/ excerpt.shtml*. Copyright © 2005 USCCB, Washington, D.C. All rights reserved.

To view copyright terms and conditions for Internet materials cited here, log on to the home pages for the referenced Web sites.

During this book's preparation, all citations, facts, figures, names, addresses, telephone numbers, Internet URLs, and other pieces of information cited within were verified for accuracy. The authors and Saint Mary's Press staff have made every attempt to reference current and valid sources, but we cannot guarantee the content of any source, and we are not responsible for any changes that may have occurred since our verification. If you find an error in, or have a question or concern about, any of the information or sources listed within, please contact Saint Mary's Press.

Endnotes Cited in Quotations from the *Catechism of the Catholic Church,* Second Edition

Section 1
1. Joshua 3:10; Psalm 42:3; etc.

Section 2
1. *Unitatis redintegratio* 22 § 2.
2. Cf. *Lumen gentium* 10.
3. Byzantine Liturgy, Pentecost Vespers, Troparion.

Section 3
1. *Lumen gentium* 11.
2. *Sacrosanctum concilium* 47.
3. Saint Augustine, *En. in* Psalm 85, 1: J. P. Migne, ed., Patrologia Latina (Paris: 1841–1855) 37, 1081; cf. General Introduction to *Liturgy of the Hours* 7.
4. *Lumen gentium* 11.
5. Saint Justin, *Apol.* 1, 65–67: J. P. Migne, ed., Patrologia Graeca (Paris, 1857–1866) 6, 428–429; the text before the asterisk (*) is from chap. 67.
6. Paul VI, *Mysterium fidei* 39.

7. Saint Justin, *Apol.* 1, 66, 1–2: J. P. Migne, ed., Patrologia Graeca (Paris, 1857–1866) 6, 428.

8. *Sacrosanctum concilium* 7.

9. Saint John Chrysostom, *prod. Jud.* 1:6: J. P. Migne, ed., Patrologia Graeca (Paris, 1857–1866) 49, 380.

10. Saint Ignatius of Antioch, *Ad Smyrn.* 8:1; Sources Chrétiennes (Paris: 1942–) 10, 138.

11. St. Augustine, *Sermo* 272: J. P. Migne, ed., Patrologia Latina (Paris: 1841–1855) 38, 1247.

Section 4

1. Saint Augustine, *Contra Faustum* 22: J. P. Migne, ed., Patrologia Latina (Paris: 1841–1855) 42, 418; Saint Thomas Aquinas, *Summa Theologiae* I–II, 71, 6.

2. Tertullian, *De Pœnit.* 4, 2: J. P. Migne, ed., Patrologia Latina (Paris: 1841–1855) 1, 1343; cf. Council of Trent (1547): Denzinger-Schönmetzer, *Enchiridion Symbolorum, definitionum et declarationum de rebus fidei et morum* (1965) 1542.

3. Cf. Council of Trent (1551): Denzinger-Schönmetzer, *Enchiridion Symbolorum, definitionum et declarationum de rebus fidei et morum* (1965) 1712.

4. John Paul II, *Reconciliatio et paenitentia* 31, 5.

5. Council of Trent (1551); Denzinger-Schönmetzer, *Enchiridion Symbolorum, definitionum et declarationum de rebus fidei et morum* (1965) 1698.

6. Council of Trent (1551); Denzinger-Schönmetzer, *Enchiridion Symbolorum, definitionum et declarationum de rebus fidei et morum* (1965) 1694.

Section 5

1. *Roman Pontifical*, Ordination of Bishops 26, Prayer of Consecration.

2. *Roman Pontifical*, Ordination of Priests 22, Prayer of Consecration.

3. *Roman Pontifical*, Ordination of Deacons 21, Prayer of Consecration.

4. Piux XII, encyclical, *Mediator Dei*: Acta Apostolicae Sedis, 39 (1947) 548.

5. Cf. *Presbyterorum ordinis* 2.

6. Byzantine Liturgy, *Euchologion*.

7. Byzantine Liturgy, *Euchologion*.

8. *Gaudium et spes* 50 § 1; cf. Genesis 2:18; Matthew 19:4; Genesis 1:28.